Minnesota 150

AMERICAN INDIAN MOVEMENT

...PORTS * ATMOSPHERE * ANN BANCROFT * MARGARET CULKIN BANNING * JOHN BEARGREASE * CHARLES

...ENDER * PATTY BERG * HARRIET BISHOP * CHARLES K. BLANDIN * NORMAN BORLAUG * BOUNDARY

...CANOE AREA * FANNY BRIN * BRYAN V. ITASCA COUNTY * PAUL BUNYAN * BURMA-SHAVE ROAD SIGNS *

...OR VICTIMS OF TORTURE * CHARTER SCHOOLS * F. MELIUS CHRISTIANSEN * THE CLOQUET/MOOSE LAKE

...918 * CONFLUENCE OF MISSISSIPPI AND MINNESOTA RIVERS * GRATIA ALTA COUNTRYMAN * COURAGE C

...EYMOUR CRAY * BETTY CROCKER * DAN PATCH * DANZA MEXICA CUAUHTEMOC * DESTRUCTION OF THE

...OLITAN BUILDING * WALTER H. DEUBENER * DON MIGUEL * IGNATIUS DONNELLY * DULUTH LYNCH

...OB DYLAN * ENSILAGE HARVESTER * ETHNIC PRESSES * WILFORD H. FAWCETT * FINKELSTEIN AND RUBEN

...MINNESOTA VOLUNTEER INFANTRY REGIMENT * F. SCOTT FITZGERALD * WILLIAM WATTS FOLWELL * WANDA

...VERNE GAGNE' * CASS GILBERT * ROBERT R. GILRUTH * GLACIATION * JAMES MADISON GOODHUE *

...PORTAGE * GRASSHOPPERS * GREYHOUND BUS COMPANY * WENDELIN GRIMM * GUTHRIE THEATER

...BROTHERS NEW ORLEANS JAZZ BAND * HAZELDEN * HERTER'S, INC. * HIGHWAY 61 ALONG THE NORTH S

...AMES J. HILL * THE HONEYWELL PROJECT * THE HONEYWELL ROUND THERMOSTAT * HUBERT H. HUMP

...MMIGRANTS * INDIAN BOARDING SCHOOLS * JOHN IRELAND * IRON ORE * ITASCA STATE PARK * JEFFERS PETRO

... FREDERICK MCKINLEY JONES * J. R. WATKINS MEDICAL COMPANY * HAMILTON HARRIS JUDSON * GA

...EILLOR * OLIVER H. KELLEY * SISTER ELIZABETH KENNY * KENSINGTON RUNESTONE * THEODORE F.

...SINCLAIR LEWIS * CHARLES A. LINDBERGH JR. * RON AND AL LINDNER * MAUD HART LOVELACE * LUTHERA

...VARREN MACKENZIE * PAUL MANSHIP * MARKET HUNTING * MAYO CLINIC * EUGENE J. MCCARTHY * FRE

...MCGHEE * L. DAVID MECH * MINNEAPOLIS TRUCKERS' STRIKE, 1934 * MINNESOTA MINING AND MANUFACT

...MINNESOTA MULTIPHASIC PERSONALITY INVENTORY * MINNESOTA ORCHESTRA * MINNESOTA STATE

...VILHELM MOBERG AND OLE E. RØLVAAG * WALTER F. MONDALE * GEORGE MORRISON * MOUNT ZION

...CONGREGATION * MUNSINGWEAR * BRONKO NAGURSKI * NEAR V. MINNESOTA * KNUTE NELSON * FLOYD B

... THE OLYMPIC HOCKEY TEAM, 1980 * BRADFORD PARKINSON * GORDON PARKS * THE PHYLLIS WHEATL

...HALLIE Q. BROWN COMMUNITY CENTERS * PILGRIM BAPTIST CHURCH * PIPESTONE * VEDA PONIKVAR * C. S

...POTTER * POWWOWS * PRINCE * ELIZABETH C. QUINLAN * RAPIDAN DAM * RED RIVER TRAILS * RELIGIOUS

... JOSEPH RENVILLE * MARTHA RIPLEY * HENRY HASTINGS SIBLEY * SKYWAYS * SNOWMOBILES * SOCIALIST

...HOUSE * SOUND 80 * SOUTHDALE CENTER * SPAM * ALLAN SPEAR * SPLIT ROCK LIGHTHOUSE * HAROLD E. S

... STATE OF MINNESOTA V. PHILIP MORRIS * TEN THOUSAND LAKES OF MINNESOTA ASSOCIATION * JOHN T

...TONKA TRUCKS * TREATY OF 1837 * CLARA UELAND * UNIVERSITY OF MINNESOTA FRUIT-BREEDING PRO

...UNKNOWN CHAMPIONS * U.S.-DAKOTA WAR * XANG VANG * JESSE VENTURA * OWEN H. WANGENSTEEN * WA

...NTER FOR CHILDREN * WCAL * WEBSTER COOPERATIVE DAIRY ASSOCIATION * PAUL WELLSTONE * W

KATE ROBERTS

MINNESOTA

150

*The People, Places, and Things
that Shape Our State*

MINNESOTA HISTORICAL SOCIETY PRESS

www.mhspress.org

The Minnesota Historical Society Press is a member of the Association of American University Presses.

Printed in Canada

10 9 8 7 6 5 4 3 2 1

∞ The paper used in this publication meets the minimum requirements of the American National Standard for Information Sciences— Permanence for Printed Library Materials, ANSI Z39.48-1984.

International Standard Book Numbers
ISBN 13: 978-0-87351-594-8 (paper)
ISBN 10: 0-87351-594-3 (paper)

Library of Congress Cataloging-in-Publication Data

Roberts, Kate
    Minnesota 150 : the people, places, and things that shape our state / Kate Roberts.
        p. cm.
    Includes bibliographical references and index.
    ISBN-13: 978-0-87351-594-8 (pbk. : alk. paper)
    ISBN-10: 0-87351-594-3 (pbk. : alk. paper)
    1. Minnesota—History. 2. Minnesota—Biography. 3. Minnesota—Description and travel. I. Title. II. Title: Minnesota one hundred fifty.
    F606.5.R63 2007
    977.6'0503—dc22
                                                    2007023575

Cover and text design by Brad Norr Design

To Nick and Matt, my top picks

Contents

CONTENTS

CONTENTS

CONTENTS

Preface

In September 2005, a new page was launched on the Minnesota Historical Society (MHS) website. The goal of the page was simple: to invite members of the public to nominate a person, place, thing, or event originating in Minnesota that had promoted real, lasting change within or beyond the borders of the state. Those nominators who made a convincing argument would see their topics interpreted in an exhibit, *Minnesota 150,* scheduled to open in fall 2007 at the Minnesota History Center in St. Paul. Over the next eleven months, several hundred nominations came in via the web, voicemail, and the U.S. mail and through a variety of workshops conducted by MHS staff throughout the state.

Thanks to the generosity of the Minnesota State Fair Foundation, MHS staff and volunteers were able to work the crowds at the 2006 Minnesota State Fair. A major media campaign coincided with the twelve-day fair, and as a result, nomination counts soared. By the end of December 2006, we had received 2,760 nominations for hundreds and hundreds of topics, great and small, famous and obscure, with arguments ranging in length from a few words to multiple-page essays with supporting documents.

As it turned out, soliciting nominations was the easy part. Narrowing them down to a final 150 topics was a challenge. First the exhibit team (as the exhibit developer, I worked closely with Andy Wilhide, outreach coordinator and research assistant; Wendy Jones, education specialist; John Lindell, exhibit designer; and Jack Rumpel, graphic designer) winnowed the selected topics down to roughly 400 that met predetermined criteria: we wanted a final group with a broad distribution across time, across subject matter, and across the state, with subjects that could be developed into lively, thought-provoking exhibit elements. Above all else, each successful nominator needed to convince us that the chosen topic truly had promoted change. We defined change as follows:

Change occurs when something or someone is fundamentally different as a result of experiencing an event; being influenced or affected by a person's actions; and/or using or interacting with a place or thing.

We then circulated our group of 400 nominations to a range of educators, historians, and others for evaluation. Each member of the group read through the nominations and provided comments, which we combined and tallied. Armed with this input, the exhibit team met with outside advisors (Dan Spock, director of the History Center Museum; Annette Atkins, professor of history at St. John's University; and Marx Swanholm, independent historian) to make our final choices.

We talked. We argued. We laughed. We cajoled, wheedled, and whined. We got off track and had to rein ourselves in. We were at times ridiculously narrow-minded. We each had to let go of topics that we thought were slam dunks. (Can you believe that the rest of the group didn't buy my argument for the Bundt pan?)

And in the end, we came up with The List. Some of the choices seem obvious; others might surprise you. Together, they provide a glimpse into what was on the minds of Minnesota history–minded people in the years leading up to our state's sesquicentennial. *Minnesota 150* has been a great experiment; I hope you enjoy the results.

Acknowledgments

I've been influenced by many, many people while writing this book—it's one of those topics on which just about everyone has an opinion. Here are just a few people whose strong research skills, good company, and challenging questions kept me going over the course of this project: Marx Swanholm, Andy Wilhide, John Lindell, Jack Rumpel, Wendy Jones, Annette Atkins, Brenda Child, Julie Davis, Heather Hawkins, Mary Jacobson, Shelly Weimann, and Doug Wilhide. A special thanks, as well, to Pam McClanahan of the Minnesota Historical Society Press, who is a wonderful editor and, even more important, a truly good person. Thanks to all of you, and to everyone who has offered their two cents about this project.

MINNESOTA

150

American Indian Movement

Bettering lives by fighting the establishment

A s I look around at the Indian situation," said Cherokee scholar and activist Robert K. Thomas in 1964, "it looks like one big seething cauldron about ready to explode." Over the next decade, American Indian groups across the country mounted angry demonstrations and occupations fueled by long-standing resentments over a host of issues, including racial discrimination and federal Indian policies.

> **"We put out a bumper sticker, 'AIM for Sovereignty.' Most of our people didn't even know what the word meant. Now they know." Vernon Bellecourt, 1973**

During these tumultuous years, one of the nation's largest concentrations of urban Indians was centered on Franklin Avenue in Minneapolis. There, in 1968, American Indian community activists, led by George Mitchell, Dennis Banks, and Clyde Bellecourt, gathered for the first time. Their goal was to draw national attention to the rights guaranteed Indian nations by treaties, by their sovereign status, and by the U.S. Constitution—rights that were too often overlooked or misunderstood by those in power. At that first meeting, the group of activists chose a name: the American Indian Movement, or AIM.

AIM's first public act was to outfit "Indian Patrol" cars to monitor police who were working in Minneapolis's Indian neighborhoods. In 1969, AIM gained national attention by joining an occupation of Alcatraz Island in San Francisco Bay. A series of public acts followed, culminating in AIM's 1973 occupation of Wounded Knee, South Dakota, a violent, seventy-one-day siege that drew worldwide attention. This militant approach has not been without controversy. In Gerald Vizenor's opinion, a writer and member of the White Earth Band of Chippewa, "the American Indian Movement has raised good issues through the press, but it has seldom followed through to negotiate. . . . It takes more than a rifle and symbolic willingness to die to bring about institutional changes that will benefit tribal people."

With AIM now in its fourth decade, its legacy is best seen in Minneapolis, where "firsts" run by and for Indians—schools like Heart of the Earth Survival School, housing programs such as Little Earth of United Tribes, and health providers like the Indian Health Board— were founded through AIM's efforts. "Inherent in the spiritual heart of AIM," reads the organization's website, "is knowing that the work goes on because the need goes on."

Ancient Tropical Sea

What goes around, stays around

The past truly is all around us. Nominator David Stevens, public programs coordinator at Mill City Museum in Minneapolis, explains: "500 million years ago during the Ordovician period, a shallow tropical sea covered much of North America, and its sandy seashore extended diagonally across the southern part of what is now Minnesota. At that time, Minnesota was near the equator. An abundance of aquatic life lived in this sea, including corals, trilobites, clams, and snails. Over millions of years, the carbonate shells from these marine organisms deposited on the ocean floor and accumulated to form the limestone that is so familiar in southeastern Minnesota.

"This limestone is an important part of the Twin Cities story. A layer of Platteville [limestone] eventually formed the shelf over which St. Anthony Falls dropped, creating the

> "First quarried commercially in St. Paul in 1856 and in Minneapolis in 1864 . . . [Platteville limestone] underlay much of the two downtowns, and builders often simply quarried it on or near the construction site. The casual removal of stone eventually became such a problem that the city of St. Paul passed an ordinance forbidding people from quarrying it in the streets." Larry Millett, *Lost Twin Cities*

waterpower for the manufacturing center of Minneapolis and the head of navigation at St. Paul. Moreover, limestone was quarried and used as a building material. The buff and gray color of Minnesota limestone can be seen all over the Twin Cities, from hundreds of basement foundations, to its earliest territorial buildings, to nineteenth-century landmarks like the Washburn A Mill, the Pillsbury A Mill, and the Stone Arch Bridge. It continues to be a favored building material, especially the Kasota Stone visible on the Wells Fargo Tower, LaSalle Plaza, the Federal Reserve Bank, and the new Target Plaza. One doesn't have to go far in Minneapolis and St. Paul to find the remains of the sea creatures that inhabited our state hundreds of millions of years ago."

Stone Arch Bridge, Minneapolis. Millions of years ago, the same limestone that now elevates people over the waters of the Mississippi River was formed under the waters of a tropical sea.

Elmer L. Andersen (1909–2004)

A lifelong commitment to serving others

As Minnesota's governor (from 1961 to 1963), and especially as a private citizen, Elmer Lee Andersen saw public service as both a privilege and a necessity. He truly believed in the importance of each life and in the idea that each of us can make a difference. His own life was an inspiring demonstration of those beliefs.

Born in Chicago in 1909, Elmer Andersen graduated from the University of Minnesota in 1931 with a degree in business administration. In 1934, he went to work for H. B. Fuller Company, a St. Paul–based manufacturer of adhesives. Six years later, Andersen bought the business for $10,000, eventually building it into a global, Fortune 500 company. Andersen believed that a company should enrich the lives of its employees—or "associates," as he preferred to call them—and its community. Under his guidance, H. B. Fuller enacted ground-breaking medical and retirement programs and parental-leave policies and contributed 5 percent of before-tax profits to local charities.

As a state senator (from 1949 to 1958), Andersen worked hard to pass the Fair Employment Practices Act, which made Minnesota the nation's fifth state to outlaw racial and religious discrimination in the workplace. As governor, he signed a companion bill banning discrimination in housing sales and rentals.

A self-described "searcher," Andersen made his greatest contributions to the people of Minnesota in the four decades after he left public office. He served on the University of Minnesota's Board of Regents, played a key role in the creation of the university's Landscape Arboretum, and in 1999 gave the university his eclectic collection of 12,500 rare books. One of his proudest achievements came in 1975, when, after considerable lobbying on his part, the U.S. Congress passed legislation establishing Voyageurs National Park. "There is no end to things that need doing by willing people," he wrote in his autobiography. "Selfless action is a great road to satisfaction."

> "As Robert Browning wrote, 'a man's reach should exceed his grasp, or what's a heaven for?' I am convinced that the reaching and grasping Browning refers to . . . have to do with wisdom, generosity, and love. The heaven he speaks of is not some afterlife destination. It is the here-and-now result of a life that is spent always striving for that which is good."
> Elmer L. Andersen, in *A Man's Reach*

5

Arrival of Major League Sports

Minnesota goes to The Show

The year that the Minnesota Twins and the Minnesota Vikings arrived in Minnesota, 1961, was a high point in the state's sports history. The previous year, the Minneapolis Lakers, the state's first professional basketball team, had pulled on their high-tops and headed for Los Angeles. The arrival of North Stars hockey and Muskies basketball would not happen until 1967, the year the Metropolitan Sports Center was built just north of Met Stadium in Bloomington. The events of 1961 gave Minnesota sports fans new opportunities to experience the thrill of victory and the agony of . . . well, we'll let nominator Gary Miller of St. Paul take it from here: "Like the Minnesota politicians who arrived on the national scene that decade, the 1960s Vikings and Twins helped cement our national profile. Both the presidential campaigns of the '60s and the Twins and Vikings games of the same decade forged the image of Minnesota as a place somewhere in flyover land that fielded earnest combatants battling rivals from the coasts through snowstorms, tornados, and mosquitoes. Like Humphrey, Mondale, and McCarthy, the Vikings and Twins of the 1960s showed that honesty, forthrightness, and work ethic were just enough to secure a second-place finish, whether they found their adversaries on the gridiron, on the diamond, or in the voting booth.

"The arrival of major league sports changed Minnesota in a number of other ways: it forged unbreakable bonds among its citizens.

It crystallized our budding rivalry with Wisconsin. It created our first professional sports stadiums, leading to the demolition of Memorial Stadium and an endless string of stadium debates. And it launched the modern sports media in Minnesota, complete with beefed-up newspaper sections, well-read opinion columns, talk shows, memorabilia, and, most of all, Sid Hartman.

"Even though the days of the hardy, gloveless Purple People Eaters prowling the heaterless Met Stadium sidelines are gone, the harsh lessons continue. We have seen that even the most vaunted, high-flying juggernauts will inevitably sputter and die like a car engine struggling to turn over in minus-fifty-degree windchill in January. Yet each year we venture forth struggling against our fate, and each year we end up huddled in a snowbank of gridiron defeat, like Per Hansa in Rølvaag's *Giants in the Earth,* waiting for the inevitable."

Minnesota Vikings head coach Bud Grant (above) and quarterback Fran Tarkenton (far left)

Atmosphere

Minnesota gets a whole new reputation

Producer Ant, Anthony Davis (at left), and rapper Slug, Sean Daley, of Atmosphere

Sean Daley grew up in south Minneapolis, a quiet, unusually articulate kid who used to practice his dance moves in his backyard. When Sean was eleven, his dad convinced him to enter a break-dancing competition. "Here's a kid who didn't want to be in the public eye at all," remembers his dad. "He didn't do that well, but he liked it. From then on, some of his introvertedness dissipated."

Boy, did it ever. Today, Sean Daley is known to his fans as Slug, front man for the hot hip-hop group Atmosphere. Recording on the local Rhymesayers label, Atmosphere has released a slew of CDs and made several national tours, all the while building a loyal fan base drawn to the group's charismatic leader and his soulful, intensely personal lyrics. Rhymesayers and Atmosphere have been instrumental in positioning Minnesota as underground hip-hop central. Minnesota? Cold, snow-white Minnesota? "It's not one of the first places you think of in hip- hop," says Seth Riddle, a talent scout for Rough Trade Records. "But Rhymesayers has definitely established it on the map."

Slug and Atmosphere produce what's becoming known in their industry as "conscious hip-hop." They focus on social issues—the economy, aversion to violence,

religion. Slug's music is often introspective and grounded in his own experiences as well. He once ended a concert by thanking his audience for "letting me deal with my personal shit in public. Those of you that know me know this is something I do all the time."

For many fans, including nominator Ben Heinemann, Atmosphere's music is also appealing because the band has stayed close to its roots, sticking with the local Rhymesayers label and writing songs steeped in Minnesota culture. "Atmosphere is using hip-hop as a tool for inspiration that we as Minnesotans should be very proud of," writes Heinemann. "'Shhh' pretty much says that Slug will always remember where he is from and how that has shaped his life and his music."

> "So, if the people laugh and giggle when you tell 'em where you live
> Say 'Shhh!' Say 'Shhh!'
> And, if you know this is where you wanna raise your kids
> Say 'Shhh!' Say 'Shhh!'
> If you're from the Midwest, and it doesn't matter where
> Say 'Shhh!' Say 'Shhh!'
> If you can drink tap water and breathe the air
> Say 'Shhh!' Say 'Shhh!'"
>
> "Shhh," from the album *Seven's Travels*

Ann Bancroft (1955–)

The first woman to cross the ice to the North and South Poles

In 1986, Ann Bancroft drove a dogsled 1,000 miles from the Northwest Territories in Canada to the North Pole. As the only female member of the Steger International Polar Expedition, she became the first known woman to cross the ice to the North Pole.

In 1992, she led the first American women's east-to-west crossing of Greenland.

In 1992–1993, she led the American Women's Expedition to the South Pole, a 67-day trek of 660 miles on skis by four women. It was the first all-women expedition to cross the ice to the South Pole, and Bancroft became the first woman to cross the ice to both the North and South Poles.

In 2001, she and Norwegian explorer Liv Arnesen became the first women in history to ski and sail across Antarctica's landmass— a 94-day, 1,717-mile trek.

These accomplishments are testament to Bancroft's tenacity, courage, and sheer physical abilities. But they also testify to the fact that one woman can change perceptions of what women can accomplish. Through web-based programs, young women worldwide have been able to follow Bancroft on her expeditions. "My motivation often comes from the students that follow the adventure," Bancroft writes. "On my last expedition to Antarctica, thoughts of kids all over the nation following us inspired me on tough days to stay at it."

Ann Bancroft on the Antarctica land mass in January 2001

Margaret Culkin Banning (1891–1982)

A Minnesota author stays close to her roots

She published her first book in 1920 and her last nearly sixty years later. She wrote 30 books and more than 400 essays and short stories, raised four children (for many years as a single mother), was a delegate to one Republican National Convention and an alternate to another, and was a sought-after speaker on women's rights and other social issues. She was a member of the British Information Service during World War II and worked in refugee and displaced persons camps in Austria and Germany after the war. So why, unlike her near contemporaries F. Scott Fitzgerald and Sinclair Lewis, is Margaret Culkin Banning not better known today?

"Minnesota has always been my home base as well as my birthplace," wrote Banning in 1960. "Native Minnesotans often refer to themselves as Minnesota Gophers, and I am one of that band." Banning moved away from Minnesota at intervals during her life—to attend Vassar College, from which she graduated in 1912; to live in England with her first husband; to attend to duties during World War II. But she always returned home, writing books steeped in the local color she had observed closely since childhood. "It would be easy to conclude that forgotten novelists are the

real regionalists (and that regionalism is a polite term for failure or provincialism)," writes historian Karal Ann Marling. But that's hardly the case with Banning. She was a best-selling author whose work is ripe for rediscovery.

"The machinery of the Club begins to move. The first motor rolls up for the hour is almost seven thirty and the dinner is to be served at a quarter before eight. Comments fill the air, little cries of admiration, questions. The first powder is spilled on the glass covered dressing tables in the ladies' retiring room. There seeps through the smoking room the odor of the first cigarette. . . . Everyone is here, the ones who are confident of place in the social hierarchy as well as those who are not. It is strangely at once the field for the exercise of snobbery and a rather fair tryout for those who are socially on the make." From *Country Club People*, a novel by Margaret Culkin Banning

John Beargrease (1858–1910)

Neither snow, nor rain, nor sleet, nor a balky sled dog team

Since 1980, the John Beargrease Sled Dog Marathon has attracted competitors and racers from the United States and around the world. Beginning in Duluth and running 400 miles along the north shore of Lake Superior to the Canadian border, the Beargrease is one of the longest, most grueling race routes outside Alaska.

> **"Day or night or good weather or bad made no difference with John Beargrease; he was sure to arrive some time with the mail intact. When he reached his journey's end with his faithful dog team, they would all rest up for a short while and start the return trip, regardless of the weather. Nature's wild wintry blasts had no terrors for faithful John."**
> Willis H. Raff, *Pioneers in the Wilderness*

The race takes its name from an Ojibwe mail carrier named John Beargrease, who was born in 1858 and grew up in a wigwam on the edge of Beaver Bay, the first white settlement on the North Shore. John was the son of Moquabimetem, who also went by the name "Beargrease," a leader who settled in the area with a small group of Ojibwe to work at Beaver Bay's sawmill.

The U.S. Congress ordered the beginning of mail service from Superior to Grand Portage in 1855, but service was spotty—if the lake was choppy in summer or icy in winter, the mail didn't make it through. The Beargrease family came to the rescue—first the father and then the sons picked up the job. John Beargrease and his brothers began covering a regular route between Two Harbors and Grand Marais in 1879. Occasionally, they'd make the trek all the way to Grand Portage. They completed their route at least once and sometimes twice a week, with a load of up to 700 pounds of personal mail, packages, and newspapers. In the summer, they hiked along the shore, sailed, or rowed a boat. In the winter, they made the trek by dogsled.

John Beargrease's team of four dogs could cover thirty to forty miles a day. When the bells were heard in the distance, people gathered, not only to receive long-awaited news of friends and relatives but also for reports of ice conditions, snow depths, and other vital information. For decades, until his death from tuberculosis in 1910, John Beargrease was the link to the outside world for the citizens of the North Shore.

Charles Albert Bender (1884–1954)

The first Minnesotan elected to the National Baseball Hall of Fame, 1953

The slider: it's one of the most effective tools in a pitcher's arsenal. A curveball with extra speed, it can throw off a batter's timing. Because it requires some nuanced wrist action, though, a slider can cause real wear and tear on a pitcher's forearm. Use it judiciously, and you can save a game. Use it too often, and you'd better grab an extra ice pack.

The National Baseball Hall of Fame credits Charles Albert Bender with inventing the slider. Like his patented pitch, Bender's life course was a circuitous one. He was born on the White Earth Reservation in northern Minnesota, one of at least eleven children in his family. At age seven, he left home to attend boarding school in Pennsylvania. At thirteen, he enrolled in Carlisle Indian School, where he was a member of his school's track, basketball, football, and baseball teams.

After graduating from Carlisle in 1902, Bender began pitching for the Harrisburg, Pennsylvania, semiprofessional team. Later that year, the legendary Connie Mack, who was then leading the Philadelphia Athletics, signed Bender to an $1,800 contract, and by the end of his rookie year he had won seventeen games. Throughout his major league career, which included 212 wins, his greatest strength was his consistent performance, especially under pressure. "If I had all the men I've ever handled and they were in their prime and there was one game I wanted to win above all others," Connie Mack once said, "Albert would be my man."

Bender's grace under pressure extended beyond his steady performance on the pitching mound. Though proud of his Ojibwe heritage, he was never fond of his nickname, "Chief," and endured hackneyed war cries from fans as he took the mound during games. After his shutout in the 1905 World Series brought him to national attention, he quietly stated his case to the press: "I do not want my name presented to the public as an Indian," he said, "but as a pitcher."

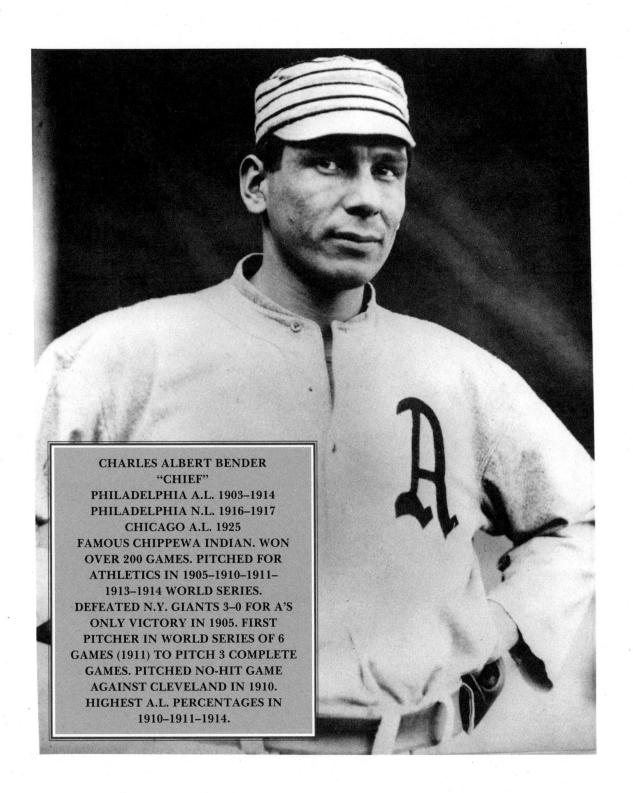

CHARLES ALBERT BENDER
"CHIEF"
PHILADELPHIA A.L. 1903–1914
PHILADELPHIA N.L. 1916–1917
CHICAGO A.L. 1925
FAMOUS CHIPPEWA INDIAN. WON
OVER 200 GAMES. PITCHED FOR
ATHLETICS IN 1905–1910–1911–
1913–1914 WORLD SERIES.
DEFEATED N.Y. GIANTS 3–0 FOR A'S
ONLY VICTORY IN 1905. FIRST
PITCHER IN WORLD SERIES OF 6
GAMES (1911) TO PITCH 3 COMPLETE
GAMES. PITCHED NO-HIT GAME
AGAINST CLEVELAND IN 1910.
HIGHEST A.L. PERCENTAGES IN
1910–1911–1914.

Patty Berg (1918–2006)

Paving the way for female athletes

Born in Minneapolis in 1918, Patricia Jane Berg started out fast and never slowed down. An all-around athlete, she took up golf after her parents persuaded her to give up the quarterback position for her

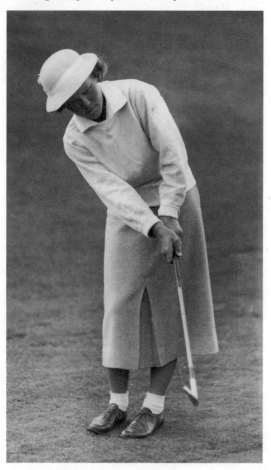

neighborhood football team, the 50th Street Tigers. At age sixteen, she won the Minneapolis City Championship. She won twenty-eight more golf titles before turning pro in 1940.

In 1948, Berg became a founding member and the first president of the Ladies' Professional Golf Association. She then entered her professional prime, winning fifty-seven tournaments on the LPGA tour and, in 1959, became the first woman to hit a hole-in-one in a U.S. Golf Association competition.

Berg battled back from setbacks throughout her life—a 1941 car accident that sidelined her for eighteen months, a bout with cancer, and hip and back surgeries. Through it all, she continued to rack up victories, conduct clinics, and live up to her nickname, "Dynamite." "If I could do it all over again, I'd do it the same way," she once said of her career.

The University of Minnesota established the Berg Scholarship Fund in 1976, which helps cover tuition, textbook fees, and room and board for female student-athletes. The LPGA established the Patty Berg Award in 1978 to recognize people who embody Berg's "diplomacy, sportsmanship, goodwill and contributions to the game of golf."

Harriet Bishop (1817–1883)

Minnesota's first schoolteacher

On Harriet Island, a small spot on the Mississippi River just across from downtown St. Paul, there is a paddleboat-shaped play area sheltered by a replica of the city's first schoolhouse. It's a lovely setting and a fitting tribute to the island's namesake, Harriet Bishop. As the city's first schoolteacher, Bishop dedicated her life to transforming the rugged outpost she first encountered into a thriving, civilized town.

Bishop moved from Vermont to St. Paul in 1847, fresh from her training with Catharine Beecher, a reformer (and sister of Harriet Beecher Stowe) who believed that women needed to be well educated in order to devote themselves to the moral development and education of their children and to their homes. As part of Beecher's program to train women to help educate and civilize frontier children, Bishop answered a call from Minnesota missionary Thomas S. Williamson. In addition to founding a school (her first schoolhouse was a former blacksmith's shop), she became involved in all sorts of other "firsts," including the First Baptist Church, the Baptist Sewing Society, the Territorial Temperance Society, the Ladies Christian Union, and the Minnesota Woman Suffrage Association. She pioneered St. Paul's first Protestant Sunday school and acted as the first state organizer of the Woman's Christian Temperance Union. Throughout her endeavors, Bishop "sought to enhance the stability and morality of Minnesota, establish a society of like-minded individuals, and improve the lot of Christian women like herself," according to Katie McKee and Judith Hentges, who portray Harriet Bishop through the Minnesota Historical Society's "History Players" program. She wrote two books that outlined her philosophies while encouraging others to join her in her adopted home. "If earth has a paradise," wrote Harriet Bishop of St. Paul, "it is here."

Harriet Bishop *paddlewheel boat, St. Paul*

15

Charles K. Blandin (1872–1958)

A commitment to rural Minnesota

BLANDIN FOUNDATION

Charles Blandin was twelve years old when he took his first part-time job, at a weekly newspaper. He went on to a career in publishing, including management of the St. Paul Pioneer Press/Dispatch Printing Company. In 1916, the *Dispatch*'s owner bought the Itasca Printing Company in Grand Rapids, Minnesota. After his death, his widow offered Blandin half the company stock and a chance to manage both the printing company and the paper mill. Blandin took her up on her offer. But when newsprint production became unprofitable, he pioneered the manufacture of high-quality coated paper instead. In 1927, Blandin sold the *Pioneer Press/Dispatch* but kept the paper mill. Two years later, it became the Blandin Paper Company.

Over the years, Charles Blandin became increasingly attached to the Grand Rapids community. In 1941, he established the Blandin Foundation to aid in the economic development of his adopted hometown and the surrounding area. He stipulated that the foundation change with the times as it supported projects leading to the "betterment of mankind." When Blandin died in 1958, his foundation had assets of approximately $1 million.

The Blandin Paper Company was sold in 1977; as a result, the Blandin Foundation's assets increased and it became an entity separate from the paper company. By 1982, the foundation's assets had grown to $100 million; today, its trust is worth more than $300 million. The foundation's support of Minnesota's communities is wide-ranging: recent initiatives include Get Broadband, dedicated to increasing the use of broadband-based technologies; Vital Forests/Vital Communities, which promotes the connections among forest-based economies, forest ecosystems, and healthy communities; and Invest Early, which supplements early education programs for at-risk children in Itasca County. Through each of these projects and many more, Charles Blandin's dream of better lives for rural Minnesotans is being realized.

George Thompson (left) and Charles K. Blandin, 1915

Norman Borlaug (1914–)

A lifelong commitment to ending starvation

Have you ever had one of those "what if" moments, when a seemingly insignificant decision on your part led to profound change in your life and the lives of those around you? For Norman Borlaug, an Iowa farm boy who enrolled at the University of Minnesota in 1933, that moment occurred when he decided to attend a lecture titled "These Shifty Little Enemies That Destroy Our Food Crops." A forestry major, Borlaug shifted his studies to plant pathology, receiving a PhD in the field from the university in 1942.

Borlaug's change in focus changed the fates of millions of hungry people throughout the world, leading to his oft-repeated designation as "the father of the green revolution." He and his colleagues introduced three key innovations—wheat varieties resistant to rust, a destructive pest; dwarf wheat varieties that didn't fall over, even when fertilized to achieve maximum yields; and a technique called "shuttle breeding," which allowed a region's farmers to grow two successive plantings in a single year. What does all this mean in practical terms? From 1950 to 1992, a 150 percent increase in the world's grain output. Borlaug first proved his theories in Mexico, but it was his work in India, where the wheat yield nearly doubled from 1965 to 1970, and in Pakistan, which was self-sufficient in wheat production by 1968, that led to his winning the Nobel Peace Prize in 1970.

Scientific advances are one thing. Convincing others to embrace them is another. As Borlaug once put it, "You can't eat potential." He was—and remains—tireless in his efforts to change the thinking of decision makers throughout the world. "Behind the outstanding results in the sphere of wheat research of which the dry statistics speak, we sense the presence of a dynamic, indomitable, and refreshingly unconventional research," said Mrs. Aase Lionaes, chair of the Nobel Committee, in her 1970 presentation speech. "Dr. Borlaug is not only a man of ideals but essentially a man of action. Reading his publications on the green revolution, one realizes that he is fighting not only weeds and rust fungus but just as much the deadly procrastination of the bureaucrats and the red tape that thwart quick action. The following warning reminds us of this: 'a strangulation of the world by exploding, well-camouflaged bureaucracies is one of the great threats to mankind.'"

> Borlaug's ties to Minnesota run deep—he was a varsity wrestler for the University of Minnesota and met his future wife in a Dinkytown coffee shop where they both worked. Borlaug Hall, the largest building on the university's St. Paul campus, is named for him, and, in 2006, Minnesota governor Tim Pawlenty declared September 16 Norman Borlaug Day in Minnesota.

Boundary Waters Canoe Area

A long fight to preserve the wilderness

On July 8, 1977, ecologist and author Sigurd Olson addressed a crowd of 1,000 people that was gathered at Ely High School to participate in a congressional hearing. Shouting over boos and catcalls, with an effigy of himself swinging from a nearby post, Olson defended a bill sponsored by Congressman Donald M. Fraser that would become the Boundary Waters Canoe Area Wilderness Act of 1978. "This is the most beautiful lake country on the continent," Olson said. "We can afford to cherish and protect it. Some places should be preserved from development or exploitation for they satisfy a human need for solace, belonging, and perspective."

That's the Boundary Waters for you: on the one hand, a place of unmatched beauty that inspires odes to peace and solitude, and, on the other hand, arguably the state's most controversial piece of land. This million-acre wilderness area within the Superior National Forest in northern Minnesota became the subject of broad public debate in the 1920s, when environmentalist Ernest C. Oberholtzer mounted a successful opposition to logging companies seeking to build dams in the region. Henrik Shipstead, U.S. senator from Minnesota, sponsored the Shipstead-Newton-Nolan Act in 1930, which was an early statute ordering that the land be retained as wilderness. In 1949, airspace over the area was restricted. The push-and-pull between preservationists and industrialists continued until President Lyndon Johnson signed the Wilderness Act of 1964. Sponsored by Senator Hubert H. Humphrey, the act designated the BWCA as a place where vehicles were not allowed, where no permanent structures could be built, and where wildlife would be kept in as primitive a setting as possible.

If the second chapter in the story of the BWCA was the signing of the BWCA Wilderness Act, then the third was the signing of the Boundary Waters Canoe Area Act fourteen years later. The third act banned logging, mineral prospecting, and mining; all but banned snowmobile use; limited motorboat

Keep the BWCA open to Everyone

Support the
Boundary Waters Conservation Alliance
Our goal . . .

1. to preserve a 700,000 acre wilderness area in Northern Minnesota for the wilderness experience . . . for those who want to canoe, hike, backpack, and cross country ski.

3. to keep open 400,000 acres of lakes and forests for family camping, where a fisherman can take his boat and motor, where snowmobiles can venture.

2. to keep the forests healthy by fighting forest fires, insects, and disease.

4. to prevent additional government take-over of private property.

You can help!
Support Congressman Oberstar's efforts to keep the BWCA open to everyone.

Contribute to the
Boundary Waters Conservation Alliance
222 Phoenix Building
Duluth, Minnesota 55802

use; and officially changed the name of the region to the Boundary Waters Canoe Area Wilderness. It also provided stipends for resort owners and outfitters who stood to lose customers due to stricter regulations.

But the third chapter in the story of the BWCA is still being written. Canoeists and motorboat owners, cross-country skiers, and snowmobilers continue to debate the region's best use. In the mid-1990s, mediators helped reach a compromise on whether trucks could be used to carry boats across portages between motorized lakes. As outfitter Bill Hansen put it in 2003, "Full wilderness status for the Boundary Waters is a very open goal. Having that happen the next year? Probably not. You know, next decade? Probably not. In our lifetimes? Probably not. But, eventually."

The poster (opposite left) highlights the tension between preservation and use that has surrounded the Boundary Waters Canoe Area. (Left) Wilderness advocate Ernest Oberholtzer (front of canoe) and friend Pinay, Big Turtle trip, 1995; (top right) portaging near Hungry Jack Lake, BWCAW, 2006

Fanny Brin (1884–1961)

A commitment to worldwide peace

I n 1963, the Minneapolis section of the National Council of Jewish Women began furnishing a "Fanny Brin Room" in Jerusalem's Hebrew University High School. How did it happen that a group of women from Minnesota dedicated themselves to this project? And who was Fanny Brin?

Fanny Xeriffa Fligelman was born in 1884 in Romania. When she was three months old, her family immigrated to the United States, settling in a Romanian Jewish neighborhood in Minneapolis. After graduating from Minneapolis South High School and the University of Minnesota, Fanny embarked on a high school teaching career.

After her 1913 marriage to Arthur Brin, Fanny never again held a paying job. She devoted her life to her family and to the service of others. She was involved in woman suffrage, German-Jewish relief efforts, and aid to new immigrants, but her greatest contributions were in the advancement of world peace. Like many of her contemporaries, Brin believed that women's organizations could and should be a force for change. "Women can do a great deal to arouse the people to the gravity, the magnitude, and the urgency" of important causes, Brin said in 1941, in an address to the National Council of Jewish Women (an organization for which she served as president from 1932 to 1938). Over the course of her life, Brin used her involvement in women's organizations, combined with her gifts as a public speaker and as a motivator of others, to further her cause, even in the darkest days of World War II.

The highlight of Fanny Brin's career as a peace activist came in March 1945 when she was appointed as a delegate to the United Nations Conference in San Francisco. Present at the signing of the UN Charter on June 26, 1945, Brin saw that her life's work, along with others' efforts, had made a difference. She had delivered speeches worldwide, had made radio addresses and written countless editorials, had spoken out against war, and had supported the Zionist movement. Still, she knew that, although the creation of the United Nations was a milestone, it was but a single step in a struggle that would continue long after she was gone. "We face a great task," she once said. "It is a long-term task. One which neither we nor our children, nor our children's children will complete. In the words of the Talmudic sage, 'It is not incumbent upon us to finish the work; neither is it permitted to us to desist from it.'"

Bryan v. Itasca County

Changing the stakes for Minnesota Indians

Nominator Kevin Washburn, associate professor of law at the University of Minnesota and an enrolled member of the Chickasaw Nation of Oklahoma, writes of a Minnesota legal battle that started small but ended up affecting American Indians nationwide: "In June 1972, an Indian named Russell Bryan received a tax bill from Itasca County for $147.95 for taxes levied on his mobile home on the Leech Lake Indian Reservation in northern Minnesota. Bryan refused to pay the tax, arguing that state tax and regulatory laws did not apply to an Indian living on an Indian reservation. When the county and state disagreed, Russell Bryan's legal aid attorneys took their case all the way to the U.S. Supreme Court. Following a remarkable argument by the late Bernard (Bernie) P. Becker, a University of Minnesota Law School alum and professor at William Mitchell College of Law, Russell Bryan's case prevailed, winning a unanimous Supreme Court decision authored by Justice William Brennan in 1976.

"The Bryan case became the cornerstone for the legal principle that states cannot regulate the activities of Indians and Indian tribes on Indian reservations without explicit authority from Congress. Soon, high-stakes bingo operations began to spring up on Indian reservations in Minnesota and across the country, from Florida to California. In 1988, Congress enacted the Indian Gaming Regulatory Act, intended to give states a modest role in Indian gaming by requiring tribes to negotiate compacts with states before conducting gaming. Minnesota was the first state to sign tribal-state compacts with tribes.

"Since then, Indian gaming has lifted many Indian communities from poverty. And even on reservations where poverty is still common, revenue from gaming has alleviated some of the worst of the suffering. Said one Indian leader: 'We had tried poverty for 200 years. We decided to try something different.'

"Indian gaming revenues nationwide now exceed $20 billion a year. The legal authority for the whole industry was established by one stubborn Minnesota Indian who challenged an illegal county tax assessment of $147.95 on his mobile home."

Paul Bunyan

Minnesota's biggest booster

Forget what you've heard about the glaciers. Minnesota's lakes were formed when Paul Bunyan and Babe, the blue ox, stomped across the region. The Grand Canyon? Same story. The Black Hills? Ditto.

Paul Bunyan's exact origins remain a mystery. Did he start out as "Jean Bonjean," hero of stories told by French Canadian lumbermen? Was he originally Paul Bunyon, supersized hero of the Papineau Rebellion of 1837, in which French Canadians revolted against their English queen? Or was he the invention of James McGillivray, who in 1910 wrote a story for a Detroit newspaper about a heroic lumberjack?

Ever since 1914, when William Laughead wrote and illustrated the first in a series of Paul Bunyan advertising pamphlets for Minneapolis's Red River Lumber Company, Minnesotans have embraced Paul and his cohorts. Laughead reported that he based some of his stories on tales he had heard in a Bemidji lumber camp; others were based on his own experiences, no doubt greatly exaggerated. Laughead's first two pamphlets were reasonably successful, but his third, published in 1922, was a hit at home and abroad.

In 1937, a giant statue of Paul was built in Bemidji. Soon after, Paul loomed large near Brainerd. A twenty-five-foot Paul bends down to greet visitors in Akeley. His sweetheart, Lucette, stands tall in Hackensack, where a copy of the pair's marriage license is displayed in the Chamber of Commerce office. Paul's anchor is in Ortonville, his rifle is in Blackduck, and he is buried in Kelliher. Whatever his origins may be, one thing is clear—Paul Bunyan may not have been born in Minnesota, but he certainly found a warm welcome here.

(Top) Postcard illustrated by Ray Bang, 1939; (bottom) statue of Paul Bunyan bowling in Brainerd

Burma-Shave Road Signs

A revolution in American advertising

The year was 1925. Clinton Odell and his sons, Allan and Leonard, had a problem. Their company, Burma-Vita, had just perfected the formula for a shaving cream that could be applied without a brush. Known as Burma-Shave, it was a great product—but no one was buying it.

Then Allan had a brainstorm. Inspired by a series of gas station signs he had seen in Illinois, Allan suggested that successions of road signs carry Burma-Shave jingles. Clinton put up $200 for reclaimed lumber; Allan and Leonard painted the first signs, which went up between Minneapolis and Albert Lea and between St. Paul and Red Wing. While Allan negotiated with farmers to place signs on their land, Leonard dug the postholes. The signs were one hundred feet apart, for easy reading at thirty-five miles an hour.

Within a year, Burma-Shave sales had increased from next to nothing to $68,000. The signs spread first across the Midwest. Within ten years, more than 7,000 signs were distributed across the United States. By the early 1950s, when Burma-Shave sales peaked, there were some 35,000 signs lining the nation's highways.

The Eisenhower-era development of the interstate highway system—and the accompanying increase in speed limits—meant that by the early 1960s, Burma-Shave signs had been left in the dust. Some ended up in the hands of collectors; others were recycled as shelving in farm outbuildings. But they were never completely forgotten. They're an indelible part of the American cultural landscape.

> **Angels**
> **Who guard you**
> **When you drive**
> **Usually**
> **Retire at 65**
> **Burma Shave**

Center for Victims of Torture (established 1985)

Finding a safe harbor far from home

It all began with a conversation between Minnesota governor Rudy Perpich and his son, a student at Stanford Law School, who was active in Amnesty International. Rudy Jr. urged his father to use his position to address the world's human rights inequities. With characteristic zeal, Rudy Sr. got to work.

Governor Perpich assembled a team of local human rights advocates, which presented ten ideas for local action. First on the list was the establishment of the first treatment center for victims of torture in the United States. Intrigued by the idea, Perpich visited the Rehabilitation Center for Torture Victims in Copenhagen, Denmark. On his return, he appointed a task force to determine whether Minnesota could support such an organization.

Minnesota's Center for Victims of Torture was founded in May 1985 as an independent, nonprofit organization. Initially, the center was located at St. Paul Ramsey Medical Center, but many clients found the institutional setting intimidating. In 1987 it moved to a small house on the University of Minnesota campus, and in 1991 the center moved to a three-story house in Minneapolis overlooking the Mississippi River. In renovating the house, designers took the needs of torture victims into account. Comfortable furnishings, large windows, and soft, rounded corners combine to make settings inviting and nonthreatening. In 2003, the organization opened the St. Paul Healing Center in a residential neighborhood.

The Center for Victims of Torture provides medical and psychological services directly to torture survivors. Staff members also train others to work with torture survivors and refugees; they conduct research and publish their findings on the effects of torture; and they advocate for public policy changes in Minnesota and worldwide. In 2006, the American Psychological Association recognized the center for its five-year effort to provide mental health services to thousands of refugees fleeing civil unrest in Sierra Leone and Liberia.

CVT counseling hut, West Africa (top). Every year on June 26—the U.N. International Day in Support of Victims of Torture—messages of hope are planted along with trees at CVT (left). University of Minnesota professor Dr. Steven Miles commemorates June 26, 2007 (bottom)

Charter Schools
Changing public schools nationwide

Charter schools give parents, teachers, and others the chance to design a school to meet students' needs, without direct control of local school districts. Each of these new schools is granted a "charter" that defines goals and sets limits on how the school is run. Like any public school, a charter school must be open to all, is publicly funded, and involves no discrimination, no tuition, and no teaching of religion. Minnesota is the nation's leader in charter school education.

That's the big picture. But the real impact of the national movement that started in Minnesota is best seen up close, by looking at how a charter school can change a student's life. David Kraft had tried, with little success, to thrive at a number of Twin Cities public and private schools before he discovered St. Paul's Avalon School, sponsored by Hamline University. David struggles with the effects of Asperger's syndrome, an autism spectrum disorder that makes it difficult for him to stay organized and focused on meaningful work. He was the classic smart kid who couldn't succeed in a mainstream educational environment.

Avalon follows a college-preparation curriculum, with individualized learning plans and project-based lessons. Not only did David complete his high school requirements at Avalon, but in his senior year, he was a key member of the school's State Academic Decathlon team. A self-described "eclectic geek," David, along with his teammates, took the state championship in the small-school category (less than 650 students). With 120 students, Avalon was the only charter school that participated in the competition. "Avalon really gives us the liberty to do what we want and the responsibility to follow through on our education," said David's teammate Eowyn Ward.

Today, there are 1,000,000 students enrolled in 3,700 charter schools in 40 states and the District of Columbia. And within those schools are countless students, like David Kraft, who have found their way to academic success.

Twin Cities Academy, one of the many St. Paul charter schools

F. Melius Christiansen (1871–1955)

Minnesota's Lutherans find their voice

It is a simple, haunting hymn, the kind that seems to rise directly from the soul of the person singing it. The words are translated from a German hymnbook; the melody is a Silesian folk tune. It is called "Beautiful Savior," and it is the signature piece of the St. Olaf College Choir.

"Beautiful Savior" is one of many choral arrangements by F. Melius Christiansen, a Norwegian-born musician who studied in Leipzig, Germany, before moving to Northfield, Minnesota. His first job was as organist at Northfield's St. John's Lutheran Church, which was affiliated with St. Olaf College. In 1903, he was also hired to teach music and direct the band at the college. He soon reorganized the church choir, filling out the ranks with St. Olaf students and faculty. In 1912, before his choir made its first extended tour to Wisconsin, he renamed it the "St. Olaf Lutheran Choir."

Christiansen became a recognized pioneer in arranging and conducting a cappella choral music. Through his influence, Minnesota became the acknowledged home of the Lutheran choral tradition in America. He trained hundreds of choral conductors, who spread his influence nationwide, including his sons Olaf, who succeeded him as director of the St. Olaf Choir, and Paul, who directed the Concordia College Choir in Moorhead, Minnesota, from 1936 to 1986.

Today, "Beautiful Savior" is always the final song performed at the St. Olaf Choir's popular Christmas festivals. Audience members, including many former choir members, hum or sing along quietly with the choir. "At the end of each concert, as the applause dies away," writes Joel Hoekstra, St. Olaf class of 1992 and former choir member, "it wells up out of nowhere: a rich humming sound that settles over the hall like a velvet blanket."

The Cloquet/Moose Lake Fires of 1918

Within hours, a region's history is rewritten

On the afternoon of October 10, 1918, a farmer named Steve Koskela and his neighbor, John Sundstrom, were collecting wood near a railroad siding fifteen miles northwest of Cloquet, Minnesota. As a passenger train left the siding, Koskela and Sundstrom saw smoke rising. They soon discovered a fire, about twenty feet across, burning through dry grass and piles of wood near the siding. Though Koskela, his neighbors, and local railroad crews worked through the night and into the following day, they were unable to contain the fire.

By October 12, a series of devastating fires had swept through northern Minnesota. A convergence of conditions—a dry summer, a rapid drop in humidity, high winds, and a lack of firefighting equipment—led to the rapid progression of fires through the wooded areas surrounding Cloquet and the peat bogs to the south, particularly around Moose Lake. Towns and rural areas in southern St. Louis, Pine, and Carlton counties were struck, as well as areas in Aitkin, Itasca, Cass, Crow Wing, and Wadena counties. More than 1,500 square miles of land burned. Cloquet, Brookston, Moose Lake, Automba, Kettle River, and at least 30 other towns were destroyed. More than 450 people died as a result of the fires, and another 106 soon succumbed to the influenza epidemic sweeping the country. More than 11,000 people lost their homes, and 2,100 people were treated for injuries. Property loss was estimated at $73 million, including 4,089 houses, 6,366 barns, 41 school buildings, 54,083 chickens, and 4,295 animals.

Relief organizations, including the Minnesota Forest Fires Relief Commission and the Red Cross, aided 50,000 refugees over the next several years. Eventually homes were rebuilt, businesses were reopened, and new routines were established. In a 1930 speech, Anna Dickie Olesen, a politician who survived the Cloquet fire, said, "I never heard one person during that night of fire, or in the years of misery that followed, ever murmur or complain about this loss. They just went to it to try to start their work again." Olesen supported the fire victims in their lawsuits against the railroad and the federal government, which were ultimately successful with the passage of federal legislation in 1935.

This pocket watch (top) survived the 1918 Cloquet fire.

27

Confluence of Mississippi and Minnesota Rivers

A place like no other

At present-day Mendota, near the place where the Mississippi and Minnesota rivers cross, an archaeologist found a 9,000-year-old flint spear point. The five-inch weapon, used to hunt giant bison, was made from limestone quarried seventy miles away. Its presence near the rivers' confluence underscores the importance of the site for traders, for worshippers, and for travelers. Long before the U.S. government acquired land near the confluence and construction began on Fort Snelling, it

was a place of rare and enduring significance for the region's people. After the fort was established, the confluence continued to be a meeting place for diverse cultures, where Dakota and Ojibwe people, traders, and soldiers came together.

Nominator Aaron Novodvorsky of Minneapolis sees in this place the story of the Dakota people who were held as prisoners of war at Fort Snelling after the U.S.–Dakota War of 1862: "The confluence has been changed by

time and by people. Today it is barely noticed by the travelers in cars, planes, or boats, but the spirits of the people who look down upon it from Pilot Knob, the spirits of those who were buried face down and with eyes closed in the internment camp, the spirits of those who have drowned in the waters, still hold this place important, cherished, and sacred. The confluence of the Mississippi and Minnesota rivers helped to shape, to change Minnesota simply by being where and what it is. Elementally and physically, it exists here because of the geological changes in the bedrock in which the rivers lie and flow. Culturally, the confluence has been the backdrop for attempted extermination and major change throughout time."

(Opposite) Edward K. Thomas, Fort Snelling, ca. 1850;
(above) aerial view of Fort Snelling, 1962

Gratia Alta Countryman (1866–1953)

Creating a library for all

I n June 1922, the Minneapolis Public Library book wagon made its first trip from Minneapolis to Excelsior, a small village on Lake Minnetonka. Riding aboard the book wagon was Gratia Countryman, the library system's visionary director. Born in Hastings, Countryman moved to Minneapolis with her parents, her sister, and two adult relatives in 1884, when she enrolled at the University of Minnesota. She joined the Minneapolis Public Library staff in 1889, just after her graduation from the university. As she worked her way up through the ranks at the library, she led a successful campaign for legislative support of public libraries throughout Minnesota. By the time she was named the library's third director, in 1904, she had forged a reputation as an effective leader who worked tirelessly to expand the library's services. "How to reach the busy men and women, how to carry wholesome and enjoyable books to the far-away corners of the city, how to enlist the tired factory girls . . . these are some of the things which I conceive to be my duty for study, if I would help this public library to become what it is for," she wrote in her 1905 annual report.

Through Countryman's efforts, collections and reading rooms were carved out in Minneapolis fire halls, factories, and hospitals. She established an open-air reading area in Gateway Park at Hennepin and Nicollet and introduced the nation's first children's reading room at the main library. She also understood the importance of the library in the lives of immigrants. By 1914, the collection included books in twenty languages, and both the main library and the branches offered services for those who sought U.S. citizenship.

In 1934, Countryman was elected president of the American Library Association. It was the worst of times for the nation's libraries—Depression-era budgets were being slashed everywhere. With characteristic determination, though, Countryman enlisted her 200,000 library patrons in a campaign for county and state support that would become a national model. The following year, the *Minneapolis Journal* summed up her efforts: "Minneapolis loves and honors Gratia Countryman most because she traveled and tramped its streets in the early days to study the reading needs of each of its little outlying districts; because she has had thought for the bedbound, the povertybound, the trouble-bound, and has offered them her greatest solace, books; because she has believed and still believes that taking books to people who need them is her job; because she does that job with the sympathetic understanding which makes a book a benediction."

(Far left) Gratia Countryman helps a patron at the bookmobile, Minneapolis, 1920s; (top left) Countryman in 1917; (bottom right) Countryman at the Minneapolis Public Library, ca. 1945

Courage Center

One size doesn't fit all

Founded in 1928 as the Minnesota Society for Crippled Children and Adults (MiSCCA), Minneapolis-based Courage Center is a nonprofit rehabilitation and resource center. Courage Center has a legacy of improving independence and quality of life for people with disabilities. Its full continuum of care includes rehabilitation therapies, transitional rehabilitation, pain management, vocational and community-based services, and camping and sports and recreation programs for people of all ages and abilities.

Courage Center has a history as a national leader in advocating changes in public policies and private attitudes toward people with disabilities. In 1961, MiSCCA received a grant from the U.S. Office of Vocational Rehabilitation for the nation's first survey of architectural barriers. Three years earlier, Henry Haverstock Jr., a Minneapolis attorney and early patient of Sister Elizabeth Kenny, had outlined the necessity of such a survey in MiSCCA's newsletter: "It is simply amazing how many . . . public buildings are still being built with a long line of stairs leading up to them. . . . This is a form of discrimination which our committee intends to militate against, so all of our citizens are given easy access to public places."

(Top) Courage Center campers; (bottom) using an adaptive stovetop

Nominator Robert Schwanke, associate professor emeritus in the University of Minnesota's School of Public Health, directed the survey. He notes that one key change in public policy resulting from the survey occurred on June 27, 1963, when Minnesota governor Karl Rolvaag signed the first accessibility law in the United States. "We got the law amended and broadened in 1965," Schwanke writes, "and the project subsequently resulted in the incorporation of accessibility standards into the 1966 Minnesota building code, decades before the federal Americans with Disabilities Act was passed." And, in 1967, Southwest State University in Marshall, the first four-year college in the nation built without barriers, opened.

Seymour Cray (1925–1996)

The world's first supercomputer

Seymour Cray at the CDC 1604 in 1959

Young Seymour Cray had a problem. He had rigged up a Morse code device for post-bedtime communications between his bedroom and his sister's. But when the late-night clicking disturbed the rest of the household, Seymour's father told him to shut down his system. Some kids might have been daunted, but the budding inventor was spurred on to greater innovation. He converted his clickers to lights and kept right on chatting.

Born in Chippewa Falls, Wisconsin, in 1925, Cray earned a bachelor of science degree in electrical engineering from the University of Minnesota in 1950 and a master of science degree in applied mathematics a year later. After graduation, he joined Engineering Research Associates (ERA) in St. Paul, where he quickly became a whiz at developing digital computer technology.

In 1957, Cray and other ERA employees founded Control Data Corporation. While at CDC, he led the design of the world's first commercial supercomputer, the CDC 6600. He went on to design a string of computers that were known for their elegance and simplicity but most of all for the speed at which they responded to their users' needs. In 1972, he left CDC to found Cray Research in Minneapolis and Chippewa Falls, Wisconsin, which, by the late 1970s, was the world's leading maker of supercomputers.

The problem-solving talents that Cray displayed in his early years served him well throughout his life. Known as an idiosyncratic, quirky genius, he shunned meetings and preferred to work in solitude. His ability to avoid distractions was legendary. Once, when someone ordered a phone for him after noticing that he didn't have one, he was asked where he wanted it installed. "On a tree, outside my office," Cray answered with a smile.

Betty Crocker

A Minneapolis company invents an American icon

1936

1955

1965

1968

1972

1980

1986

1996

Despite rumors to the contrary, Betty Crocker was never a real person. She was cooked up by the folks at Washburn Crosby Company in Minneapolis (the forerunner to General Mills) as part of a promotional scheme.

In 1921, Washburn Crosby offered homemakers free flour-sack pincushions for completing a jigsaw puzzle. Successful entries flooded the mailroom, along with hundreds of questions about recipes and baking techniques. Advertising manager Sam Gale saw in these questions an opportunity to promote Washburn Crosby as a trusted friend of homemakers. But form-letter answers just wouldn't do—he needed an approachable expert to lend a personal touch to his correspondence.

And so along came Betty Crocker: a friendly, familiar first name attached to the surname of William G. Crocker, the company's recently retired director. Washburn Crosby employees were invited to submit sample signatures for Betty—and the winner is still in use today.

Betty found her voice in 1924, when daytime radio's first food service program hit the airwaves via WCCO, the "Gold Medal Station" of Washburn Crosby Company. An instant success, the "Betty Crocker Cooking School of the Air" soon became a network program, dispensing tasty recipes and up-to-the-minute advice for the next twenty-four years.

A name, a signature, and a voice. But how do you picture the person whose timely tips saved your last dinner party from disaster? In 1936, the first portrait of Betty Crocker was commissioned from Neysa McMein, a well-known artist whose work had appeared on the covers of *McCall's* and The *Saturday Evening Post*. McMein blended the features of several General Mills Home Service Department staffers into an image of culinary competence that was the official Betty Crocker for nearly twenty years.

Over the years, a succession of Betty Crockers followed. The eighth and most recent portrait was unveiled in 1996 to accompany the eighth edition of *Betty Crocker's Cookbook*. Her looks may have changed with the times— but where food preparation and nutrition are concerned, you can still trust Betty Crocker every time.

Dan Patch (1896–1916)

A pacing horse that never lost a race

Dan Patch advertisement, 1905

Sired by a champion pacer, Dan Patch was bred to be a racehorse. At first glance, though, his chances didn't look too good. He had long legs, knobby knees, and, worst of all, a sweet disposition—not considered an asset in the hypercompetitive world of harness racing. "I thought all he would be good for would be hauling a delivery wagon," said his first owner.

Luckily, a stable owner took an interest in the little charmer and began training him for a life on the track. After four years, he was ready—and once he started running, he never looked back. Dan Patch was a pacer, a horse that pulls his driver in a wagon in harness races. He lost only two heats in his career and never lost a final race. So fast that other owners eventually refused to race their horses against him, Dan Patch spent most of his career running against the clock.

By December 1902, when Minneapolis businessman Marion Savage bought him for $60,000 (about $1.2 million today), Dan Patch was famous in horse-racing circles. Savage's friends questioned his extravagance, but Savage had a plan for recouping his investment. Savage's company, International Stock Food, was a large operation that sold feeds and tonics to midwestern farmers and ranchers. Dan Patch was soon featured in the company's

advertisements, and within a year Savage's annual sales had risen from $1 million to $5 million.

Decades before images of sports figures began appearing on cereal boxes and in TV commercials, Dan Patch began "endorsing" everything from cigars to cars to washing machines. Under Savage's watchful eye, he was transformed from a racetrack wonder into a household name. Adding to his reputation was his continued high level of performance at exhibitions. On Saturday, September 8, 1906, Dan Patch made horse-racing history when he set a new world record by pacing a mile in one minute and fifty-five seconds. Savage changed the name of his farm in Savage, Minnesota, to the International 1:55 Stock Food Farm, and his horse's record stood until 1938. Dan Patch died on July 11, 1916. Marion Savage died just thirty hours later.

Danza Mexica Cuauhtemoc

Instilling pride through dance

Danza Mexica Cuauhtemoc (DMC) is one of several branches of a national community of people dedicated to the preservation and promotion of indigenous Mexican culture, ceremonies, dance, history, and traditions. It is the first Aztec dance group in Minnesota and the first traditional Aztec dance circle in the Midwest.

DMC is located on East Lake Street in the heart of Minneapolis's thriving Mexican American community. It holds gatherings throughout the Twin Cities and southern Minnesota that are free of charge and open to all, where children and adults can learn traditional dances; practice drumming, martial arts, and outdoor survival; and study culture and history. "DMC has brought the face of indigenous Mexico to the front of the Latino community," writes nominator Papalotl Almanza Lopez. "Its members have worked for over ten years to incorporate Latino youth in all of their movements. The DMC youth recently successfully helped in organizing the Honor the Youth Run to bring awareness to Native American youth suicide and have been bridging and facilitating cooperation between young people of different cultures.

"The work DMC does in the region is truly tireless and its members are committed to making all Latino youth proud of their ancestry and who they are."

Destruction of the Metropolitan Building (1961)

The wrecking ball strikes an architectural gem

Twin Cities Tear Down the Old to Make Room for the New," proclaimed the *Engineering News-Record* in 1962. The article was the ninth in a series about urban renewal efforts in American cities, from Los Angeles to Philadelphia to Jacksonville, all of which were rehabilitating aging neighborhoods. "The biggest thing, by far, going on," according to the *News-Record,* "is the 22-square block redevelopment Minneapolis has named—as did Pittsburgh name its famed redevelopment—Gateway Center. As was Pittsburgh's, this is a bold and progressive venture designed to reshape the image of downtown Minneapolis." When all was said and done, nearly 200 buildings—40 percent of Minneapolis's historic central business district—had been demolished. The area had fallen into disrepair, and the city's solution was to wipe the slate clean and start over.

The most notorious casualty of the city's "bold and progressive venture" was the Metropolitan Building, also known as the Northwest Guaranty Loan Building, a seventy-one-year-old red sandstone monument to Minneapolis's late-nineteenth-century building boom. "The most magnificent office building in the whole round world," according to the *Minneapolis Journal,* the twelve-story Metropolitan, located at Third Street and Second Avenue South, sported a marble entrance, glass floors, and a remarkable central court fashioned with elaborate iron grillwork. The Metropolitan Building had its boosters— a group of architects, historians, and others who did their best to spare it from demolition. But it was not to be. The building was considered beyond repair, and the renovation of historic buildings was not yet commonplace. The demolition was, according to architectural historian Larry Millett, "perhaps the most inexcusable act of civic vandalism in the history of Minneapolis."

Walter H. Deubener (1887–1980)

How would we get along without them?

Some things are so commonplace that we forget there are inventors behind them. In 1918, Walter and Lydia Deubener were operating a small grocery stand in the Kresge dime store in downtown St. Paul (where the World Trade Center is today). They were part of a new trend in grocery sales—the cash-and-carry method had begun to replace home delivery during World War I, due to a depleted workforce and rising prices. Ordinary brown bags were the norm, but for savvy retailers like the Deubeners, they just didn't hold up. "Many times a day I would notice that a customer's purchases were limited by her arms rather than by her pocketbook," Walter Deubener later told a *Scientific American* reporter.

Deubener tried various methods, including wrapping customers' purchases together with heavy string attached to a wooden handle or supplying customers with market baskets, but nothing worked.

"Month after month we wrestled with the problem," recalled Deubener.

Finally, genius struck. Deubener imagined his invention one night, and the next day he quickly made a paper prototype with cord

handles. He patented his invention in 1919. When it could carry fifty pounds of groceries without a hitch, Deubener knew he had struck gold. He and Lydia sold a million handled bags at five cents each in 1919 and more than ten million in 1927. They moved their booming business to Indianapolis in 1928.

Walter Deubener went on to invent other things, from the "Jingleloon" musical balloon to a wastepaper compactor. After selling their shopping bag business in the 1930s, he and Lydia became real estate developers and philanthropists. In 1937, they built Deep in the Pines, a vacation area for family and friends in northern Minnesota. In 1971, their family resort became Courage North, a camp operated by Courage Center to serve children and adults with physical disabilities and sensory impairments.

A handy solution (right). Promotional shots of Lydia Deubener, ca. 1921 (opposite)

Don Miguel (Howard H. Hathaway) (1924–2001)

An innovative teacher brings the world home to Minnesota

Don Miguel performs

If you are lucky, there's a teacher who has made a difference in your life—the art teacher who told you it was okay to color the sky green, the band teacher who smiled with encouragement as you and your friends massacred your school's fight song, the math teacher who finally helped you make sense of geometry. Nominator Dorie Hathaway of St. Paul tells us about her husband, a born teacher who touched thousands of lives: "If you are in your late forties or fifties and grew up in Minnesota, most likely your grade-school memories include Don Miguel. His classroom was a television program produced in the 1960s at KTCA/Channel 2. Through it, Don Miguel introduced Spanish and the Spanish-speaking world to over 150,000 students of Minnesota and the upper Midwest during times when most Minnesota citizens didn't do much traveling. Three days a week, a black-and-white television set—can you imagine figuring out how to teach colors on a black-and-white TV screen?—was rolled into school classrooms for Don Miguel's innovative show. In one year, approximately 30,000 fourth, fifth, and sixth graders were registered in the program. At that time, Don Miguel's student count was more than the entire enrollment of the University of Minnesota.

"Don Miguel's students are now in their late forties and fifties, but their early experience with Spanish is a vivid memory to many of them. Some remember Don Miguel visiting the Twins stadium to interview famous Spanish-speaking baseball players Tony Oliva and Camilo Pascual, or they remember the live animals he brought in to teach vocabulary. Childhood songs and greetings used in the TV classroom and the dialogues of the dolls, Paco and Maria, continue to be sung and repeated throughout our state."

Once his program went off the air, Howard Hathaway became supervisor of World Languages and Cultures Education for the St. Paul Public Schools. In his twenty years in that position, he received Minnesota's first grant for bilingual education, initiated the first English as a Second Language program in St. Paul schools, and, in 1986, started the state's first language immersion program at Adams Spanish Immersion School.

Ignatius Donnelly (1831–1901)

A brilliant malcontent leaves his mark on the world

Over the course of his long, colorful life, Ignatius Donnelly was known as the Sage of Nininger, the Prince of Cranks, and the Apostle of Discontent. And that's just for starters—at various times he assumed such roles as lieutenant governor (1859 to 1863), U.S. congressman (1863 to 1869), Populist Party vice presidential candidate (in 1900), and best-selling author. Possessed of a lively mind and a penchant for attracting controversy, Donnelly was one of Minnesota's first national celebrities—or instigators of causes célèbres, depending on your point of view.

Born in Philadelphia, Donnelly was admitted to the bar in 1852. Five years later, he moved to Minnesota, where he and several partners founded the community of Nininger City on the Mississippi River, seventeen miles south of St. Paul. Hoping to attract immigrants who shared his vision of cooperative living, Donnelly instead found himself deeply in debt after the country was swept into a depression in 1857.

His next step was to enter politics. He served as Minnesota's lieutenant governor from 1859 to 1863, was elected to the U.S. Congress as a Republican in 1863, and then served several terms in the Minnesota legislature between 1874 and 1898. As time went on, he found himself increasingly at odds with the political establishment. He became involved in the National Grange movement, which was then in its infancy, and was an organizer of the Minnesota Farmers' Alliance, which advocated the organization of farmers to ensure fair prices for their crops. The Populist Party, which grew out of the national Farmers' Alliance movement, nominated Donnelly as its vice presidential candidate in 1900. He ran unsuccessfully on a platform that called for, among other things, the abandonment of the gold standard, the abolition of national banks, a graduated income tax, and an eight-hour workday.

During his years on the national political scene, Donnelly was also well known as the author of a number of best-selling, if controversial, books. In *Atlantis: The Antediluvian World*, published in 1882, he advanced his theories that the lost city of Atlantis had existed and was the antecedent for all known ancient civilizations. Six years later, he published *The Great Cryptogram: Francis Bacon's Cipher in Shakespeare's Plays*, in which he wrote that the true author of some of the Bard's plays was actually Francis Bacon. In 1890, he published *Caesar's Column*, a futuristic science-fiction novel in which a workers' revolt results in the formation of a utopian society. Always one to look ahead and never content with the status quo, it is fitting that Ignatius Donnelly died on January 1, 1901, the first day of the twentieth century.

Duluth Lynchings (1920)

A pivotal moment in Minnesota race relations

On the evening of June 15, 1920, Isaac McGhie, Elmer Jackson, and Elias Clayton—three young African American men who had been accused of raping a white woman—were pulled from their jail cells in Duluth, Minnesota, and lynched by a mob of thousands of people. The United States was going through a time of violent racial conflicts in 1920, and discrimination was rampant against southern African Americans who migrated north seeking employment. The violence in Duluth was shocking, but it was hardly isolated. From 1889 to 1918, at least 219 people were lynched in northern states; during the "Red Summer" of 1919, 15 whites and 23 blacks were killed in Chicago riots alone.

> "This event is the most visible moment in Minnesota's unfortunate racist history. Maybe no better or worse than any other state, Minnesota nonetheless has a self-image as a progressive, open-minded place. While that is true, it is also true that Minnesota had one of the most active and virulent Ku Klux Klan chapters in the country and has a long and sad history of racism and anti-Semitism. Facing all of our history is a good thing for all of us and our future."
> Robert Garfinkle, St. Paul

The three men were "roustabouts," passing through Duluth with a traveling circus. A total of six circus workers were jailed for the alleged rape; after McGhie, Jackson, and Clayton were killed, Governor J. A. A. Burnquist ordered the Minnesota National Guard into Duluth to protect the three surviving prisoners. The streets of Duluth may have appeared calm, but not everyone felt safe. The city's small number of black residents locked themselves indoors, fearful of further violence.

The press covered the lynchings in great and often lurid detail. Some condemned the act— the *Minneapolis Journal* accused the lynch mob of putting "a stain on the name of Minnesota"— but others saw it as necessary. The *Ely Miner,* for example, wrote that "while the thing was wrong in principle, it was most effective."

Duluth district judge William Cant convened a grand jury two days after the lynchings. On August 8, nineteen men were indicted, eight of whom were tried. Three were convicted of riot-

TH HERALD

JUNE 16, 1920.

30 PAGES

THREE CENTS.

YNCHED IN DULUTH

**POLICE HEADQUARTERS
M LYNCHED THREE NEGROES
ERIOR OF BUILDING IS WRECK**

GRAND JURY IS CALLED
TO FIX RESPONSIBILITY
FOR HANGING OF MEN

**NEGROES ATTEMPTED
ASSAULT WHILE SHOW
WAS AT SOUTH BEND**

South Bend, Ind., June 16.—
Negroes employed by the same
circus as those who were lynched
in Duluth last night following an
attack on a white girl, attempted
to assault Helen Penrod of
South Bend when the show was
in this city June 7. The assail-
ants of the South Bend girl escaped, being hidden by com-
panions, the police said here today.

TROOPS SENT
TO DULUTH BY
THE GOVERNOR

**Acts in Response to Tele-
graphic Request by
Sheriff Magie.**

**Two Companies Arrive at
8 A. M. From Fort Snell-
ing Camp.**

**Accompanied by Adjt.-Gen.
Rhinow and Other
Officers.**

**Mob Seeking Vengeance for
Assault on Girl Accom-
plishes Its Aim.**

**Thousands Watch Exciting
Scenes From Early Eve-
ning Until Midnight.**

**Judges of District Court
Issue Order Calling for
Investigation.**

The lives of three human
beings were snuffed out, several
policemen injured and police
headquarters wrecked as the result of action by a mob which
sought vengeance for the assault
made on a West Duluth young
woman by negro employes of the
circus which exhibited here on
Monday evening. Thousands
filled Superior street near the
police station all evening, culminating in an attack on headquarters and seizing of the three negroes who were taken to the
corner of East First street and
Second avenue and there strung
up to an electric light pole.

EFFORTS OF PRIESTS,

TAKES THREE
POLICE STATION
M TO LIGHT POLE

, Tuesday Evening, Force Way
ts and Bars and Drag
Their Doom.

ing, and each served less than fifteen months of
their five-year sentences in prison. No one was
convicted of murder. Seven black circus workers
were indicted for rape. Five were acquitted and
two went to trial; one was sentenced to thirty
years in prison.

Horrified by the lynchings, many African
Americans left Duluth. From 1920 to 1930, the
city's already-small black population dropped by
16 percent. Those who stayed formed a local
branch of the National Association for the
Advancement of Colored People. Throughout
Minnesota, African Americans supported a state
antilynching bill. Nellie Francis, a St. Paul
activist, led the campaign. Signed into law on
April 21, 1921, the bill provided for the

removal of police officers who were found
negligent in protecting against lynchings and
stipulated that damages be paid to the
dependents of victims of lynchings. Despite
further efforts, a national antilynching bill was
never passed.

For years, the burial locations of McGhie,
Clayton, and Jackson were unknown. In 1991,
it was learned that their bodies lay in unmarked
graves at Duluth's Park Hill Cemetery. In a
ceremony later that year, the graves were
marked with granite headstones bearing
their names and the inscription "Deterred but
not defeated."

(Top left) Front page from The Duluth Herald *of June 16,
1920; (above) Clayton, Jackson, McGhie Memorial dedicated in
downtown Duluth, 2003.*

Bob Dylan (1941–)

"The Times They Are A-Changin'"

With his unconventional voice and hard-edged lyrics, Bob Dylan made a name for himself as a folksinger whose 1962 "Blowin' in the Wind" set a standard for protest songs. Born Robert Zimmerman, he grew up in Hibbing, Minnesota, and moved to Minneapolis in 1959 to attend the University of Minnesota. He attended few classes, spending most of his time listening to music and performing in coffeehouses. Zimmerman—soon known as Dylan—dropped out of the university after his freshman year and headed for New York City.

Within a few years, Dylan had released two albums and had a string of hits. But he soon resisted being a spokesperson for his generation, and his music reflected his ambivalence. His 1965 album *Bringing It All Back Home* departed from the sense of social concern that had marked his earlier work. Equally shocking to his fans was his movement away from the purely acoustic sound of most folksingers—an electric band backed half the songs on his new album.

Dylan's stubborn refusal to be pinned down—or even tracked down—continues. Now a best-selling memoirist with a Grammy and an Oscar, he still defies categorization. Even on the subject of his early influences, he's like quicksilver. "I'm North Dakota–Minnesota–Midwestern," he said in 1997. "I'm that color. I speak that way. I'm from someplace called the Iron Range." Yet, five years later, in a conversation with a *National Geographic* reporter, he said, "I never was a kid who could go home."

Bob Dylan contemplates, 1962

Ensilage Harvester (patented 1915 by Adolph Ronning)

Streamlining farm work

In many ways, Adolph Ronning was a typical Minnesota farm boy. One of nine children, he grew up on a farm near Boyd, in Lac qui Parle County, and graduated from Dawson High School in 1912. He took violin lessons in school, tinkered with his family's farm equipment, and used some of his free time to earn extra money.

But, unlike many rural teens, Ronning wasn't saving up for a set of wheels or a bus ticket to the big city. His earnings funded a patent application for his ensilage harvester, which he had started designing at age seven. He was nineteen years old when he and his brother Andrean filed the patent, and it was the first of dozens he was to receive throughout his life, all with the goal of making mechanical work easier and more efficient.

The ensilage harvester improved on standard practices for harvesting and storing crops. Its basic design, largely unmodified, is still used by agricultural implement companies worldwide. The Ronnings' machine cuts corn, grinds it into silage, and stores it in a side- or rear-drawn wagon as the field is harvested. When the wagon is full, it is detached from the harvester and pulled to a silo, where a mechanism propels the silage up and into the silo. Meanwhile, a second wagon is attached to the harvester so that the cutting and grinding can continue.

Ronning soon moved to Minneapolis, where he founded a company to make and sell ensilage harvesters and other machines, including a power road grader. In 1925, he sold his business to International American Harvester Company of Minneapolis. The following year, he sold some of his tractor patents to International Harvester, including one for what the company dubbed the "Farmall System of Horseless Farming." After that, he later recalled, "I had more time to myself." His inventiveness was seemingly boundless, and for a fifty-year period, beginning in 1913, Ronning had a continuous succession of patents pending. His brainstorms ranged from headlight dimmers to tractor-powered golf course mowers (sold to Toro Corporation) to a stick power control for army tanks.

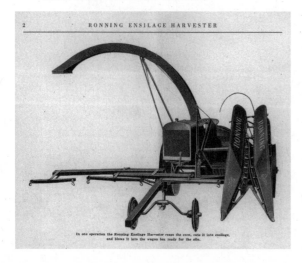

2   RONNING ENSILAGE HARVESTER

In one operation the Ronning Ensilage Harvester reaps the corn, cuts it into ensilage, and blows it into the wagon box ready for the silo.

Ethnic Presses

News from Home

There were many newspapers printed in the languages of the subscribers," writes nominator Marlene Wisuri of Duluth. "They kept immigrants informed of the news of the day and helped people maintain ethnic connections. I remember clearly my grandparents with their copies of *Minnesotan Uutiset,* published in New York Mills."

Chinese Press weekly newspaper, Minneapolis, 1925

When you're putting down roots in an unfamiliar place, a newspaper printed in your own language, filled with news about your old and your new homes, can be a lifeline. Countless ethnic newspapers have been published throughout Minnesota over the years, with new ones established each year. Most arise from communities with a strong common bond. Take

the *Minnesotan Uutiset* (Minnesota News), for example. By the 1890s, New York Mills was attracting large numbers of Finnish immigrants, who farmed in the summer and cut railroad ties and cordwood in the winter. Finnish-language newspapers were instrumental in drawing settlers to the area. Carl Parta and Adolph Lundquist, both experienced newspapermen, founded the *Uutiset,* which by the 1950s boasted the largest circulation of any Finnish American newspaper in the United States.

One of Minnesota's newest ethnic newspapers is *Hmong Today,* published in St. Paul since 2003. In an early issue the newspaper's publisher described its goals:

> "As we, the Hmong, move along to the next phase of our cultural awakening, it has become crucial that we find answers to the cultural ills that linger from our past.
>
> "At the same time, we are losing those cultural attributes that have uniquely kept us resilient, artistic and vibrant—those things that make us Hmong.
>
> "I envision *Hmong Today* to act as a forum for community growth . . . for visions to be transported to the next generation of Hmong who will, hopefully, take us all as a strong, united people, to the next phase."

Wilford H. Fawcett (1885–1940)

From Captain Billy to Captain Marvel

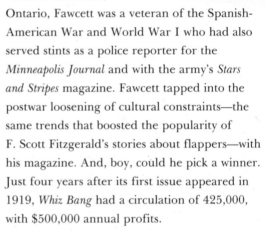

O
h, we've got trouble," sings slick salesman Harold Hill in *The Music Man,* Meredith Willson's 1962 musical, "right here in River City." Hill continues his shtick, designed to frighten River City's impressionable parents into buying into his proposal to outfit their sons with spendy band instruments and uniforms, by asking a series of shocking questions: "Is there a nicotine stain on [your son's] index finger? A dime novel hidden in the corn crib? Is he starting to memorize jokes from *Captain Billy's Whiz Bang*?"

It's that third question that causes the fair mothers of River City to swoon. *Captain Billy's Whiz Bang* was a bawdy joke magazine filled with double entendres and racy poems. And here's the truly shocking part—it was published by a company located not in some cesspool of a city on one of the coasts but right here in America's heartland—Robbinsdale, Minnesota.

"Captain Billy" was Wilford Hamilton Fawcett. Born in Brantford, Ontario, Fawcett was a veteran of the Spanish-American War and World War I who had also served stints as a police reporter for the *Minneapolis Journal* and with the army's *Stars and Stripes* magazine. Fawcett tapped into the postwar loosening of cultural constraints—the same trends that boosted the popularity of F. Scott Fitzgerald's stories about flappers—with his magazine. And, boy, could he pick a winner. Just four years after its first issue appeared in 1919, *Whiz Bang* had a circulation of 425,000, with $500,000 annual profits.

Fawcett Publications went on to a string of other successes in the magazine world, from *True Confessions* to *Mechanix Illustrated.* In the 1930s, its headquarters moved to New York City and Greenwich, Connecticut; after Wilford's death, in 1940, his sons continued to build the company. They introduced Captain Marvel through their Fawcett Comics, and they launched a hugely successful line of paperback originals, Gold Medal Books, featuring popular authors like Louis L'Amour, John D. MacDonald, and Mickey Spillane. But it was Captain Billy who started it all, and he's still feted each year during Robbinsdale's Whiz Bang Days.

Mr. and Mrs. Wilford Fawcett at their Breezy Point Resort near Brainerd, 1926

Finkelstein and Ruben

Hollywood comes to Minnesota

(Top) Moses L. Finkelstein with son Leonard, Isaac Ruben, and actor Gary Cooper at Paramount Picture Studio, 1929; (below) State Theater, 1938

Nominator Dave Kenney, author of the book *Twin Cities Picture Show: A Century of Moviegoing,* brought to light the story of two lesser-known Minnesotans who, on their way to making a buck, also transformed our view of the world:

"When Minnesotans went to the movies during the 1910s and 1920s, chances are they did so at a theater owned by Moses Finkelstein and Isaac Ruben. Finkelstein was a Lithuanian immigrant who arrived in St. Paul during the 1880s and quickly established himself as one of the city's most successful jewelers. Ruben, a native of upstate New York, was the owner of a small movie theater in Des Moines, Iowa. Aware that Finkelstein owned a prime piece of property in downtown St. Paul, Ruben proposed that they team up and build a motion picture house on the site. Finkelstein was hesitant at first, but he eventually agreed.

"In the summer of 1910, the two men opened the Princess, the finest movie theater in Minnesota. In the years that followed, Finkelstein and Ruben steadily expanded their holdings, assembling one of the largest regional theater chains in the United States. By the end of the 1920s, the two partners owned 120 theaters in 27 upper Midwest cities. The Finkelstein and Ruben circuit included three of the most magnificent picture palaces of the silent-movie era: the Capitol (later the Paramount) in St. Paul; and the State and the Minnesota (later Radio City) in Minneapolis.

"Finkelstein and Ruben introduced countless Minnesotans to a new form of entertainment that was stamping itself on the nation's collective consciousness. And because they ranked among the most powerful regional exhibitors in the country, they were able to make sure that Minnesotans—unlike the residents of other heartland states—saw all the same movies that audiences in New York, Chicago, and Los Angeles saw."

First Minnesota Volunteer Infantry Regiment

Ordinary men who made an extraordinary sacrifice

They were farmers, loggers, clerks, teachers, students, and lawyers. Many were fairly recent arrivals in Minnesota from eastern states. Some were born abroad. They were young—most were in their late teens to mid-twenties. What united them was their commitment to serving their country during the Civil War.

On April 13, 1861, the day after the fall of Fort Sumter signaled the Civil War's beginning, Minnesota governor Alexander Ramsey volunteered 1,000 men to defend the nation. Thus Minnesota, the Union's newest state, became the first to volunteer troops. When word of Ramsey's pledge reached eligible Minnesotans, they stepped forward. Their motivations were

varied, but many most likely felt their service would help preserve the Union. Minnesotans had voted overwhelmingly for Abraham Lincoln in the 1860 election, and although the issue of slavery was certainly on their minds, the possibility of southern states' secession was a more pressing concern. Minnesota sent eleven infantry regiments, four artillery batteries, a company of sharpshooters, and several cavalry companies to the war. It was one of the highest enlistment rates of any state.

The First Minnesota participated in many battles, including Bull Run, the Peninsula Campaign, Antietam, Fredericksburg, and Chancellorsville. But it was for its role at Gettysburg on July 2, 1863, that it is best remembered. On the second day of the battle, members of the First Minnesota were ordered to charge Confederate soldiers who were close to breaking Union lines. They marched down an open slope and plugged a gap to prevent Confederate troops from rushing through and breaking the Union line. Their commander, General Winfield Scott, later wrote: "I knew they must lose heavily and it caused me pain to give order for them to advance. . . . No soldiers, on any field, in this or any other country, ever displayed grander heroism." Nor was the battle over for the First. On the next day, the soldiers were called upon again, this time to stem

Pickett's Charge, thus playing a significant part in breaking the momentum of the Confederacy.

The Union forces went on to win at Gettysburg, and the battle changed the course of the Civil War. But for the First Minnesota, the outcome was grim. Out of the 289 soldiers in the First Minnesota at Gettysburg, 163 were killed or wounded on July 2; the next day, another 70 were added to the toll. Their casualty rate was 82 percent—the highest for any battle during the war. The remaining few went from Gettysburg to New York City, where they were posted to quell draft riots. During that time, a woman who had watched them leave Fort Snelling just two years before saw them march through Brooklyn. She sent a description of the scene to the *St. Paul Press*: "Their bronzed faces looked so composed and serious. There was a history written on every one of them. . . . The music of the band, as the men went through the changes of the drill, was very sweet, but it seemed to me all the while like a dirge for the fallen."

(Opposite left) First Minnesota Volunteers drum; (opposite top) 28th Virginia Regiment flag, captured by the First Minnesota Volunteers at Gettysburg; (bottom) Company D, First Minnesota Regiment, Minneapolis, 1861

F. Scott Fitzgerald (1896–1940)

Great American novelist

His story reads like a slightly maudlin short story—he was a writer of great and early promise who penned one of the best-known works of American literature. Yet, plagued by alcoholism and conflicted because of his strong devotion to his mentally unstable wife and with a penchant for high living that often landed him in the gossip pages, he was considered less than a serious writer. He died in relative obscurity, his novels by then poor sellers.

F. Scott Fitzgerald was born in St. Paul in 1896. His first short story was published when he was thirteen, while he was a student at St. Paul Academy. In 1918, while stationed in Alabama during a stint in the U.S. Army during World War I, he met Zelda Sayre. The

Fitzgeralds were married in 1920, the same year his first book, *This Side of Paradise,* was published to broad critical acclaim. The couple moved to New York City, where their highly publicized partying made them icons of the 1920s Jazz Age.

In addition to working on his novels, Fitzgerald continued to publish short stories in the *Saturday Evening Post*—throughout his life, in fact, it was the sale of his stories, many tales of young, free-thinking women who defined the term "flapper," that provided most of his income. He published *The Great Gatsby,* a tale of the complex interactions between middle-American values and East Coast urbanity, in 1924. Soon afterward, he and Zelda moved to

> "I came across F. Scott Fitzgerald's stories in the Anoka library when I was 14, and devoured them, fascinated that the man who wrote them was a Minnesotan, a Saint Paul boy, who had lived through our winters and summers, walked the same streets, watched the Mississippi flow by, and looked at the golden horses on the capitol dome. He was, and still is, a hero of mine." Garrison Keillor, in 1996, the centenary of Fitzgerald's birth

own in a 1936 essay, "The Crack Up": "I began to realize, that for two years my life had been drawing on resources that I did not possess, that I had been mortgaging myself physically and spiritually up to the hilt."

Hopelessly in debt, in poor health, and nearly estranged from his wife and their only child, a daughter named Scottie, F. Scott Fitzgerald moved to Hollywood where, in 1937, he won a contract to write for Metro-Goldwyn-Mayer. But his alcoholism continued to get the better of him, and he was frequently fired from studio jobs. He suffered a heart attack and died in 1940, at age forty-four, a failure in his own mind.

Europe, where living costs were lower. He continued to write, but his alcoholism, coupled with Zelda's increasing instability, caused problems. From 1930 on, Zelda lived in and out of institutions. Scott wrote about her struggles in *Tender Is the Night*, published in 1934, and about his

(Opposite) F. Scott and Zelda Fitzgerald, 1921; (above) F. Scott Fitzgerald, 1920

William Watts Folwell (1833–1929)

A visionary educator and scholar

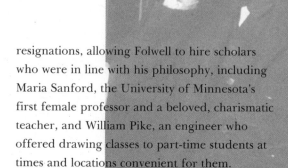

William Watts Folwell was just thirty-six years old in 1869, when he was appointed the first president of the University of Minnesota. With eight faculty members and less than one hundred students, and only recently reopened after suspending teaching during the Civil War, the university was in its infancy. But Folwell was confident that it could grow into a valued contributor to Minnesota's culture. In his inaugural address, he described its ultimate purpose. Higher education, he said, "will put bread into no man's mouth directly, nor money in his palm. Neither the rains nor the sunshine do that, but they warm and nourish the spring grass, and ripen the harvest. So higher education, generous culture, scholarship, literature inform, inspire, and elevate communities."

Folwell's "Minnesota Plan" for the university included offering college courses as well as graduate and professional programs. At the time, this idea was met with skepticism by traditionalists, who preferred that the university follow an undergraduate and graduate curriculum that emphasized Greek and Latin. An 1879 faculty protest led to several resignations, allowing Folwell to hire scholars who were in line with his philosophy, including Maria Sanford, the University of Minnesota's first female professor and a beloved, charismatic teacher, and William Pike, an engineer who offered drawing classes to part-time students at times and locations convenient for them.

"Uncle Billy," as Folwell was unofficially known, resigned from the presidency in 1884 but continued as a political science professor and librarian, retiring in 1907. He then went on to make another remarkable contribution to the state by writing a comprehensive, four-volume history of Minnesota that is a lasting example of rigorous scholarship and lively writing. Folwell witnessed firsthand many of the events he chronicled, and he wasn't one to sugarcoat his opinions. On the passage of a 1916 resolution to present a statue of Minnesota politician Henry M. Rice for placement in Statuary Hall in the U.S. Capitol, Folwell wrote: "There were abounding eulogies by each of the ten representatives from Minnesota. . . . That departures from historical accuracy, chiefly in details, were numerous was probably due to hasty perusal of secondary authorities for the perfunctory duty."

Folwell's elegant typewriter

Wanda Gág (1893–1946)

A multitalented artist known by children worldwide

The oldest daughter of Bohemian immigrants, Wanda Gág began writing and illustrating to support her family after her father's death in 1908. She went on to international fame as an author and artist. She's best known for her children's books *Millions of Cats* and *ABC Bunny,* both of which received Newbery Honor awards.

Here's how Gwenyth Swain, author of *Wanda Gág: Storybook Artist,* describes Gág's remarkable life:

"What story would you like to hear? The one about the child who grew up speaking German, at her home in New Ulm in the late 1800s, only to become a beloved author of classic read-aloud children's books, all written in English? Or the one about the girl who adored her artist father, only to lose him when she was just fifteen, taking to heart his last words, 'What Pap was unable to accomplish, Wanda will have to finish,' and vowing to become an artist in her own right? Or the story of the daring teenager who bucked popular opinion which said girls didn't need to be well-educated and stayed in high school after her father's death and her mother's breakdown, even when it meant going hungry and freezing in a house without coal? Or the story of the big sister who sold hand-drawn postcards and Valentine's Day cards at the local drugstore in order to buy shoes and school supplies for her younger siblings, helping them all, eventually, to graduate from high school, too? . . . Or the story about the struggling artist in New York City who, having taken a job with a small graphic design company, spent her spare time telling the owners' children stories, including one about 'millions and billions and trillions' of cats? Or perhaps you'd prefer to hear the story of how that struggling young artist met an editor of children's books in 1928, submitted a story called *Millions of Cats* complete with rich, black pen-and-ink illustrations that leapt across two-page spreads and revolutionized the picture book form, and saw that book become an instant classic? Take your pick. They're all wonderful stories, and they're all about Wanda Hazel Gág, a pioneering artist in the field of children's books.

"But perhaps the best story to tell is the one that still unfolds, here and there, across the country and in translation around the world of a child hearing for the first time the story of 'hundreds of cats, thousands of cats, millions and billions and trillions of cats' and seeing a bedraggled kitten grow sleek and well-fed in a warm, cozy, and loving home."

Verne Gagne (1926–)

A quiet Minnesotan moves out of the ring and into sports history

When we think of Minnesota's influence on the performing arts," writes nominator Mitch Vars of Minneapolis, "we may think of the Guthrie, Prince, Garrison Keillor, or maybe Josh Hartnett. I believe the most overlooked Minnesotan who has had a lasting influence on the performing arts nationally would be Verne Gagne, former owner/promoter of the American Wrestling Association (AWA), based in Minneapolis. Gagne's work through the AWA as a wrestler and wrestling promoter shaped the early days of professional wrestling and set the stage for pro wrestling's eventual growth into a multi-billion-dollar industry."

Verne Gagne grew up on a Minnesota farm, was an outstanding athlete at Robbinsdale High School, and enjoyed a successful amateur wrestling career as a student at the University of Minnesota. He turned pro in 1949 and soon wowed fans with his flawless technique and smooth maneuvers. Through the new medium of television he became a national sports star, and, in addition to capturing several heavyweight titles in the 1950s, he was one of the nation's highest-paid wrestlers.

In 1960, Gagne formed the American Wrestling Association as a promotional vehicle for his sport—and, overnight, became its biggest star. He was awarded the AWA's first World Heavyweight Championship and would go on to win the title nine more times before retiring in 1981. An understated, soft-spoken man, Gagne was nevertheless a tireless promoter whose public "feuds" with such archrivals as The Crusher and Dr. X drew unprecedented crowds. Never much for show, he simply laced up his boots, entered the ring, and got the job done. He left the theatrics to some of the more notorious members of the AWA, including Hulk Hogan (Gagne's biggest draw in the 1980s) and Jesse Ventura (who wrestled with the AWA in the early 1980s).

In 2004, Verne Gagne was inducted into the Professional Wrestling Hall of Fame by his son, Greg, one of dozens of young wrestlers he trained over the years. In an interview preceding the induction ceremony, Greg was asked to assess his dad's early impact on wrestling: "It's funny, it seems like wherever we go in the country, people recognize my father from way back then. The people are a bit older, of course, but they still recognize him and they recognize that that's when wrestling first hit the [television] networks. And he was a major, major part of that."

Cass Gilbert (1859–1934)

The architect of Minnesota's capitol building

May 9th 1901

One of America's first celebrity architects, Cass Gilbert is best known as the architect of the Woolworth Building in New York City. Completed in 1913, it was a pioneering design—a soaring steel frame clad in a lively, neo-Gothic shell. Gilbert might not have received this plum commission, however, were it not for one of his earlier designs—the third Minnesota State Capitol, commissioned in 1895 and completed ten years later.

Born in Ohio, Gilbert moved to St. Paul as a boy. When he was seventeen, he dropped out of school and joined a local architect's office. He later completed his architectural studies at the Massachusetts Institute of Technology and then, like many of his peers, took a grand tour of Europe, where the classical styles so much in evidence were to shape his designs throughout his career. Returning to the United States, he worked with the prestigious New York firm of McKim, Mead, and White until 1884, when he established a practice in St. Paul with James Knox Taylor.

Gilbert designed a number of office buildings, churches, and Summit Avenue houses before receiving the State Capitol commission. His design expresses the best of the Beaux Arts tradition—a grand, stately image for a state coming into its own. The building's placement on Wabasha Hill (known today as Capitol Hill) near downtown St. Paul was within viewing distance of the future site of the Cathedral of St. Paul, forming a pairing of church and state that dominated the St. Paul skyline.

The Capitol's design attracted national attention, and in 1899 Gilbert received the commission for the U.S. Custom House (now the George Gustav Heye Center) in New York City. Gilbert soon moved his practice to New York City, but he remained keenly interested in his largest Minnesota project and stayed involved in the smallest details regarding furnishings and landscaping: "The miscellaneous correspondence" about the project, writes historian Neil B. Thompson, "sounds a bit like the private conversations of a young couple furnishing their first home." Minnesotans flocked to the new Capitol when it opened on January 2, 1905, and have viewed it with pride ever since. Gilbert's artistic vision and attention to detail have paid off.

Robert R. Gilruth (1913–2000)

The man responsible for launching America's space program

As he tracked Charles Lindbergh's historic 1927 solo flight from New York to Paris, young Robert Gilruth of Nashwauk, Minnesota, became fascinated by flight. Four years later, he enrolled in the University of Minnesota, where he completed both a bachelor of science and a master of science degree in aeronautical engineering. A year later, he joined the National Advisory Committee for Aeronautics—the predecessor of NASA—and his career really took off.

Gilruth's earliest assignments involved rocket research. After World War II, he led a team of engineers in the development of rocket-powered aircraft. All the while, though, America was racing the Soviet Union into space. In 1957, Gilruth's professional focus shifted from rockets to spaceships. "I can recall watching the sunlight reflect off of Sputnik as it passed over my home on the Chesapeake Bay," Gilruth said in 1972. "It put a new sense of value and urgency on things we had been doing."

In 1958, Gilruth was transferred to the newly formed NASA, where he was assigned the task of putting men in space. He and his team worked around the clock on a top-secret assignment later known as Project Mercury, the first U.S. human space flight program. Gilruth was personally responsible for designing the Mercury capsule and its propulsion systems;

he also established the requirements for astronaut qualifications and mission control procedures and training.

Gilruth's team and responsibilities expanded as the U.S. space program gained credibility and funding. As director of the Manned Spacecraft Center (later the Lyndon B. Johnson Space Center) in Houston, Texas, Gilruth conceived and developed the Gemini Program and was also responsible for the spacecraft design and the selection and training of the astronauts and ground crews for the Apollo missions. He directed twenty-five manned space flights, including Alan Shepard's first Mercury flight, the first lunar landing by Apollo 11, and the dramatic rescue of Apollo 13.

"There is no question that without Bob Gilruth there would not have been a Mercury, Gemini, or an Apollo program," said Gilruth's NASA colleague George Low. "It is clear to all who have been associated with him that he has been the leader of all that is manned space flight in this country."

Apollo 11 lunar module pilot Edwin "Buzz" Aldrin climbs down to the Moon's surface

Glaciation

The shape of things to come

Like much of the Minnesota landscape, the beautiful curves of the St. Croix River Valley were created by glaciation.

Ever wonder why the Red River of the North flows north? Why sections of the Red River Valley are so flat you can see across them for miles? Why, despite numerous dams and dikes, the river overflows its banks after heavy rains and rapid snow melts? Much of this has to do with geological events that occurred thousands of years ago, when glaciers melted and slowly retreated from the land that would become Minnesota. Nominator David Borchert of Duluth explains: "Down a well of time only twice as deep as the pyramids of Egypt, a continental glacier was receding from Minnesota. It left a blasted landscape of bedrock, boulders, gravel, sand, silt, and water. A land made by ice. Plants, animals, and eventually Lutherans colonized and scratched at the surface of the land, but the power of the glaciers still dominates our physical environment and profoundly shapes our work lives and our recreation.

"Glacial Lake Agassiz left a fertile lake bottom now known as the Red River Valley and a large overflow valley that now contains the meandering Minnesota River. Another great glacial meltwater stream carved the beautiful St. Croix River Valley to the east. The scoured bedrock of northern Minnesota became the stunning lakes of the BWCA. Further south and west, the random plowing of soil by moving ice and the deposition of sand and gravel around remaining chunks of ice created our recreational lakes for weekend trips and prairie potholes that facilitate continent-wide migrations. This glacially produced hydrological chaos of lakes, ponds, and marshes provides us with our greatest common enemy, the mosquito.

"I'm writing this note looking out over Lake Superior and the Duluth Harbor. The Great Lakes are arguably the most amazing creation of glaciation on our planet. I watch oceangoing ships and 1,000-foot ore boats pass into Duluth Harbor. Over 1,000 miles from the ocean, Minnesota has the most remote seaport in the world. If we Minnesotans have to choose between creation by fire and ice, I think that ice will best suffice."

James Madison Goodhue (1810–1852)

Shaping a new state's image

Editor of Minnesota's first newspaper, the *Minnesota Pioneer*, James Goodhue was born in New Hampshire and arrived in St. Paul in 1849, just after Congress established Minnesota Territory. Like many men of his era, Goodhue made his way west over a number of years. Along the way he worked as a farmer, lawyer, and novelist before landing a job as a newspaper editor in Wisconsin. But he kept a close eye on political developments in Minnesota, and when territorial status was announced,

Goodhue and his young family boarded a steamboat and headed west once more.

Goodhue printed his first issue of the *Minnesota Pioneer* on April 28, 1849. For the next three years, he used the paper as his public mouthpiece, airing his views on everything from politics to the weather with skill and wit. Newspaper writing in the mid-1800s was very different than it is today—editors used their newspapers to express their personal views, and readers expected candor and bias. "The columns of his paper were like a terrific storm in mid-summer amid the Alps," wrote Rev. Edward D. Neill, a contemporary of Goodhue. "One sentence would be like the dazzling arrowy lightning . . . the next like a crash of awful thunder; and the next like the stunning roar of a torrent of many waters."

Above all else, though, Goodhue's newspaper reflected his strong and unwavering commitment to attracting settlers to Minnesota. He was "the precursor to the modern-day Chamber of Commerce," according to one writer. His words formed images of his adopted home in an era when few photographs and no moving pictures were in circulation. "I dwell upon Minnesota and St. Paul," he wrote, "for they are ever in my thoughts and a part of my very existence. There is not a party tie or political association, that I would not instantly sever, to promote their welfare."

"Let an editor slash away—anything but salve, salve, salve, when the dissecting knife is needed. The journal that does nothing but paddle along with public opinion, without breasting the current of popular errors, is of no value—none whatever." James Goodhue, *Minnesota Pioneer*, April 15, 1852

Reputed to be the press upon which James Goodhue printed the first issue of the Minnesota Pioneer, *the first newspaper printed in Minnesota territory, April 28, 1849*

61

Grand Portage

A commercial venture leads to cultural change

From 1600 to 1850, a widespread system of exchange fueled the economy of the region. Known today simply as the fur trade, it was at heart a simple proposition: American Indians exchanged furs, especially beaver pelts, for all sorts of manufactured goods provided by European traders.

Grand Portage, at the very northeastern point of what is now Minnesota, was a key location during the fur trade era. Karl Koster, of Armstrong, Iowa, explains why the North West Company established headquarters at Grand Portage: "The company may have been based in Montreal, but the key was having that location in Minnesota. The company's most successful years, when it was five times larger than the Hudson's Bay Company, were all at Grand Portage. From there [Scottish fur trader and explorer] Sir Alexander Mackenzie reached the Pacific before Lewis and Clark, and also reached the Arctic Ocean. Geography, exploration, and economics came together in one place and that explosion opened half a continent."

Location, location, location. According to fur trade historian Alan R. Woolworth, "No fewer than three geographical features ensured the Grand Portage locality of its place in fur trade history." The bay was deep and sheltered, perfect for building a trading post. It was a relatively short and easy portage to the Pigeon River. And the river was an excellent natural waterway to the network of lakes to the west. The area's advantageous natural features supported an empire.

Like many of Minnesota's most storied places, Grand Portage was a gathering spot long before Europeans arrived on the scene. Ojibwe Indians had traveled to this nexus for centuries, and the nine-mile trek used by traders to avoid a waterfall and rapids on the Pigeon River was first navigated by Ojibwe, who called the place Kitchi Onigaming, or "great carrying place." Today, Grand Portage State Park—the only state park land not owned by the State of Minnesota—is located within the Grand Portage Indian Reservation.

(Left) North Shore trapper in winter, 1875. (Middle) For centuries, Grand Portage has allowed travelers to safely bypass potential boat hazards such as the Pigeon River Falls in Cook County.

Grasshoppers

A Minnesota farm crisis

Works Progress Administration workers mix grasshopper poison for distribution to farmers in 1937

A cloud was over the sun. It was not like any cloud they had ever seen before. It was a cloud of something like snowflakes, but they were larger than snowflakes, and thin and glittering. Light shone through each flickering particle.

"There was no wind. The grasses were still and the hot air did not stir, but the edge of the cloud came on across the sky faster than wind. . . .

"Plunk! Something hit Laura's head and fell to the ground. She looked down and saw the largest grasshopper she had ever seen. Then huge brown grasshoppers were hitting the ground all around her, hitting her head and her face and her arms. They came thudding down like hail.

"The cloud was hailing grasshoppers. The cloud was grasshoppers. Their bodies hid the sun and made darkness."

From Laura Ingalls Wilder, *On the Banks of Plum Creek,* 1937

Every summer from 1873 to 1877, midwestern farmers saw flourishing crops vanish as swarms of grasshoppers descended on their fields. There had been earlier infestations in the 1850s and 1860s, and more were to come in the 1930s. But the five-year plague in the 1870s was particularly devastating, leaving thousands of families without the basic necessities, including seed for the next year's crop.

"In the 1870s, the media campaign behind the losses to wheat farmers began a long-enduring process of designating farmers as disaster victims and generating numerous forms of disaster relief," writes nominator Bob Quist, site manager at the Oliver H. Kelley Farm, a Minnesota Historical Society Historic Site and working farm near Elk River, Minnesota. Relief was slow in coming, however—initially, farmers were expected to look to their families and communities for help, and it was only after the plagues stretched on for several years that state and federal resources kicked in.

Changes wrought by the grasshopper plagues are still with us, not only in the form of farm-relief programs that have eased burdens during droughts and other disasters, but in other, less obvious, ways. Bob Quist explains: "Piles of grasshopper poison were later bull-dozed into pits across western Minnesota as the pests departed, creating leaking hazardous waste sites into the twentieth century."

Greyhound Bus Company (founded in Hibbing, 1914)

The world's largest intercity passenger carrier

It all started when Hibbing's Carl Eric Wickman and Andrew Anderson pooled their resources and bought a Hupmobile, hoping to sell it at a profit. When that plan failed, they decided to run the car as a "jitney," a passenger car used to shuttle folks between towns. The first route of Wickman and Anderson and their partner, C. A. A. Heed, was between Hibbing and Alice, another iron-mining town. They charged fifteen cents a trip; round-trip fare was a quarter.

Business was brisk, and soon the company began acquiring buses, running on fixed schedules, and merging with other jitney companies, changing names many times in the process. By 1922, Wickman had relocated to Duluth; he soon bought a number of sleek, gray buses, made in Michigan and nicknamed

M67—Greyhound Bus Depot, Minneapolis, Minn.

Greyhound Bus Depot, 1940

64

"greyhounds." Eight years and several mergers later, Wickman's coast-to-coast operation was renamed the Greyhound Corporation, with a running dog as its logo.

Greyhound stayed afloat during the Depression by showing the same entrepreneurial spirit that had marked its early days. In 1933, for example, the company became the official transportation carrier of the Century of Progress, held in Chicago. The company gambled on the success of the fair, reserving 2,000 hotel rooms and launching a campaign offering lodging and transportation to the fair

on a single ticket. The promotion earned more than $500,000.

Over the years, Greyhound marked many more milestones, becoming the primary stateside carrier of troops during World War II, setting industry standards by being the first

In 1961, a group of activists known as the "Freedom Riders" boarded Greyhound and Trailway buses headed to southern states to protest state-sponsored segregation in interstate transportation facilities. Buses were firebombed and protesters stormed terminals, but the company, backed by Attorney General Robert Kennedy, continued its course. Later that year, the Interstate Commerce Commission outlawed segregation in interstate bus travel.

carrier to install such niceties as air conditioning and lavatories in its buses, and standing firm against racial discrimination among its workers and its riders.

Wendelin Grimm (c. 1817–1890)

Through seed saving, the Dairy Belt was born

I n the 1850s and 1860s, farmers from Germany and Sweden began settling in the east-central region of Minnesota. One of those immigrants was Wendelin Grimm, who, along with his wife, Julianna, bought acreage near Chaska in northern Carver County in 1857.

Among the few possessions that Grimm brought with him from Germany was a box of alfalfa seed. Grimm tended his alfalfa crop closely that first year, laboriously gathering the seeds from the plants that survived the winter. He repeated this seed-saving process over the next fifteen years, until he had a full crop of alfalfa capable of surviving Minnesota's weather extremes. He called his crop *ewiger Klee*, or everlasting clover. It was the first winter-hardy alfalfa in North America.

Neighboring farmers took notice of Grimm's flourishing crops and well-fed cattle

and gradually switched to his seed strain as a source of fodder and nourishment for the soil. Over time, Grimm Alfalfa (officially acknowledged by the U.S. Department of Agriculture in 1903) became the dominant strain of this forage crop grown in the Midwest. It is the source of all modern varieties of alfalfa, now grown on more than twenty-five million acres in the United States.

The Grimms' farmstead, built in 1876 of Chaska brick, was placed on the National Register of Historic Places in 1974. Today, it is used for agricultural education programs.

Third crop of Grimm Alfalfa, Carver County, 1910

Guthrie Theater

A new model for regional theaters

(Top) Opening of the Guthrie Theater on May 8, 1963; (bottom) the new Guthrie opened in 2006 on the Minneapolis riverfront.

I t all started with an article on the drama page of the *New York Times,* September 30, 1959. "Stage Unit Slated Outside of City," the headline read. "Guthrie among Planners of Permanent Company That Would Perform Classics."

The article described a plan by "three prominent show people," including director Tyrone Guthrie, to cultivate artists and build audiences beyond the increasingly commercialized Broadway networks that dominated the theatrical world. Guthrie and his colleagues proposed a regional theater with a resident company that would maintain the highest professional standards and seven cities expressed interest in supporting one: Waltham, Massachusetts, Cleveland, Chicago, Detroit, Milwaukee, San Francisco . . . and Minneapolis.

Four years later, George Grizzard took the stage in the title role of the Guthrie Theater's inaugural production of *Hamlet,* accompanied by Ellen Geer as Ophelia and Jessica Tandy as Gertrude. "The Guthrie Theater is off to a happy start," wrote Dan Sullivan of the *Minneapolis Tribune.* Sullivan noted that Tyrone Guthrie made "audacious use of his semi-arena stage," a reference to the theater's distinctive thrust stage, partially surrounded by seating. This innovative design, which extended to the building's starkly modern exterior, resulted from a collaboration between Guthrie and

Ralph Rapson, a leading Modernist architect who headed the University of Minnesota's School of Architecture.

Flash forward forty-three years. The spirit of Sir Tyrone Guthrie looms large over the Minneapolis riverfront, where his image is one of several emblazoned on the exterior walls of the new Guthrie Theater. It is, in the words of artistic director Joe Dowling, "a permanent reflection of the incredible spirit of openness and respect for the art of theater that [Guthrie] found here in the early 1960s and that continue to delight and amaze me every day."

> "But the river is what most charmed and amazed us. It had not yet frozen over and was flowing with a lively sparkle through winding gorges which are still beautiful, although here, as everywhere else, the convenience of the waterway has been exploited. . . . Of course it will not always be so. Eventually the Twin Cities will realize that their river can be, and ought to be, a wonderful and life-giving amenity without losing any of its utility."
> Sir Tyrone Guthrie, *A New Theatre,* 1964

Hall Brothers New Orleans Jazz Band

Bringing sweet sounds to Minnesota

You might not think of the Twin Cities as a center for the kind of music you'd hear on a hot summer night in the Deep South, but thanks to a talented bunch of musicians, our jazz scene is alive and well. Nominator Dick Parker explains: "In the late 1950s, Stan Hall, Charlie DeVore, Don Berg, and others formed a band to play old jazz in the authentic New Orleans style, thanks largely to DeVore's studies during Navy service in New Orleans about fifty years ago. By the 1960s, they were playing concerts and jobs in the Twin Cities area at Brady's Bar on Hennepin Avenue and had begun a cultural link to the other end of the Mississippi River, bringing old New Orleans musicians to the Twin Cities to give Minnesotans a taste of the real roots of jazz.

"One landmark occasion was the 1964 Guthrie Theater concert by the Preservation Hall Jazz Band with pianist Sweet Emma Barrett. From 1966 to 1991, the Hall Brothers band, as business partners, owned and staffed the Emporium of Jazz in Mendota, continuing to bring to Minnesota the last of the musicians who had lived and performed during the Jazz Age in New Orleans, New York, and Chicago.

"Stan and Russ Hall are retired from music, but some members of the band are still working in the Twin Cities and beyond: cornetist/musicologist Charlie DeVore; trombonist/bassist Bill Evans; pianist/clarinetist Butch Thompson; drummer Don 'Doggie' Berg; and pianist/saxophonist Mike Polad. Around them has grown a battalion of musicians who make up the traditional-jazz scene in Minnesota today."

Hazelden

The Minnesota Model becomes a symbol of hope

t was incorporated on January 10, 1949, as "a sanatorium for curable alcoholics of the professional class" based in Old Lodge, a farmhouse retreat for men only in Center City, Minnesota. Today, Hazelden is an international provider of addiction treatment, a publisher, a research center, and an educational facility with branches at several Minnesota sites and in Oregon, Illinois, and New York. More than 180,000 men, women, and adolescents have been treated at Hazelden.

Hazelden's early treatment was based on the Twelve Steps program pioneered by Alcoholics Anonymous. In the 1960s, a more holistic, multidisciplinary approach evolved—known today as the "Minnesota Model." A team, including nurses, doctors, psychologists and psychiatrists, addiction counselors, fitness specialists, and spiritual advisors, delivers Hazelden's groundbreaking residential treatment.

William Cope Moyers is vice president for external affairs at Hazelden. He's also a recovering alcoholic and substance abuser who is living proof of the effectiveness of the Minnesota Model. When asked to explain Hazelden's philosophy in a 2006 interview following the publication of his memoir, *Broken,* Moyers summed it up this way: "We're good at what we do. But part of what we do is not just treat people or publish materials. . . . Our mission is to educate every generation around addiction, treatment, and recovery issues. . . . I go all over the country sharing not just my story, but the messages of hope that come from the reality that this is an illness that does have a way out. It's called treatment, it's called recovery, it's called personal responsibility."

(Top) The original Hazelden Historic Lodge; (bottom) Hazelden's nearly 500-acre campus of today

Herter's, Inc.

Boosting Minnesota's image with outdoorsmen worldwide

Anybody know of a mail-order company called Herter's?" Thus begins a query to the Kountrylife.com website. The writer continues, "They sold gear for hunters, guides, trappers, etc. I bought a skinning knife from them some 40 years ago, still have it, and it's a good one. I can't remember now if they were in the USA or Canada. Like to get a catalogue if they are still around." Many people responded to this query, including other owners of Herter's gear, a former Herter's employee, and several people who directed the writer to Cabela's website, which features products with a Herter's label.

Like many other long-gone stores, Herter's, Inc., a sporting-goods store once located in Waseca, Minnesota, lives on through its products. But the quantity of goods still in use is only one indicator of Herter's influence on Minnesotans and on the sporting-goods industry. Nominator Doug Lodermeier explains: "What singular experience has affected Minnesota sportsmen more than any other from both a cultural and a business perspective? Standing in the showroom of Herter's, Inc., of Waseca.

"This Minnesota institution (and the world-wide catalog that promoted it) changed hunting and fishing in the state in three dramatic ways: It caused an explosion in the popularity of these activities by making them even more attractive and accessible. It put Minnesota on the map as a sportsmen's paradise. And it dramatically changed the economics of retail throughout the state.

"Whether you were ten or one hundred, a pilgrimage to Herter's captured every sportsman's imagination through the latter half of the twentieth century. You'd step through the doors to find every hunting and fishing item known to man under one roof. Though we take this concept for granted now (thanks to

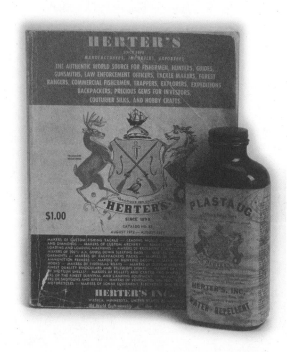

Cabela's, not to mention Wal-Mart), it was absolutely revolutionary in the mid-1930s.

"Of course, it wasn't just the showroom. Herter's catalogs reached nearly every corner of the globe—peddling not only a massive array of products, but subconsciously promoting Minnesota as the hub of sportsmen's knowledge and innovation. (Would that famous *Time* magazine cover with Wendell Anderson have happened without Herter's? I doubt it.)

"Herter's is not without controversy. While sportsmen firmly approved of its innovative approach to retail, the existing 'Mom and Pop' shops did not. Like all big-box retailers, Herter's was the beginning of a model that is still being perfected today and has caused a rapid decline in smaller, family-owned stores.

"To put it plainly, hunting and fishing has always defined Minnesota, and today, every Minnesotan knows Cabela's. What they don't know is that Cabela's wouldn't exist without Herter's."

(Opposite) Herter's 1973 catalog included Swiss Plastaug water repellent. (Bottom) Herter's duck decoys

Highway 61 along the North Shore

King of the roads

I nominate the completion of Highway 61 along the North Shore in the 1930s," writes Doug Wilhide of Minneapolis. "First of all, it was a substantial engineering feat, involving blasting tunnels through solid rock, building roadways along steep precipices above Lake Superior, and handling the logistics of a major construction project in what was substantially wilderness. It opened up the North Shore to tourism, making Minnesota a major destination for vacationers from throughout the Midwest and the rest of the country. It effectively linked Minnesota to Canada for motorists, with benefits for people on both sides of the border. And

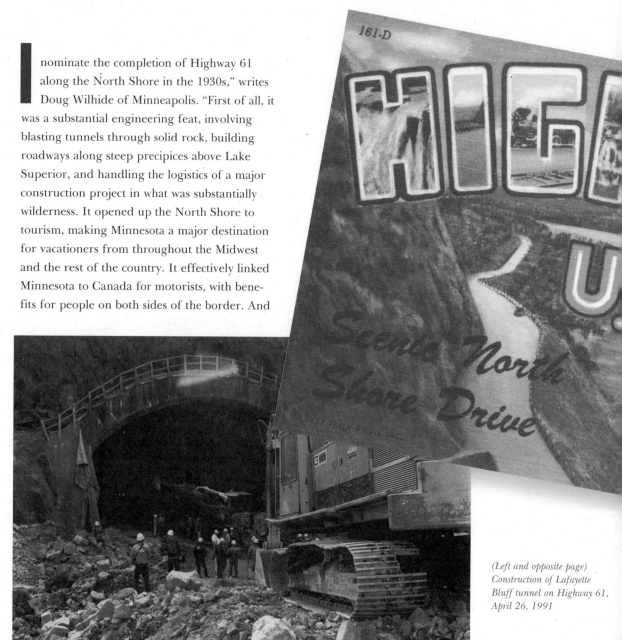

(Left and opposite page) Construction of Lafayette Bluff tunnel on Highway 61, April 26, 1991

it was essential in building an economy in a part of the state that—after the lumbering and mining bottomed out in the 1960s and 1970s—had virtually none."

Hugging the rocky shoreline of Lake Superior for more than 150 miles, Highway 61—also known as the North Shore Scenic Drive—winds through spectacular and varied

scenery, from wooded hills to dramatic waterfalls, from Split Rock Lighthouse to Glensheen Mansion in Duluth. The drive has been named an All-American Road, along with twenty-eight other roads, including the Pacific Coast Scenic Byway in Oregon and Louisiana's Creole Nature Trail, and it is considered not just a way from Point A to Point B but a destination in itself, a road worth traveling for the sheer pleasure of it.

"Glaciers have marked and grooved many of the rock formations of the area. In earlier geological periods these were gigantic ranges; today only a few precipitous slopes remain . . . boulders are scattered over much of the area.

"This region is the most rugged in Minnesota. The rough topography is the result of complicated geological processes; a huge fault (slipping of rock masses) left the depression now filled by Lake Superior."
From *Minnesota: A State Guide,* written by the Federal Writers' Project of the Works Progress Administration, 1938

James J. Hill (1838–1916)

Building a fortune while connecting the nation

On May 30, 1916, the *New York Times* announced that on the previous day James J. Hill had died at his St. Paul home. "Leaving as a monument of his life's work more than 6,000 miles of railroad, with gross earnings of $66,000,000 from carrying 15,000,000 tons of freight annually, along whose line in six different States of the great Northwest are scattered 400,000 farms, with 65,000 acres of improved land worth $5,000,000,000, James Jerome Hill was called the greatest empire builder of the new world."

The *Times* is not given to hyperbole, of course, and though the figures cited in Hill's obituary seem staggeringly large, their real impact lies in their accuracy. James J. Hill

was Minnesota's answer to the Rockefellers, the Carnegies, and other Gilded Age magnates—a hard-working, driven, fiercely competitive businessman whose great wealth was matched only by the impact its accumulation and dispersal made on Minnesota and the upper Midwest.

Hill was born on what one of his biographers called "a stingy farm in the backwoods of Ontario" in 1838. After only nine years of formal education, he went to work, first as a bookkeeper in Canada and then, at age seventeen, as a bookkeeper for a steamboat company on the St. Paul levee. In 1878, after twenty years spent working in shipping on the Mississippi and Red rivers, Hill turned his attention away from water transport and toward the land, when he and several partners bought the nearly bankrupt St. Paul and Pacific Railroad. Renamed the Great Northern Railway in 1890, Hill's railroad eventually extended north to Canada and west across the Rocky Mountains to the Pacific Ocean. It was the only transcontinental line built with neither public

money nor land grant—and it was the only transcontinental that avoided bankruptcy.

Not content simply to run one of the nation's largest transportation companies, Hill also sold homesteads along his rail lines to immigrants, developed businesses in railroad towns, and had financial interests in mining, shipping, banking, milling, and farming. He was an avid art collector—in 1892, the *New York Journal* called the collection of paintings and sculpture installed in his Summit Avenue mansion "a model art gallery of an American private palace"—and he also funded community projects, including the St. Paul Public Library, the James J. Hill Reference Library, and the St. Paul Seminary. His wife, Mary, a devout Roman Catholic, made significant contributions to the construction of the St. Paul Cathedral. Hill was a self-made man who was justly proud of the mark he made on his city and on the United States. "When we are all dead and gone," he said to his employees in 1880, "the sun will still shine, the rain will fall, and this railroad will run as usual."

The Honeywell Project

A lifelong commitment to promoting peace

(Above) Marv Davidov, speaking; (left) Davidov, in corner chair, Honeywell Project office

On October 7, 1998, fifty-three people were arrested outside Alliant TechSystems in Hopkins, Minnesota. The group was conducting the first of its protests against the company's production of land mines for the U.S. military.

One of the protesters arrested was Marv Davidov, Minneapolis's best-known practitioner of civil disobedience. Recently described as "the world's oldest protester—almost," Davidov

launched the Honeywell Project in 1968, at the height of the Vietnam War. The Honeywell Project's goal was to convince the board and management of the Honeywell Corporation to convert their weapons manufacturing business to production of nonmilitary devices. At the time the state's largest military contractor, Honeywell made cluster bombs

and guidance systems for nuclear weapons and for military aircraft.

In its early days, the Honeywell Project sponsored educational events that were coupled with large demonstrations outside Honeywell headquarters in south Minneapolis. In the 1980s, the group turned to large events of nonviolent civil disobedience, including a 1983 protest that made headlines when more than 500 people were arrested, including Erica Bouza, wife of Minneapolis police chief Tony Bouza.

In September 1990, just as the Project was winding down, Honeywell formed a new company, Alliant TechSystems, to handle its military contracts. Though the company's management denied that the Honeywell Project's activities had any bearing on its decision, longtime activists disagreed. In 1996, Marv Davidov and activists from Women against Military Madness, the Sisters of St. Joseph of Carondelet, and others protested for the first time at Alliant's headquarters. Their group, officially named AlliantACTION in 1998, scheduled regular protests for several years.

The Honeywell Round Thermostat

A design recognized around the world

It all started in 1885 with a little device called a "damper flapper," which helped to regulate a room's temperature—especially important for those who wished to sleep through the night without having to adjust their furnaces. The damper flapper was invented by Albert Butz, who sold his patents to a company that in turn was bought by William R. Sweatt, who merged his company with one founded by Mark Honeywell, all leading to the eventual founding of Honeywell, Inc., one of Minnesota's oldest and most successful businesses.

Honeywell is notable for all sorts of reasons, but none is more significant than the development of the T86 Round—the round thermostat introduced in 1953. Through an aggressive advertising campaign that advanced the Honeywell Round as the perfect complement to streamlined, post–World War II homes, the company's little wonder soon made its way into millions of American homes. Today a digital version remains a top seller, and the original design was included in a 1997 exhibit at the Cooper-Hewitt National Design Museum in New York.

The Honeywell Round's distinctive look and user-friendly dimensions were the brainchild of Henry Dreyfuss, who also designed telephones for Bell (including the famous Princess phone), tractors for John Deere, and cameras for Polaroid. Dreyfuss was a practical, form-follows-function type who designed with real people and real homes in mind. "If people are made safer, more comfortable, more eager to purchase, more efficient—or just plain happier—the designer has succeeded," he wrote. Based on those criteria, the Honeywell T86 Round is a smash.

Honeywell Round thermostats ready for final check and packaging, Golden Valley, 1955

Hubert H. Humphrey (1911–1978)

Civil rights champion

Late on the last day of the 1948 Democratic National Convention in Philadelphia, Hubert Humphrey, mayor of Minneapolis, Minnesota, took the podium. He began by warming up the crowd with a joke about a talking cow. Some listeners guffawed; others glanced sideways at each other. Few had ever seen or heard of him.

Over the next few minutes, Humphrey made sure that he would not be forgotten. He delivered a fiery, impassioned speech urging the delegates to include a civil rights plank in the Democratic platform. He cared deeply about the issue, and it showed. Minneapolis, which in 1946 had been described as "the capital of anti-Semitism in the United States," had, under Humphrey's leadership, just enacted the nation's first municipal fair employment law. "I realize that I am dealing with a charged issue," Humphrey said to the Democratic delegates. "I realize that there are those here—friends and colleagues of mine, many of them—who feel as deeply as I do about this issue and who are yet in complete disagreement with me."

Midway through his speech, Humphrey hammered his message home. "There are those who say to you," he shouted, "we are rushing this issue of civil rights. I say we are 172 years late." He paused to let the roar of the crowd die down. "There are those who say—this issue of civil rights is an infringement on states' rights. The time has arrived for the Democratic Party to get out of the shadow of states' rights and walk forthrightly into the bright sunshine of human rights."

Humphrey's words—"fiery prairie Progressivism fused with an untrammeled gift of gab," as one of his biographers put it—were instrumental in spurring the convention to add a civil rights plank to its platform. Later that year, Hubert Humphrey was elected to the U.S. Senate—the first Democrat ever sent there from Minnesota. He served in the Senate until 1964, when he was selected as Lyndon Johnson's running mate in the presidential campaign. His vice presidency was possibly the roughest time in his political career—he was torn between his allegiance to Johnson and his misgivings about the U.S. position in Vietnam. His ambivalence cost him dearly, and he narrowly lost the race for president in 1968. He returned to Minnesota, was elected to the U.S. Senate in 1970, and served there until his death in 1978.

For all the controversy that surrounded his last years in public office, Hubert Humphrey remains one of Minnesota's most influential and beloved politicians. In the words of one admirer, he was "one of the most engaging, certainly one of the most decent, politicians in recent American history." He had charisma and he had brains, but most of all, he had the courage to face whatever life dealt him, from political defeat to personal struggles. During his final struggle against terminal cancer, he remained upbeat and optimistic to the end. "He taught us how to hope and how to live, how to win and how to lose," said his friend Walter Mondale at his funeral. "He taught us how to live, and, finally, he taught us how to die."

(Top) Hubert H. Humphrey, 1946; (far left) Humphrey revised his typewritten speech before delivering it at the 1948 Democratic National Convention; (bottom) Walter Mondale (left) and Humphrey, 1975

79

Immigrants

From around the world to Minnesota

Nominator Nathan Huerkamp of Minneapolis writes, "There is nothing that has had a greater impact on Minnesota.

"Immigrants claimed land from the native people in what is now known as America. Past as well as present cannot escape the role immigrants continue to have in shaping Minnesota. Many a fur trader, lumberjack, and miner have come and gone, while laborers of all types now come here seeking those same opportunities and ultimately a better life.

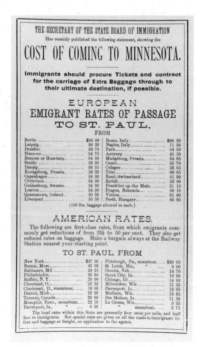

"Now people arrive to gain a better education and access to health care, along with the tried-and-true of oh, so many freedoms for themselves, their children, and their children's children. Freedom can mean a million things, from that of speech and religion to simple things like self-expression and walking down the street without fear. Immigrants have brought with them new ideas, an eagerness to succeed, and cultural flair, all of which positively impact everything in small-town Minnesota and in Minneapolis and St. Paul."

In recent decades, an increasing number of people have come to Minnesota as refugees from countries torn by war, famine, and political unrest. The family of Saida Hassan, a student at St. Paul's Central High School, for example, came here after fleeing Somalia during its civil war, then spending several years in a refugee camp in Kenya. Hassan moved to Minnesota in 2000. Five years later, she recalled the difficulties of leaving her home in Mogadishu: "That was the hardest thing that I've ever had to do. I mean for a moment I even thought to sneak away and no one would see me and I wouldn't have to go onto that plane." What she found at Central High School was a diverse student body made up of people with life stories similar to her own. "It was amazing to me," she remembered. "I didn't know that there was so much in this world that you could learn about people. I met a girl from Hungary, and we became very good friends . . . we are from opposite sides [of the world] but still we can come to one place and share it."

"These days, I too know
 That if people were to ask me,
 What am I doing in this life?
 My response is predestined
 By the people I was born into:
 I walk in life
 Because that's what the Hmong people
 Used to do. . . .

"I salute the spirit of my communities
 And am spending my years
 Learning how to read
 The shades of their dreams,
 Shaping the wave
 That will take us all
 To a true American shore
 Of peace, justice, and equality."
 From Pacyinz Lyfoung,
"Walking Manifesto #2"

(Far left) Broadside from about 1872, when states still competed to lure immigrants, listing rates from various European ports and promising bargain overland routes. (Top) Graduation, Lao Family Community Center, St. Paul, 1981; (bottom) immigrants taking the oath of citizenship, Minneapolis Council of Americanization, 1925.

Indian Boarding Schools

Nighttime was the worst

When he was six years old, Jim Northrup was sent from his home on Minnesota's Fond du Lac Reservation to the Pipestone Indian School in Pipestone, Minnesota. Life at Pipestone was hard, and homesickness and loneliness soon overwhelmed Northrup and his fellow students. "Nighttime was the worst," Northrup, now a successful author and humorist, recalled. "On one end of the room, a young kid would start to cry in his bed. It was like a domino effect; soon the whole room was sobbing. The next day everyone would carry on like nothing happened." Northrup tried running away from Pipestone several times and eventually completed his schooling at a Christian boarding school in Hot Springs, South Dakota.

Why was Jim Northrup sent to Pipestone at such a young age? By the late 1800s, most American Indians were living on reservations, since much of their land base had been ceded to the U.S. government through treaties. Indians supported themselves by living off the land when possible, getting jobs wherever they could, and, if necessary, leaving their families and moving to cities in search of employment. To solve what federal officials often called the "Indian problem"—rampant unemployment, poor health, and few prospects—the government enacted a general policy of assimilation, from a belief that American Indians should suppress their own cultural practices, including speaking in their own languages and worshipping in traditional ways, and instead adopt the ways of America's majority culture. As part of this policy, boarding school attendance was mandated for American Indian children nationwide. When children arrived at boarding

schools, they were given haircuts and European-style clothing and were expected to adhere to strict practices that, in an oft-repeated description from Captain Richard C. Pratt, founder of Carlisle Indian School, would "kill the Indian and save the man."

The first building at Pipestone Indian School was completed in 1892. Soon children began arriving from throughout Minnesota and across the Midwest. As in other federal Indian schools, students usually spent half of each day in the classroom and the other half learning occupations such as farming, masonry, carpentry, cooking, baking, and nursing. This vocational training was resented by many Indians, who saw their children being prepared for little else than lives of menial labor.

Life for many boarding school students was bleak, but not all experiences were negative. Some former students recall compassionate teachers, character-enhancing sports programs, and strong bonds forged through common experiences. Overall, however, strict assimilation programs were deemed a failure, and, over time, boarding schools closed or changed their curricula to better reflect their students' backgrounds and beliefs.

(Opposite page) Children on the steps of the Indian School at Pipestone, 1893; (top) young girls playing at an Indian boarding school, 1900; (bottom) Mille Lacs students leaving for Pipestone Indian School, 1940

John Ireland (1838–1918)

Committed to church and state

Born in County Kilkenny, Ireland, in 1838, John Ireland came to St. Paul with his parents in 1852. He was ordained a Catholic priest in 1861, served briefly as chaplain for the Fifth Minnesota Regiment in the Civil War, and was appointed bishop in 1875. By the time he was appointed archbishop of St. Paul in 1888, he was one of the city's most prominent citizens, and he was responsible for recruiting Irish immigrants to settle in communities throughout Minnesota, including Clontarf, Adrian, Graceville, and Ghent. Nominator Kevin Duchschere of St. Paul picks up the story from here: "John Ireland was a builder, a politician, a colonizer, an orator, a writer, a diplomat, and a friend to presidents, an Irishman who loved America and a true believer in the promise of Minnesota—and that's before you get to his accomplishments as arguably the state's outstanding religious leader.

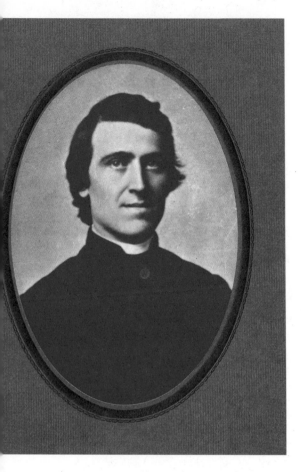

for the American way, and at least once he needed James J. Hill to bail out his personal finances—but his legacy is still evident today. He founded the state's largest private college, the University of St. Thomas, in 1885. And he built two massive cathedrals in the Twin Cities, the Cathedral in St. Paul and the Basilica of St. Mary in Minneapolis, among Minnesota's most remarkable architectural and religious monuments, which still move and inspire visitors and have long since become indelible parts of the Twin Cities' skyline.

"It's not too farfetched to suggest that Minnesota became familiar to many Americans at the turn of the last century because of Archbishop Ireland. 'I thought he had a fine name,' Ernest Hemingway wrote of the archbishop in *A Farewell to Arms*, 'and he came from Minnesota which made it a lovely name: Ireland of Minnesota.'"

"From the 1870s until his death, Ireland led the Catholic church in Minnesota and won national fame for his work in the temperance movement and in settling southwestern Minnesota with Irish immigrants like himself. He was a highly intelligent, voluble, and hyperactive man who fought the widespread prejudice that Catholics couldn't be good Americans. He was an outspoken Republican and intimate of McKinley, Roosevelt, and Taft at a time when the political sympathies of American Catholics rested largely with the Democratic Party. Ireland's leadership was not without its flaws— he was famously impatient with immigrants being unwilling to trade in their old traditions

(Top) Archbishop John Ireland, 1862;
(opposite page) the St. Paul Cathedral

Iron Ore

Buried treasure or not?

When you take in the vast expanse of the Hull-Rust-Mahoning Mine in Hibbing, Minnesota, it's easy to see why it's sometimes called the "Manmade Grand Canyon of the North." The world's largest open pit mine, it spurred the formation of U.S. Steel, once the world's largest corporation. At its peak production during World Wars I and II, the mine supplied one-fourth of all the iron ore mined in the United States. It is no longer a working mine, but the breathtaking sweep of the Hull-Rust-Mahoning site symbolizes the huge significance of iron ore for northern Minnesota. This natural resource drew waves of immigrant workers, led to the development of close-knit Iron Range communities, and drove the region's economy for decades.

Over billions of years, geological forces left behind three major ore deposits—the Vermilion Range between Tower and Ely, which is underground; the Mesabi Range between Grand Rapids and Babbitt; and the Cuyuna Range in Crow Wing and Aitkin counties, both of which sites are open pit. Prospectors came to Lake Vermilion in the 1860s looking for gold but moved on when they discovered ore instead. Pennsylvanian Charlemagne Tower saw the value in the ore, however, and bought up huge amounts of land on the Vermilion Range. In 1884, he shipped his first ore from the Soudan Mine to eastern ports. In 1890, Duluth's Merritt brothers laid the groundwork for their Mountain Iron Mine, the first on the Mesabi Range. Cuyler Adams opened the Cuyuna Range in 1904.

The rapid rise in Iron Range mining led to large waves of new arrivals in the region—immigrants from Cornwall, Finland, Sweden, Slovenia, and Croatia, who joined people from dozens of other countries and created the state's great melting pot. They built churches, synagogues, social halls, and schools in town sites close to the mines. Crosby, Ironton, Eveleth, Gilbert, Hibbing, and, later, model towns, including Coleraine, Marble, and Taconite, all owed their beginnings to the presence of iron ore.

From 1900 to 1980, the Mesabi Range—including the Hull-Rust-Mahoning Mine—contributed about 60 percent of the country's total iron ore output. Production peaked in the 1940s, when more than 600,000 tons were shipped out

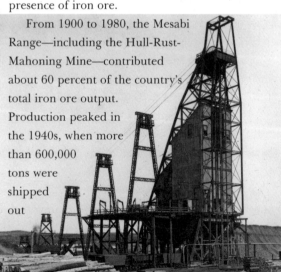

and sent to fuel the war effort. But the ore was depleted by the early 1960s. Enter Professor Edward W. Davis and his colleagues at the University of Minnesota, who developed a process to mine taconite, a low-grade ore that could be concentrated into pellets. The region's economy was revived, new towns, including Babbitt and Silver Bay, were incorporated, and by the 1970s taconite was the area's primary export.

But fortunes shifted once again in 1972, when the U.S. government sued taconite processor Reserve Mining Company, alleging that the company was disposing of harmful waste materials, called taconite tailings, in Lake Superior. The case dragged on until April 1974, when Judge Miles Lord, raised on the Iron Range, made the difficult decision that Reserve Mining should be shut down. Just like that, 3,000 jobs were lost. Though the company appealed and production continued for a time, this well-publicized victory for environmentalists spelled disaster for many Iron Range workers. Today, with the bustling mines and processing plants a distant memory, the region is reinventing itself again as a tourist destination—Tower-Soudan underground mine is open for tours, visitor centers have been built at Hull-Rust-Mahoning and other mines, and Ironworld, a living history museum, draws 20,000 visitors a year. And iron ore is once again, as it has been for more than a century, at the center of it all.

(Opposite top) Power shovel for strip mining, 1940; (opposite bottom) Sibley Mine headframe, Ely, 1905; (bottom) Miners and car in the pit, Tower-Soudan Mine, 1890

Itasca State Park

Minnesota's first state park

Come to the beginning of a river
A river known for long-time traveling
Come to the beginning of a river
Itasca and the Mississippi."

From *Itasca: A Place of Beginnings,* written by Charlie Maguire for the grand opening of the Jacob V. Brower Visitor Center at Itasca State Park, 2000

On April 20, 1891, Minnesota governor William R. Merriam signed into law a bill creating Itasca State Park—the first piece of Minnesota land to be designated a state park. But, as historian Roy Meyer writes, "as was to be the case many times in later years, the legislature's passage of an act authorizing a park did not mean that a park existed." The State of Minnesota owned only a small portion of the parkland described in the legislation. The rest, including the headwaters of the 2,552-mile-long Mississippi River, was owned by the federal government, by railroads, and by logging companies.

And so, over the next decades, a struggle ensued to acquire the land that would eventually become one of Minnesota's most popular destinations. The federal lands were turned over with little fanfare, and eventually the state legislature appropriated funds to begin

HEADWATERS

HERE 1467 FEET ABOVE THE OCEAN

THE MIGHTY MISSISSIPPI BEGINS TO FLOW ON ITS

WINDING WAY TO THE GULF OF

MEXICO, 2546 MILES

purchasing some of the land from private companies. Meanwhile, though, Itasca's valuable
resources—notably its trees—continued to be
harvested. One particularly notorious moment
in the struggle between conservationists and loggers occurred in 1900, when loggers dammed
the Mississippi and flooded Lake Itasca, which
they filled with cut timber. This went on for
three years, until Mary Gibbs, a young woman
who had taken over as state park commissioner
after her father's death, served a warrant to loggers—despite death threats—that forced open
the dam gates and relieved flooding on the lake.

Large-scale logging finally ended in Itasca
State Park in 1920. In the 1930s, with the help
of the Civilian Conservation Corps, the park
was spruced up—trees were planted, a
dam was built to stabilize the lake level,
and the log buildings and lodges still in
use today were built. Today, the park
totals more than 32,000 acres with
more than 100 lakes, including Lake
Itasca, which draws close to a half
million visitors a year.

Jeffers Petroglyphs

Minnesota's oldest stories, etched in stone

J effers Petroglyphs is where Minnesota's recorded history began," writes nominator Tom Sanders, Jeffers Petroglyphs Historic Site manager for the Minnesota Historical Society. There are more than 2,000 petroglyphs, or rock carvings, made between 5,000 and 250 years ago, on a 150-by-1,000-foot expanse of quartzite in Cottonwood County, in the southwestern part of the state.

The carvings "represent the prayers of people seeking spiritual guidance and record their parables and historic events," Sanders continues. "They document the perseverance of the people, including the Cheyenne, Dakota, Arapaho, Otoe, and Iowa, who thrived on this prairie for thousands of years because of their deep understanding and intimate relationship with their physical and spiritual world."

Some of the symbols carved at Jeffers depict weapons, such as an atlatl, a handheld tool that was used by hunters to propel a spear. There are also images of spear tips used by hunters, as well as a range of symbols from thunderbirds to dragonflies, turtles to buffalos. Why were the carvings made? No one is completely certain, but it's likely that they were used to record events and to accompany prayers and ceremonies.

"Today American Indians visit and pray at this sacred place. In fact, Jeffers Petroglyphs may be one of the oldest continually used sacred sites in the world. It provides a rare and profound experience for non-Indians seeking to understand American Indian culture and history."

These two stick-figure carvings hold atlatls, spear-throwing hunting tools.

Frederick McKinley Jones (1892–1961)

Making Minnesota even colder

When you read the story of someone like Fred Jones, it's hard not to feel like a slacker by comparison. A self-taught mechanic, Jones held more than sixty patents, most for refrigeration systems. But he also invented a portable X-ray machine, an automatic ticket-taker, a sound-track movie projector, and a self-starting gas motor.

Born near Cincinnati to a poor African American family, Jones was orphaned and on his own by the time he arrived in Kittson County, Minnesota, in 1912. He started inventing early, building radios, the portable X-ray machine, and improved surgical equipment for local doctors. Stationed in France during World War I, he worked as an electrician. He returned home to Hallock, Minnesota, where he worked as a garage mechanic and raced cars. In 1929, Joe Numero, who sold equipment for the movie industry, persuaded Jones to come work with him in Minneapolis. It was during that time that Jones invented a box-office device that automatically distributed tickets and change to customers (patented in 1939).

One hot summer night in 1935, the story goes, Jones talked to a trucker who was frustrated because a load of chicken he was carrying spoiled before he could reach his destination. Drawing on his mechanical know-how, Jones built a refrigeration unit for trucks that was compact, shockproof, and automatic. Jones and Numero founded Thermo King Company to market their products, which soon included systems for trains and ships as well as for trucks. Today, Thermo King is the world's largest truck refrigeration company. So, next time you enjoy fruit in the middle of winter or salmon shipped fresh from Seattle, think of Fred Jones.

J. R. Watkins Medical Company

A new standard for customer satisfaction

"If not fully satisfied, your money cheerfully refunded." We take statements like this for granted today, but when twenty-eight-year-old entrepreneur Joseph Ray Watkins of Plainview, Minnesota, put that message on a bottle of his Red Liniment, he was a trailblazer. In 1869, a year after Watkins first sold his patented combination of Asian camphor and red pepper extract, he bottled it in patented Trial Mark bottles, which showed how much of a product could be used before returned for a refund.

The secret to Watkins's success lay not only in his money-back guarantee but also in his sales force, a well-trained, highly motivated bunch that sold his products door-to-door. In 1885, the rapidly expanding company moved its headquarters to Winona, Minnesota. Ten years later, the company expanded its line of natural remedies to include gourmet cooking items: vanilla extract, black pepper, and cinnamon. In 1913, Watkins went international by opening a branch office in Winnipeg, Manitoba, and within two years, it had become the world's largest direct-sales company.

By 1940, Watkins's 10,000 sales associates—more than those employed by the better-known Fuller Brush Company—were offering 200 products, including vitamins, herbal remedies, and a range of baking goods. In 1978, multimillionaire businessman Irwin Jacobs bought the company from the Watkins family. Jacobs's son Mark is now president of Watkins, Inc., and sales are good. And what of J. R. Watkins's Red Liniment? It's still available, now through the company's website as well as from sales representatives. And it's still sold in a Trial Mark bottle.

C. A. Lawrence, Watkins' Remedies salesman, 1900

Hamilton Harris Judson (1849–1920)

Connecting Minnesota's farmers to the world

The Farmington, Minnesota, post office had been in operation for almost three decades in 1884, when Hamilton Harris Judson was appointed its ninth postmaster. He took his job seriously, arriving at 7 AM seven days a week and staying until 10 PM. During harvest season, he kept the post office open even later to accommodate area farmers.

In August 1896, Judson and Israel Herrick, publisher of the *Dakota County Tribune,* were asked to design several rural delivery routes in the Farmington area. The U.S. Congress was testing the concept of Rural Free Delivery—an expansion of postal duties that meant direct, daily delivery to farmers. The Farmington post office was only the second one in the nation to attempt Rural Free Delivery.

Judson and Herrick submitted three twenty-five-mile routes to Congress, and all were accepted. In early 1897, a fourth route was added. Rural Free Delivery in Farmington was off and running. The *Dakota County Tribune* wrote, "A promiscuous variety of mail boxes may now be seen near the entrance of door yards in which the mail carrier collects and delivers mail. We hope this experience will be a successful one as it is very handy to have our mail delivered daily." Newspaper publisher Herrick knew a good thing when he saw it, too. "Rural mail delivery will begin in a short time now," he wrote in the November 19, 1896, issue of the *Tribune.* "Subscribe for a daily newspaper now and have it left at the house every day. To new subscribers, the *Tribune* will give the daily *Minneapolis Tribune* and the *Dakota Country Tribune* one year for five dollars."

The Farmington experiment was a success, paving the way for other rural Minnesotans to experience the convenience and reliability of Rural Free Delivery. Hamilton Judson kept at his job until 1914. "Mr. Judson steps down and out with a record rarely attained by anyone, with none better," wrote the *Tribune.* He died six years later. His obituary said it best: "Hamilton Harris Judson, although modest of manner and declining in accepting honor where honor was due, was the greatest of all our citizens." Today, the Farmington post office is named for Judson.

Garrison Keillor (1942–)

Tuning in to Minnesota culture

In November 2006, Garrison Keillor opened a bookstore in a quiet, upscale St. Paul neighborhood. The news of the opening, like most news related to the "Old Scout," elicited much and varied commentary. Here's one blogger's reaction: "Opening a bookstore, eh? I suppose the progression makes good sense: writer, radio performer, novelist, public radio mogul, screenwriter, movie star—now, bookstore owner! Only one slot left after that: the Pope of Minnesota."

Okay, the point is well taken: Garrison Keillor is a resounding success in a number of fields, and that success is due in large part to his acute observations of the local scene. Keillor doesn't just happen to be from here—he's a performer who trades on being from here. Keillor has given the world an interpretation of Minnesota life that some view as accurate while others say evokes a time that never was. But love it or loathe it, Keillor's Minnesota is known worldwide. Ask anyone who's recently returned to Minnesota from far-flung travels, and you'll get the same story: when the subject of Minnesota comes up, people mention Prince, the Mall of America, and Garrison Keillor—and not necessarily in that order.

How did this happen? Gary Edward Keillor was born in 1942 in Anoka, Minnesota, a small town about a half hour's drive from downtown St. Paul. He graduated from the University of Minnesota with a bachelor's degree in English in 1966; three years later, he began working for Minnesota Public Radio, hosting the morning drive-time show, *A Prairie Home Companion.* From 1974 until 1987, and again from 1993 to the present, Keillor has hosted a successful radio variety show that showcases his folksy, carefully crafted stories of life in the fictional town of Lake Wobegon. Along the way, he has published several best-selling books and made regular appearances in the *New Yorker* and, more recently, on websites, including *Salon.com*; in 2006, he wrote the script for and appeared in Robert Altman's last film, *A Prairie Home Companion.*

Today, Keillor's radio show reaches millions of listeners each week via more than 600 public radio stations. He's at the top of his game but insists that he will retire soon, content to spend his time at home with his family and in his St. Paul bookstore. It could happen; or, perhaps, in the life of this champion storyteller, the next chapter has yet to be written.

Oliver H. Kelley (1826–1913)

Founder of the nation's largest agricultural fraternity

He was a "book farmer," a man who had learned what he knew about agriculture from reading rather than from direct experience. Born in Boston, Oliver Kelley arrived in St. Paul via steamboat in 1849, the year Minnesota was established as a territory. The following year he moved to Itasca, a small town near present-day Elk River.

Kelley was a progressive farmer, anxious to adopt the newest methods and to procure the newest equipment. He built one of the first frame barns north of St. Anthony and planted the first timothy hay. He installed an elaborate irrigation system on his farm and experimented with a variety of fruits and vegetables. He was a born leader, active in local agricultural societies and dedicated to ensuring that the area's new farmers benefited from each others' experiences.

In 1864, Kelley became a clerk for the U.S. Bureau of Agriculture. For two years, he divided his time between Minnesota and Washington, D.C. In 1867, on a bureau visit to the South, the idea of a national farmers' organization first occurred to him. "Encourage them to read and think; to plant fruits and flowers,—beautify their homes; elevate them; make them progressive," he wrote in a letter to a friend. "I long to see the great army of producers in our country, turn their eyes up from their work; stir up those brains, now mere machines . . . set them to think,—

let them feel that they are human beings, and the strength of the nation, their labor honorable, and farming the highest calling on earth."

On December 4, 1867, Oliver Kelley and six of his associates from the bureau founded the National Grange of the Order of Patrons of Husbandry. Within two years, Minnesota had forty Grange chapters and a state organization, and Granges were in the works in Illinois, Iowa, and Wisconsin.

The Grange was, in Kelley's mind, both a social organization and an advocacy group. He wrote newspaper articles that were increasingly critical of manufacturing and processing monopolies that fixed prices at rates unfair to farmers and of railroads with exorbitant freight rates. As its influence grew, so did the Grange's membership. By the end of 1873, there were 379 chapters in Minnesota and about 9,000 across the country, with a total membership of almost 700,000. Today, the National Grange has 300,000 members from 3,600 branches in 37 states.

OLIVER H. KELLEY HOME
KELLEY'S IDEA OF A NATIONAL SOCIETY FOR THE SOCIAL AND ECONOMIC BETTERMENT OF THE FARMER LED TO THE FOUNDING OF THE ORDER OF PATRONS OF HUSBANDRY AT WASHINGTON, DECEMBER 4 1867.
AS FIRST SECRETARY OF THE NATIONAL GRANGE, KELLEY MAINTAINED THE HEADQUARTERS OF THE ORDER ON THIS FARM UNTIL 1870.

Sister Elizabeth Kenny (1880–1952)

The power of one fights an epidemic

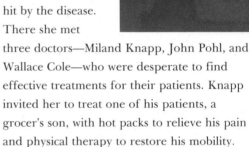

Polio, an infectious viral disease that is also called infantile paralysis, reached its peak in the United States in 1952 with 58,000 cases, causing 3,145 deaths and leaving 21,269 people with varying degrees of paralysis. Beginning in 1916, the disease had been at epidemic levels somewhere in the country each summer. Into this culture of fear and suffering stepped Elizabeth Kenny, a self-taught Australian bush nurse. Kenny, who had earned the military rank "Sister" while serving with the Australia Army Nursing Service during World War I, had developed a successful program of massage and exercise that restored polio patients' strength and mobility. But the Australian medical profession did not support her unorthodox treatments.

In 1940, she came to the United States, seeking acceptance for her practices. The American Medical Association spurned her— her term for the cause of polio-related paralysis, "mental alienation," wasn't found in any medical dictionary. Nor was her system of "muscle re-education" a standard procedure. Instead, polio patients were isolated from others, their limbs immobilized with braces or their bodies encased in iron lungs.

Kenny made her way to the Mayo Clinic, where doctors were receptive to her ideas. There were few polio patients for Kenny to treat in Rochester, however, so she went to Minneapolis, a city particularly hard-hit by the disease. There she met three doctors—Miland Knapp, John Pohl, and Wallace Cole—who were desperate to find effective treatments for their patients. Knapp invited her to treat one of his patients, a grocer's son, with hot packs to relieve his pain and physical therapy to restore his mobility.

(Opposite top) Sister Elizabeth Kenny, 1915; (opposite bottom) Sister Kenny (far right) and her niece meet actor Cary Grant at the 1946 opening of the movie Sister Kenny; *(above) dedication ceremony, Kenny Rehabilitation Institute, Minneapolis, September 17, 1942*

The treatment was successful, Knapp became a convert, and Kenny was given permission to treat patients at Minneapolis General Hospital. Fifty-five percent of her patients returned to normal function; the rest regained varying degrees of mobility.

Sister Kenny was a force to be reckoned with—a statuesque woman with snow-white hair who did not suffer fools gladly. Her zeal yielded results—she convinced a group of Minneapolis businessmen to back her efforts, each donating $412 toward what eventually became the Kenny Rehabilitation Institute. Her ideas are still in use around the world and in Minneapolis at the Sister Kenny Institute.

Kensington Runestone

For more than a century, the debate has raged on

Quick—what Minnesota treasure was described as an "important archaeological object" when it was exhibited at the Smithsonian Institution in 1948? Was it

a) a chunk of limestone found beneath St. Anthony Falls in Minneapolis;

b) a copper kettle retrieved from Lake Superior; or

c) the Kensington Runestone?

Yup—it was the Runestone. The celebrated slab was returned to Minnesota the next year and was featured in Territorial Centennial celebrations, where debates about its authenticity continued, as they had since it first came to light a half century before.

The story of the Runestone is familiar to many Minnesotans. In 1898, Olof Ohman, a Swedish immigrant who farmed near Kensington in Douglas County, said he and his son had found the stone while clearing trees on his land. Symbols—or "runes"—had been carved into the stone, which, when translated, suggested that Scandinavian explorers had left it behind in the year 1362. It was an amazing find, but when the scholarly community pronounced the runes a modern forgery, Ohman removed the stone from the spotlight and began using it as a steppingstone to his barn. In 1907, though, Norwegian American journalist Hjalmar Holand visited Ohman, took the stone

and the next year published a book declaring the Kensington Runestone's authenticity. People have been taking one side or the other in the matter ever since.

Whether we believe Ohman's story or not, the impact of the Kensington Runestone on the popular imagination over the past century has been tremendous. It traveled to the New York

Was Text of Rune Stone

George Rice, Minneapolis St[ar] writer, begins a series of articles [dis-]cussing the 56-year-old Kensing[ton]

YES J. A. Holvik, retired professor of Norse at Concordia college, Moorhead, Minn., has long believed the rune stone a fake. He contends Olof Ohman, farmer, who brought the stone to public notice, probably was the man who carved on it the runic inscription "recording" a journey of Norsemen to Minnesota in 1362.

★ ★ ★ ★

OLOF OHMAN (CEN[TER])
Soldiers stood by

World's Fair in 1965 and to Sweden in 2003, where Ohman's relatives living there viewed it for the first time. It is an object of civic pride in Alexandria, the seat of Douglas County, where a monumental runestone was erected in 1951 as a tourist attraction. The original stone is displayed in Alexandria's Runestone Museum, and the Ohman farm has been preserved as

> The inscription on the Runestone has been translated as follows: "We are 8 Goths and 22 Norwegians on an exploration journey from Vinland through the West. We had camp by a lake with 2 skerries one day's journey north from this stone. We were out and fished one day. After we came home, we found 10 of our men red with blood and dead. AVM save us from evil. We have 10 of our party by the sea to look after our ships, 14 days' journey from this island. Year 1362."

Kensington Park. A number of local organizations, including the Runestone Electric Association and Our Lady of the Runestone Catholic Church, keep the stone's image alive. It is a reminder of the power of the past and the undeniable thrill of a good mystery.

[Minneapolis Star, April 11 1955]

Before It Was Carved?

(See Page One.) Some fac-
ave led to this series of articles
d on this page.

NO Hjalmar Holand, Ephraim, Wis., is the man chiefly responsible for keeping the rune stone controversy alive since 1908, when he wrote that it was genuine record of Scandinavian penetration of North America 130 years before Columbus. His books and articles have convinced many including scholars and historians.

ONE (ABOUT 1929)
t a celebration

Theodore F. Koch (1854–1940)

The business side of European immigration

It's a life story repeated thousands of times in places throughout the United States. A European immigrant settles in the United States and convinces other immigrants to join him in his new home. It's happened over and over and it's still happening, with the result that America's cultural landscape is a patchwork of communities that hark back to their founders through their names, through the traditions they uphold in their annual festivals, and through the churches and social halls and synagogues and restaurants where community members gather. Nominator Robert Schoone-Jongen tells the story of Theodore Koch, born in Looward Castle in the Netherlands, whose sharp business sense and ability to match a good farmer with a good piece of land shaped a number of communities still going strong more than a century after their founding:

"During his twenty-five-year career as a colonizer and real estate developer in Minnesota, Koch sold in excess of 1,000,000 acres of land in more than a dozen counties to immigrants from many nations, including the Netherlands, Germany, Ireland, Sweden, Norway, and Denmark. Koch formed a vital link in the economic network that channeled cash from European investors into the state during the 1880s, 1890s, and 1900s. These investments provided much of the capital that created literally thousands of farms in every corner of the state.

"Koch, who served as vice consul of the Netherlands in St. Paul for about fifteen years, personally knew politicians and financiers and linked them to common farmers. These alliances and his connections with steamship companies and railroads on both sides of the Atlantic helped create Minnesota's rich cultural mosaic in settlements stretching from Askov in Pine County to Clara City [named for Koch's wife] in Chippewa County and Prinsburg in Kandiyohi County all the way to Lake Wilson in Murray County. Theodore F. Koch was truly one of the unsung heroes who made Minnesota the unique place it still remains."

Theodore and Clara Koch in 1937 at the fiftieth anniversary celebration of the town Mr. Koch named after his wife

Sinclair Lewis (1885–1951)

Small-town Minnesota's most subversive native son

Babbitt, noun [George F. Babbitt, character in the novel *Babbitt* (1922) by Sinclair Lewis]: *a person and especially a business or professional man who conforms unthinkingly to prevailing middle-class standards.*

It's not often that a novelist's characterizations are so sharp and well defined that new words are added to the dictionary because of them. But Sinclair Lewis was no ordinary novelist—he was a social critic who saw himself as a rebel against the constraints of American institutions and prejudice.

Lewis was born in Sauk Centre, Minnesota, in 1885. He attended Yale University, earning a bachelor's degree in 1908, and held several jobs with publishing companies and magazines. A prolific writer, he could complete a novel in a month and tried to publish at least one every year. He became famous when *Main Street*, a satirical account of a small town modeled on Sauk Centre, was published in 1920 and soon became a best seller. It was followed by *Babbitt* in 1922 and a number of other widely popular novels, including *Arrowsmith* (1925), which won a Pulitzer Prize that Lewis declined, *Elmer Gantry* (1927), and *Dodsworth* (1929).

Sinclair Lewis became the first American to win the Nobel Prize for Literature, in 1930. As the story goes, Lewis answered the telephone the morning the news broke and heard an excited man with an accent announcing that the prize was his. The caller was a Swedish newspaper correspondent, but Lewis thought it was one of his friends making a crank call. He mocked the caller, who finally hung up and asked an American friend to call Lewis instead. Once the news sunk in, Lewis was overwhelmed. Breathing heavily and somewhat dazed, he called his wife, who thought he was ill and asked him what was wrong. "Dorothy, I've got the Nobel Prize," he shouted. "Oh, have you? How nice for you," answered his skeptical wife. "Well, I have the Order of the Garter!"

"Sinclair Lewis's 1920 breakaway novel [*Main Street*], initially criticized for taking aim at the small-town status quo, is perhaps one of modern American literature's rarest gems. I say this without hesitation, especially because of the frankness and freshness with which Lewis paints a picture of small-town America's reluctance to accept change, especially coming from outsiders from the big city." **Nominator Larry Ellis Reed, Winona, Minnesota**

Charles A. Lindbergh Jr. (1902–1974)

A new law resulting from an unthinkable crime

He was the twentieth century's first international celebrity—a tall, photogenic, articulate young aviator who soared into the spotlight in 1927 when, at age twenty-five, he completed the first solo crossing of the Atlantic Ocean by air. He was Minnesota's own Charles Lindbergh—soon known around the world as "Lucky Lindy"—and his historic flight from New York to Paris on the *Spirit of St. Louis* brought him wealth, admiration, and a life in the public eye, to which he never became fully accustomed.

His solo flight may have made his a household name, but it was a later event in Lindbergh's life that was to have an even greater impact on the nation's history. On a cold, rainy night in March 1932, Charles and Anne Morrow Lindbergh's twenty-month-old son, also named Charles, was kidnapped from their New Jersey home. Sadly, after weeks of well-publicized searches, the boy's body was found near the family's estate. The search was on for his murderer.

After almost two years, Bruno Richard Hauptmann was brought to trial for the crime. Lindbergh's celebrity made the trial front-page news, fodder for sensational, invasive reporting from coast to coast. It was, in the words of journalist H. L. Mencken, "the greatest story since the Resurrection." Hauptmann was convicted

and executed in 1936, and the Lindbergh family, exhausted by the ordeal and angry with the media, left the United States in 1935 to live in England.

Beyond its lasting impact on Charles Lindbergh and his family, the effects of the trial were felt throughout the legal world. In 1937, the American Bar Association inserted a prohibition on courtroom photography into its Canons of Professional and Judicial Ethics. All but two states adopted the ban, and Congress amended the Federal Rules of Criminal Procedure to ban cameras and broadcasting from federal courts. Even more significantly, the kidnapping resulted in the 1932 passage of the Federal Kidnapping Act, popularly called the Lindbergh Law, which made it a federal offense to kidnap someone with the intent to seek a ransom or reward.

(Opposite) Anna C. Kelly reading the newspaper with headline "Lindy Baby Dead," with Hans Kelly listening to the radio, 1932; (above) Charles A. and Anne Morrow Lindbergh, 1929; (right) Charles A. Lindbergh Jr., lithograph, 1930

103

Ron and Al Lindner

Big fish in some awfully big ponds

I t all started in 1968, when brothers Ron and Al Lindner and their friend Nick Adams developed a new way of catching walleye. They came up with the Lindy Rig, an outfit whose simplicity and finesse appeals to both pros and more casual anglers. The Lindy Rig became an overnight success, in part because it works and in part because Al Lindner is an indefatigable, single-minded promoter who spent years on the road demonstrating his invention. "There's no replacing Al Lindner," said Steve Pennaz, executive director of Minnetonka's North American Fishing Club. "Almost single-handedly, he changed the way we fish."

Spurred on by the success of the Lindy Rig and other products made by their Brainerd-based Lindy Tackle Company, in 1975 the Lindners founded *In-Fisherman* magazine, filled with cutting-edge advice and plenty of tech talk. Four years later, *In-Fisherman Television,* hosted by Al Lindner, and *In-Fisherman Radio* went on the air. The company has also published a number of books and instructional videos. More important than their products and their fishing tips, according to nominator and serious recreational fisherman Jim Schreiber, is the Lindners' promotion of a catch-and-release philosophy. "They used their influence, shows, and articles to educate people about the importance of keeping a modest amount of smaller fish to eat and letting the rest go," writes Schreiber. "Fishing and the love of the northern lakes are core attributes and attractions of Minnesota. No one better represents these than Ron and Al Lindner."

Maud Hart Lovelace (1892–1980)

A storied childhood

Maud Hart Lovelace
Author of THE CHARMING SALLY

Maud Hart Lovelace's career began with a bedtime story. She used to lull her daughter to sleep with stories of her childhood in Mankato, Minnesota. The town was only forty years old when Maud was born, and what Maud remembered was playing on the hills surrounding the town, viewing the Minnesota River from atop the hills, and, of course, the friends and family members that enlivened her days.

In 1940, Lovelace published a book, *Betsy-Tacy*, based on her childhood memories. In the

book, Mankato became "Deep Valley" and Maud became "Betsy," and a host of other remembered places and people became part of her tales. Lovelace was already a published author by the time she wrote *Betsy-Tacy*. Her first novel, *The Black Angels*, was published in 1926, followed three years later by *Early Candlelight*. But it was the stories she wrote using her own diaries, letters, and prodigious memory that truly captured readers' imaginations. She never intended *Betsy-Tacy* to begin a series, but because of its success, she continued

to write. The series begins when Betsy and her friends turn five, takes them through high school and college, and ends with Betsy's wedding. A volume was published every year until 1955. Lovelace published many books in her lifetime, including thirteen in the *Betsy-Tacy* series, four others for children, and eight for adults.

In recent years, the formation of a Betsy-Tacy Society has brought renewed interest to the series. A bronze plaque on a stone bench at the top of Center Street in Mankato reads, "To honor Maud Hart Lovelace, who here began the childhood daydreams that one day would be our window to the past."

Lutheranism

Weaving the fabric of Minnesota

Architect's drawing of the Vasa Lutheran Home for Children, 1920

The faith of immigrants from Germany, Norway, Sweden, Finland, Denmark, Kenya, Tanzania, and elsewhere has shaped and continues to shape the character of Minnesota," writes nominator Kenath Harris. "Some of our state's most famous institutions—schools, colleges, universities, and hospitals—are a result of people acting out of their Lutheran faith. Lutheran Social Service of Minnesota has even shaped the culture of the state by helping to bring refugees from around the world."

The story of Lutheran Social Service, now Minnesota's largest statewide social service organization, begins with the work of Eric Norelius, a Swedish Lutheran minister who established congregations in Minnesota and Illinois. He was also one of the founders of Gustavus Adolphus College in St. Peter, Minnesota. In 1865, Norelius made a life-changing visit to St. Paul, which he later described in his autobiography: "I was notified that a family from Dalarna, Mikola Erik Erikson and his wife, had recently come from Sweden and both had died and left four children in a destitute and defenseless position. Asked if I had any advice regarding these children, it was as if a voice said to me: take them home with you. And I took them home to Red Wing, where I lived then.

"The following Sunday, I took the children with me to church service . . . and it was obvious that they needed care, clothes, and food. The congregation was immediately ready to take a collection for this purpose. The next step was to find a caretaker for the children and a place to live. The latter was found in the space under the church in Vasa, and the former found in Mrs. Brita Nilson, a devout and religious woman who came from Stockholm, Wisconsin."

Out of the Vasa congregation's generosity grew the Vasa Lutheran Home for Children and eventually Lutheran Social Service. Owned by the six state synods of the Evangelical Lutheran Church in America, the organization's mission is to express the love of Christ through its services.

Over the years, Lutheran Social Service has adapted its programs to meet the changing needs of its constituents. After World War II, its members began sponsoring displaced persons from Eastern Europe. In the 1950s, Lutheran Social Service orphanages were converted into homes for mentally challenged children and at-risk teens. In the early 1970s, Lutheran Social Service responded to the needs of political refugees from Africa and Asia by sponsoring their resettlement in Minnesota. In the 1980s, AIDS ministries were formed. Today, after 140 years of service, Lutheran Social Service employs more than 2,100 people in 300 communities throughout Minnesota.

Warren MacKenzie (1924–)

A master potter and a born teacher

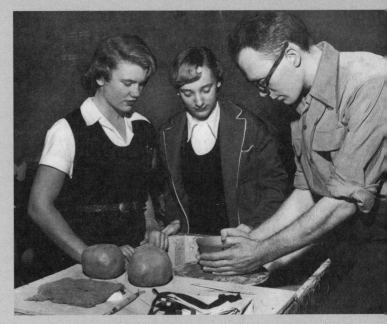

Warren MacKenzie with students Junie Stringer (far left) and Roxanne Freese, at Summit School, St. Paul, December 9, 1949

Warren MacKenzie once said that he became a potter "by the back door." Growing up in Kansas City, Missouri, and in Chicago, MacKenzie was always interested in art. His post–high school training at the Art Institute of Chicago, however, was interrupted in 1943 by his service in the U.S. Army. Returning to school on the GI Bill, he found that the painting classes he wanted to take were full and so turned to a course in ceramics instead.

MacKenzie's career shift turned out to be a fortuitous one. Today he is one of Minnesota's best-known and most prolific potters and teachers. The beauty in MacKenzie's work lies, above all else, in its functionality. While studying in Chicago, he was inspired by pottery exhibited at the Field Museum of Natural History. "The pots that really interested us," he said in a 2002 interview, "were the pots that people had used in their everyday life, and we began to think—I mean, whether it was ancient Greece or Africa or Europe or wherever, the pots that people had used in their homes were the ones that excited us. And so we thought, if those are the kinds of pots from every culture that interest us, why would we think that it should be any differ-ent in mid–North America twentieth century?"

After an apprenticeship with British potter Bernard Leach, who was known for his spare, Asian-inspired designs, MacKenzie settled into a studio in Stillwater, Minnesota. In 1953, he began his long teaching career at the University of Minnesota, where he was named a Regents Professor in 1984. He is now professor emeritus. Over the years, MacKenzie has inspired hundreds of students at the university and at summer programs throughout the country.

Paul Manship (1885–1966)

A Minnesota boy makes it in the Big Apple

St. Paul–born sculptor Paul Manship created one of the nation's most recognizable public sculptures: the soaring, golden Prometheus that adorns Rockefeller Center. Built in 1929, Rockefeller Center was meant to symbolize the hope that the United States would rebound from the economic hardships of the Depression. Paul Manship was at the top of his game when he received the commission for Prometheus in 1934, and his gravity-defying interpretation of the Titan who gave mankind the gift of fire captured the optimism that Rockefeller Center's backers hoped to present to their troubled nation.

Paul Manship was something of a golden boy himself. He dropped out of St. Paul's Mechanic Arts High School at fifteen and enrolled in the St. Paul School of Art. Always a doodler, he intended to pursue a career as a painter. But he was color-blind and thus turned to sculpture.

By the time he was nineteen, Manship had saved enough money from his work as a freelance illustrator to move to New York, where he embarked on a series of apprenticeships with the era's well-known sculptors. In 1909, at age twenty-three, he became the youngest sculptor ever awarded the coveted American Prix de Rome, which funded a three-year study trip through Italy and Greece. In Europe, especially after focusing on form in

the work of ancient sculptors, Manship found his artistic voice. He developed a streamlined, linear style that broke with what he had learned from his American mentors. When he returned to the United States, his work drew broad critical acclaim, and he soon became the toast of the New York art world.

Fame is fleeting, of course. Manship enjoyed several decades in the limelight and completed some 700 works. In the 1940s, though, Manship's style fell out of favor. He became just a footnote in art history textbooks until the 1980s, when his works were favorably reevaluated. As historian William Stott wrote in the catalog for a 1985 centenary exhibit of Manship's works at the Minnesota Museum of American Art, "Paul Manship, feeling mortal, wrote in 1943, 'I am always fearful that the old reputation will slump.' . . . On his hundredth birthday Manship can sleep easy. Reputation is fickle, but competent sculpture has a long half-life; his time has been and gone, and is coming."

(Left) Paul Manship's Cochran Park Memorial, Indian Hunter and His Dog; *(top) Manship family portrait*

Market Hunting

Bad practices lead to better wildlife management

Seven men lined up for the camera, each with a firearm, each with a steely-eyed gaze that tells us a rifle isn't just a casual accessory. Wondering what's going on? The photo's caption reveals more of the story: "Dewey Brothers, market hunters and crack shots, Fergus Falls, about 1910."

The Dewey Brothers were participants in a practice that meant big business in Minnesota at the end of the nineteenth century and into the twentieth. Nominator Doug Lodermeier explains: "Minnesota is known today as a model of smart, progressive, and pragmatic conservation policies. What most Minnesotans are not aware of is the large part that market hunting played in producing our current game-management laws and conservation movements.

"This reckless process of commercially killing and selling animals, particularly ducks, completely changed the way we approach Minnesota's natural resources today—fortunately, for the better. Three lakes in particular—Heron

Lake, known as the "Chesapeake of the West," Swan Lake in southern Minnesota, and Lake Christina to the north—once epitomized the wholesale slaughter of our natural resources. At one time, as many as 700,000 canvasback migrated through Heron Lake. Unfortunately, through practices such as baiting, punt guns, and indiscriminate harvesting, market hunting decimated this duck population in the name of fat profits from Twin Cities, Chicago, and East Coast markets."

It wasn't until 1931 that Minnesota had a Department of Conservation (renamed the Department of Natural Resources in 1971). Before then, hunting regulations were handled through a combination of governmental efforts and private initiatives. The earliest example of a private regulatory agreement came in about 1906, when a group of hunters signed the Lake Heron agreement. This act restricted shooting hours, boat traffic, and open-water hunting on the lake. Its intent was to extend opportunities to all hunters throughout the season, and it's still in effect today. The Lake Heron agreement and other such "self-policing" acts are, according to Lodermeier, "some of Minnesota's and the nation's proudest examples of recognizing destructive practices and having the courage and foresight to overcome them."

Mayo Clinic

A family's passion revolutionizes the world of medicine

On May 31, 1819, a boy was born in a small village near Manchester, England. His father died when the boy was only seven, leaving his mother to raise him and his five siblings. She worked hard to provide a good education for her children; the boy was tutored in Latin and Greek and began studies in medicine and science with John Dalton, who would later be known as "the father of modern physical science" for his groundbreaking work in developing the atomic theory of matter.

The boy grew into a man, and at twenty-seven he left Manchester for the United States.

He landed in New York and soon moved west, working as a pharmacist, a tailor, a census taker, a farmer, a newspaper publisher, a justice of the peace, a ferryboat operator, and a veterinarian before completing his medical training in Indiana in 1850 and moving to Minnesota four years later.

Thus begins the story of Dr. William Worrall Mayo, whose name is synonymous today with high-quality, compassionate health care. Dr. Mayo and his sons, William and Charles, helped put our state on the map when they founded their clinic in Rochester, Minnesota.

In 1861, William Mayo, then living in Le Sueur, Minnesota, volunteered for duty in the Union army, but his application for regimental surgeon was denied. Two years later, he was appointed the examining surgeon for an enrollment board based in Rochester that selected military recruits. In January 1864, William Mayo, his wife, Louise—a skilled milliner who would later become her husband's medical assistant— and their children settled down in Rochester for good.

From the start, the Mayos' practice was a family affair. Mrs. Mayo instructed her sons, Will and Charlie, in botany as they worked in the garden; their father taught them chemistry and anatomy, and if an emergency called for it, he invited them, their sisters, and their mother to accompany him on patient calls. "We came along in medicine like boys on a farm," Charlie later said. After earning their medical degrees—Will from the University of Michigan in 1883 and Charlie from Chicago Medical College five years later—they both returned to Rochester to join their father's growing practice.

On August 21, 1883, a devastating tornado swept through Rochester. The Mayos and other Rochester doctors soon established an emergency hospital in the town's dance hall. Recognizing the need for round-the-clock care for patients, the Mayos enlisted the help of Mother Alfred Moes and the Sisters of St. Francis. Though trained as teachers, the nuns remained at the temporary hospital until it closed. Mother Alfred didn't forget her experience, though, and she began working

with the Mayo family to establish a permanent hospital in Rochester. In 1889, St. Mary's Hospital, a three-story brick building equipped for twenty-seven patients, opened. It became the Mayo Clinic in 1914.

The practices that make Mayo Clinic an international name today were established in the early years. Teamwork—groups of specialists working together to teach, to learn, and to treat patients—is at the heart of the clinic's practice of integrated care. Dr. Henry Plummer, who joined the clinic in 1901, established other innovations. Credited with operating the clinic's first X-ray machine, Plummer was also the architect of the system of patient record keeping—in which each patient is assigned a number and a unique medical history chart—that is the foundation of today's record systems.

> "The sum-total of medical knowledge is now so great and wide-spreading that it would be futile for one man to attempt to acquire, or for any one man to assume that he has, even a good working knowledge of any large part of the whole. . . . The best interest of the patient is the only interest to be considered, and in order that the sick may have the benefit of advancing knowledge, union of forces is necessary."
> Dr. William Worrall Mayo, 1910

(Opposite page) Charles (left) and William Mayo

Eugene J. McCarthy (1916–2005)

A quiet man rallies America's young voters

He was a reluctant politician, a thoughtful, sharp-witted man who once summed up his profession by saying that "being in politics is like being a football coach. You have to be smart enough to understand the game, and dumb enough to think it's important." He was elected to the U.S. Congress and to the Senate but made his most significant contribution to the national scene during a political race that ended in his defeat.

Eugene McCarthy was born in Watkins, Minnesota, near Collegeville, and grew up in the shadow of St. John's Abbey. He graduated from St. John's University in 1935 and considered becoming a Benedictine monk. Instead he

> The maple tree that night
> Without a wind or rain
> Let go its leaves
> Because its time had come.
> Brown veined, spotted,
> Like old hands, fluttering in blessing,
> They fell upon my head
> And shoulders, and then
> Down to the quiet at my feet.
> I stood, and stood
> Until the tree was bare
> And have told no one
> But you that I was there.
> From "The Maple Tree,"
> by Eugene McCarthy

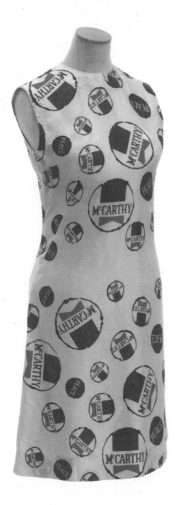

became a teacher, first in high schools, then as a professor of economics, education, and sociology at St. John's, and later at what is now the University of St. Thomas. He published seventeen books, including political studies, memoirs, and poetry.

In 1949, McCarthy joined Minnesota's newly formed DFL Party and was elected to Congress, where he served until 1959. From 1959 to 1971, he served in the U.S. Senate, forging a reputation as an outspoken critic of the Vietnam War. He ran for president in the 1968 election. In announcing his candidacy, he posited that "the issue of the war in Vietnam is not really a separate issue, but one which must be dealt with in the configuration of other problems to which it is related. And it is within this broader context that I intend to make the case to the people of the United States."

McCarthy was one of the first mainstream Democrats to break ranks with their party by protesting U.S. involvement in Vietnam. Backed by thousands of young, vocal antiwar activists who cleaned up their acts and joined his "Clean for Gene" presidential campaign, he took 42 percent of the Democratic vote in the New Hampshire primary, precipitating incumbent Lyndon Johnson's decision not to seek reelection. McCarthy's campaign came to a dramatic climax at the 1968 Democratic convention in Chicago, where protesters and the Chicago police force engaged in direct, violent confrontations. McCarthy lost the Democratic nomination to Hubert Humphrey, but he had succeeded in focusing the nation's attention on a nightmare that was still years from reaching its conclusion.

(Opposite page) Senator Eugene McCarthy on a campaign visit to St. John's University, 1968; (above) McCarthy "peace dress"

Fredrick L. McGhee (1861–1912)

A national spokesman for civil rights

One hundred years ago, Fredrick McGhee was known as one of Minnesota's most prominent trial lawyers. His road to the state's courtrooms followed a most unlikely route. He was born in Mississippi slaves' quarters in 1861, just months after the Civil War broke out. He and his family made their way to Knoxville, Tennessee, after the war, where Fredrick graduated from college, and then to Chicago, where he worked as a waiter to pay his way through law school. In 1889, he settled in St. Paul, where he became the first African American admitted to practice law in Minnesota.

Had McGhee spent all his time in Minnesota advocating for his clients, his contribution would already have been significant. He was known as a powerful, forceful orator, a formidable presence in the courtroom. But McGhee's influence didn't end there. After he converted to Catholicism, he became one of the founders of St. Peter Claver Church, still an important gathering place for St. Paul's African Americans. He became involved in national politics, first as a Republican and then as a Democrat. And in 1905 he was one of a group of thirty-two men, led by W. E. B. DuBois, who founded the Niagara Movement, which called for full civil liberties and an end to racial discrimination. The Niagara Movement was the catalyst for the 1909 founding of the National Association for the Advancement of Colored People (NAACP). McGhee founded Minnesota's first NAACP chapter. Years later, the group's chairman, Roy Wilkins, recalled that "it was through him that the NAACP reached St. Paul and [our house at] 906 Galtier Street."

"McGhee was not simply a lawyer," wrote W. E. B. DuBois in a 1912 obituary for his friend. "He was a staunch advocate of democracy, and because he knew by bitter experience how his own dark face had served as excuse for discouraging him and discriminating unfairly against him, he became especially an advocate of the rights of colored men."

L. David Mech (1937–)

Protecting a predator

L. David Mech

Early in his career, Dave Mech found himself standing fifteen feet away from a wild wolf. A graduate student in biology, Mech was following a pack of wolves through Isle Royale National Park when he had an opportunity to photograph one of them up close. As he snapped the shutter, the wolf cocked his head. "It was easy to believe that I could have reached out and petted the beast," Mech later wrote. "Although my standing face-to-face with a wild wolf had little scientific value, it certainly helped inspire me to learn all I could about the animal that had such a calm and gentle look yet earned its living by killing."

Mech's early interest developed into a lifelong passion that has resulted in his making Minnesota a national model in teaching how to live with wolves and to protect and manage wolf populations. A senior scientist with the U.S. Geological Survey and an adjunct professor in the University of Minnesota's Department of Fisheries, Wildlife, and Conservation Biology, Mech is also the founder of the International Wolf Center in Ely, Minnesota. Since 1985, the Wolf Center has given adults and children a chance to help advance the survival of wolf populations by learning about wolves, their relationship to wild lands, and the human role in their future. Today, just thirty years after the endangered animal had been driven almost to extinction in the lower forty-eight states, Minnesota is home to an estimated 3,000 wolves. The wolves were removed from the endangered list in March 2007.

"What makes Dave Mech special," writes nominator Kit Briem of Ely, "is his commitment to sharing his discoveries and knowledge with the general public as well as his peers. His insistence on accuracy and openness is crucial because people, including livestock growers in Minnesota and elsewhere, deserve the truth about these sometimes troublesome predators in order to live with and manage them successfully. Because of the positive changes he has created, from the International Wolf Center to wolf education throughout the United States and the world, Dr. L. David Mech is truly one of Minnesota's living legends."

Minneapolis Truckers' Strike, 1934

Change comes at a steep price

The 1930s were a time of intense labor activism in Minnesota, and one of the most notorious—and violent—battles between business and labor occurred in Minneapolis. The city's business leaders had managed to keep unions at bay through an organization called the Citizens Alliance. But, in 1933, activists Carl Skoglund and Vincent R. Dunne successfully organized truckers (also called teamsters) in the Minneapolis coal yards. In May 1934, their union, Teamsters Local 574, initiated a citywide strike that halted trucking

operations throughout Minneapolis. On May 25, after management accepted a federally mediated settlement that granted union recognition and wage conditions, the strike was settled.

But a clash over the terms of the settlement led to a second strike. The conflict peaked in late July, with a bloody, two-day battle at the city market, where strikers clashed with police, who were trying to open the market for farm produce to be brought in. The police force was increased, women strike supporters entered the fray, and 35,000 building trades workers went on strike in support of the teamsters. When Minnesota governor Floyd B. Olson called in the National Guard and the Citizens Alliance activated the local militia, strike leaders countered with "flying squads" of pickets. But the toll was sobering: 200 injured and 4 dead.

After lengthy negotiations over bargaining and wages, the two sides reached an agreement. The settlement was a resounding victory for the Minneapolis teamsters and for the broader labor movement. In Minneapolis and across the country, the workers' fight for a living wage and the right to organize unions and the violent opposition of business interests—all occurring

during the Depression's darkest years—spurred passage of the 1935 Wagner Act. This federal legislation legitimized and enforced the right of workers to collective bargaining through unions.

(Opposite) Police intervene in a clash between striking truckers and the Citizens Alliance, Minneapolis; (above) flag erected at the spot where Henry Ness, a striker, was slain during the riot on July 20, 1934

Minnesota Mining and Manufacturing

Changing our daily lives, one Post-it Note at a time

It's hard to believe, but Minnesota Mining and Manufacturing—the international corporation known today as 3M, with annual revenues in excess of $20 billion—got off to a very rocky start. The story goes like this: Henry S. Bryan, Dr. J. Danley Budd, Harmon Cable, William A. McGonagle, and John Dwan incorporated in 1902 at Two Harbors, on Lake Superior's North Shore. Their plan was to sell corundum, a mineral used by East Coast manufacturers for the grinding wheels used to polish products. There was only one thing standing between the five business partners and success: Minnesota's North Shore was lousy not with corundum, as they had been told, but with anorthosite, which was less useful for their needs.

Down but not out, they tried to make sandpaper from the anorthosite. When that didn't work, they finally turned a profit by making sandpaper from imported minerals, including Spanish garnet. But, in 1914, they hit another glitch when a shipment of garnet was inadvertently doused in olive oil during a rough crossing. When customers complained that the garnet

fell off the paper, the company figured out the problem, then solved it by washing and baking the garnet before making it into sandpaper. Sandpaper sales rebounded, then increased further in the 1920s when 3M introduced waterproof sandpaper.

Ingenuity and perseverance kept 3M afloat in its early years, and they are still the company's watchwords. William L. McKnight, who headed the company from 1929 to 1966, summed it up in 1948: "Mistakes will be made. But if a person is essentially right, the mistakes he or she makes are not as serious, in the long

and Post-it Notes. Each came about because its developers were allowed to dream, tinker, fiddle, mess up, dream some more, try, and try again until they achieved their goals of making products that met consumers' needs. What's the next great 3M product to hit the store shelves? Odds are that right now, somewhere within the company's headquarters in Maplewood, Minnesota, there's a scientist tinkering away, working on that very product, and dreaming of things to come.

Manufacturing 3M sandpaper, 1970s

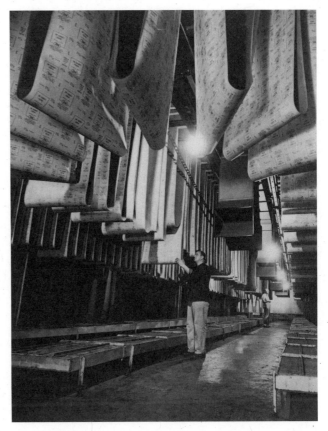

run, as the mistakes management will make if it undertakes to tell those in authority exactly how they must do their jobs."

Of 3M's 55,000 products, the best known are probably masking tape, Scotch Tape, Thinsulate,

"Who can live without Scotch Tape? Post-it Notes? 3M began as three guys in a garage trying to develop a better sandpaper. They later became the Minnesota Microsoft through our midwestern values of hard work, innovation, and entrepreneurship. Now 3M is a Minnesota-grown company that is known worldwide for all of its products that make our lives better."
Nominator Catherine Dorr, Minneapolis

Minnesota Multiphasic Personality Inventory

Getting to know you

The Minnesota Multiphasic Personality Inventory (MMPI) was developed in the late 1930s by Dr. Starke R. Hathaway, a psychologist, and Dr. J. C. McKinley, a psychiatrist, at the University of Minnesota. After years of clinical trials, it was first published and copyrighted in 1942. The MMPI and its revised second edition (MMPI-2) are assessment instruments that allow an examiner to draw some tentative conclusions about a person's typical behaviors and ways of thinking. The test outcomes can help an examiner, such as a psychologist, determine a person's outlook on life, typical mood, likely diagnoses, and potential problems in treatment. The MMPI-2 is used in a range of settings, from psychiatric assessments to criminal trials where a defendant's mental health may be of concern.

From the 1940s to the 1980s, the original MMPI was the most widely used and most intensely researched psychological assessment instrument in the world. The test was originally developed using an innovative process developed by Dr. Hathaway called empirical keying. Before the MMPI, most assessment tools used questions or tasks that the test designer assumed would realistically assess behaviors. To develop empirical keying, Hathaway and his colleagues wrote a wide range of true-or-false statements, many of which did not directly target typical psychiatric topics. The statements were given to groups of psychiatric inpatients and to others to determine which test items reliably differentiated the patients, both from each other and from the other groups. From there, the MMPI could be used to make preliminary diagnoses of some common psychiatric diagnoses.

The MMPI-2 was published in 1989. This version is based on much larger and more racially and culturally diverse community comparison groups than the original version.

Minnesota Orchestra

All together now

In 1903, a collection of Minneapolis's movers and shakers whose names are still familiar to us today, including the Pillsburys, the Peaveys, and the Pipers, formed a group known as the Philharmonic Club. Their goal was to raise $10,000 in each year to fund the newly formed Minneapolis Symphony Orchestra.

Why an orchestra? Minneapolis was a new, rapidly growing urban center at the turn of the century, and its leading citizens understood the importance of building a strong cultural base—an orchestra, museums, and the like—to accompany the economic and political infrastructures they were creating. And the new group was among a handful of groups in cities across the country that were inventing a new, uniquely American way to fund and present classical music. In Europe, state-supported orchestras and operas were the norm. But no such support existed in the United States, so business leaders and other music lovers took up the task.

The fifty-member orchestra played its first concert on November 5, 1903. On the podium was Emil Oberhoffer, a German-born musician who had landed in the Twin Cities, as legend has it, around 1885 as a member of a touring Gilbert and Sullivan troupe. When the troupe suddenly disbanded, Oberhoffer was stranded in Minneapolis. He found work as a church organist, hotel orchestra violist, and freelance lecturer and musician, until the Apollo Club, the city's leading chorus, hired him as its conductor. Four years later, the Philharmonic Club wooed him away, and from 1903 to 1922 he led the new orchestra to a national reputation.

In its early years, the orchestra (which wouldn't be known as the Minnesota Orchestra until 1968) inaugurated a number of signature programs still in practice today, from an ambitious touring schedule (they were known in Oberhoffer's time as "the orchestra on wheels") to weekend pops concerts to young people's concerts. Distinguished directors followed Oberhoffer, among them Eugene Ormandy, Dimitri Mitropoulos, Antal Dorati, and Stanislaw Skrowaczewski. The orchestra moved into Orchestra Hall in 1974. Today, the Minnesota Orchestra enjoys an international reputation, thanks to its ambitious recording and broadcast schedules and its innovative programming, including Sommerfest.

Beethoven String Quartet; (top) Orchestra Hall postcard, 1975

Minnesota State Fair

See ya there!

"T he Minnesota State Fair is our central cultural institution," wrote historian Karal Ann Marling in the preface to her 1990 book, *Blue Ribbon*, "the place where all the varied strands of immigration, agriculture, commerce, politics, aesthetic preference, and moral standards meet and mingle; the place where our collective past is preserved in the language of the premium lists and our collective future manifest in the project of the littlest 4-H'er."

Minnesota held its first territorial fair in 1854 and its first state fair five years later. Those early fairs were held primarily to attract newcomers to Minnesota, and the emphasis was on boosterism (imagine exhibits of giant vegetables grown in Minnesota's rich soil), education (imagine the region's farmers gathering to compare successes and failures in their grain crops), and entertainment (imagine brass bands, trotting horses, and balloon rides).

(Right) Butter sculptures of the winner and finalists of the annual Minnesota Dairy Princess Program are carved at the Fair. (Opposite top) The All-You-Can-Drink Milk booth is one of the most popular and affordable attractions at the Fair. (Opposite bottom) Watermelon display, Minnesota State Fair, 1895

Come to think of it, maybe things haven't changed all that much over the years. Boosterism is still very much in evidence at the State Fair, now promoted as the Great Minnesota Get-Together. And while the singular emphasis on agriculture has broadened with the years, there is still a great deal to be learned at the Fair, from the state-of-the-art displays in the Progress Center and the dealers describing late-model SUVs and ATVs on the land once dubbed Machinery Hill. And the Fair's enter-tainment offerings, from big-name performers in the Grandstand to bungee-jumping and other

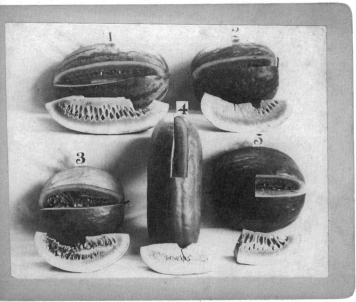

thrill rides just off the Midway, have eclipsed many of its other offerings.

Maybe that's the Minnesota State Fair's secret of success—the reason it remains one of the country's largest, most-visited fairs. It reflects the popular culture and concerns of its day while at the same time shaping them. Like one of those multi-purpose gadgets demonstrated at the Grandstand, the Fair is both a barometer and a blender. And like one of those gadgets, once we've seen it in action, we know we can't live without it.

Vilhelm Moberg (1898–1973) and Ole E. Rølvaag (1876–1931)

Telling it like it was

They were both born into humble circumstances in Scandinavian countries. One immigrated to America, where he became a scholar committed to preserving his people's culture. The other stayed home, where he became one of his country's best-known writers and social critics. Together, they gave the world an unvarnished view of what it meant to pull up stakes in one's homeland and rebuild a life in the Midwest in the late nineteenth century.

Ole Rølvaag was twenty years old when he came to the United States from his home in Norway, where he had worked as a fisherman. He settled in South Dakota, where he studied at Augustana Academy (later College). He later completed a bachelor's degree and a master's degree at St. Olaf College in Northfield, Minnesota, and then served there as a professor of Norwegian language and literature from 1906 to 1931. He began writing fiction, short stories, and poems during his early teaching years; his works are severe, dramatic, and unsparing in their accounts of the hardships of immigrant life. His best-known novel is *Giants in the Earth,* the first in a trilogy about a Norwegian family's struggles in the Dakotas.

(Above) Vilhelm Moberg; (opposite) Ole E. Rølvaag and wife, wedding picture, 1901

The book ends with a disappointing, oft-cited image of its protagonist's sad end:

> "On the west side of the stack sat a man, with his back to the mouldering hay. This was in the middle of a warm day in May, yet the man had two pairs of skis along with him; one pair lay beside him on the ground, the other was tied to his back. He had a heavy stocking cap pulled well down over his forehead, and large mittens on his hands; in each hand he clutched a staff. . . . To the boys, it looked as though the man were sitting there resting while he waited for better skiing. . . .
>
> ". . . His face was ashen and drawn. His eyes were set toward the west."

Vilhelm Moberg was born in Småland, Sweden. He worked a number of jobs, from farming to glassblowing to editing a newspaper, until he became a recognized author. Politically active throughout his life, he supported socialism and opposed Sweden's trade with Germany during World War II. His most famous work is a series of four novels—*The Emigrants, Unto a Good Land, The Settlers,* and *Last Letter Home,* all published in Sweden between 1949 and 1959, chronicling one Swedish family's migration to Minnesota in the mid- to late nineteenth century—a story that mirrored some of the author's own relatives' lives. Two of the novels in this series—*The Emigrants* and *Unto a Good Land*—were made into critically acclaimed films by Swedish director Jan Troell in 1971 and 1972, with Max von Sydow and Liv Ullmann in starring roles.

"They stood crowded together on deck like a herd of cattle," writes Moberg in the final pages of *The Emigrants,* "shackled in the narrow stalls of the byre during a whole long winter, and at last stretching their necks and turning toward the door when it began to smell of spring and fresh grass and meadows. . . . The life at sea had undermined their bodies and souls. The land-frenzy was bringing them new strength. They had again seen the green earth. As seekers of new homes they had come sailing from the earth—now they were back on the earth, and felt life returning."

Walter F. Mondale (1928–)

A new breed of vice president

The favorite son of Ceylon, Minnesota, Walter Mondale received his law degree from the University of Minnesota Law School in 1956. After a stint as Minnesota's attorney general, he was named and then elected to the U.S. Senate, where he served from 1964 until becoming vice president.

On December 9, 1976, vice president–elect Walter Mondale sent president-elect Jimmy Carter a memo titled "The Role of the Vice President in the Carter Administration." Only a month after their victory, "Grits and Fritz" had already engaged in several serious discussions about the lack of definition and chronic underutilization that had long characterized the vice presidency. As Richard Moe, Mondale's chief of staff, described it, the office was "a constitutional afterthought designed solely to provide a president-in-reserve, and for 200 years it languished in obscurity, derision, and irrelevance."

Mondale and Carter set out to change all that—and in doing so, they redefined the role of the vice president for future generations. "The biggest single problem of our recent administrations has been the failure of the President to be exposed to independent analysis not conditioned by what it is thought he wants to hear or often what others want him to hear," Mondale wrote. "I hope to offer impartial advice and help assure that you are not shielded from points of view that you should hear."

In an unprecedented move, Carter placed Mondale's office in the West Wing of the White House. He arranged for close communication and coordination between staff assigned to the two men. In the end, these changes resulted in Mondale's being a valued advisor during many of the key moments of the Carter presidency, from the Iran hostage crisis to negotiations with the U.S. Navy over the Vietnamese "boat people." Vice presidents since Mondale have continued to serve as important advisors to and collaborators with their presidents.

Walter Mondale ran for president in 1984 but lost to Ronald Reagan. He served as U.S. ambassador to Japan from 1993 to 1996. In 2002, after Paul Wellstone's death, he ran for the U.S. Senate in Wellstone's stead but lost to Republican Norm Coleman.

George Morrison (1919–2000)

A Minnesota artist, through and through

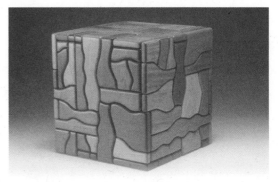

George Morrison grew up in Chippewa City, a mile east of Grand Marais on the North Shore in northern Minnesota. In a sense he never left there, despite his many years studying and teaching on the East Coast and in Europe. To say that he was inspired by nature is an understatement—Morrison was consumed by nature, completely captivated by its vitality and changeability. In his wood collages, sculptures, and paintings, Morrison incorporated abstracted images of trees, rocks, rivers, and skies. "He may have gone to Paris, painted on Cape Cod, taught at Rhode Island,"

wrote Grand Marais resident Pat Zankman, who nominated Morrison, "but he was always here."

After graduating from high school, Morrison enrolled in the Minneapolis School of Art (now the Minneapolis College of Art and Design). He continued his studies at New York's Art Students League; in 1952 he received a Fulbright Scholarship that funded a year's study in Italy and Spain. He returned to the United States the following year and embarked on a teaching career that led to various schools, including the Rhode Island School of Design and the University of Minnesota, all the while maintaining his ties to home. "He did something else of great importance in our small community," according to Zankman. "He helped to bridge the cultural/social gap between Indian and non-Indian. George Morrison, Native American, native son, serves as a role model within our schools for all our students. He has made it possible for others to excel."

(Bottom) George Morrison, 1993; (top) Cube, 1988

Mount Zion Hebrew Congregation

Minnesota's first Jewish congregation

The city of St. Paul had been incorporated for only two years when, in 1856, eight Jewish fur traders and clothing and liquor merchants founded Mount Zion Hebrew Congregation. The first services were held in a rented third-story room on Robert Street in downtown St. Paul. Mount Zion is a Reform congregation, and every Reform congregation in the Twin Cities and major Jewish organizations in St. Paul can trace their existence to the leaders of Mount Zion.

Members of Mount Zion quickly became involved in all facets of building their new city, both through their business ties and in their service to others. In 1895, the women of Mount Zion founded Neighborhood House on the city's West Side, a settlement house that welcomed the large waves of Eastern European Jews then moving to Minnesota. In 1903, Mount Zion gave Neighborhood House to the city of St. Paul, and over the years, it has served waves of immigrants and refugees that have sought new homes in Minnesota. Today,

Neighborhood House continues to involve members of Mount Zion in its programs, including providing emergency services and language classes and a host of other offerings to Minnesota's newest arrivals from Mexico, Laos, Somalia, and other countries.

In 1954, led by Rabbi W. Gunther Plaut, the Mount Zion congregation made a conscious decision to stay in St. Paul, choosing a building site on Summit Avenue in the midst of several other landmark churches. The temple board commissioned Bauhaus architect Erich Mendelsohn to design the temple. Today, 690 families gather regularly for religious services and to continue the congregation's service to its community.

(Top) Mount Zion Temple, 1958; (middle) Peter Stein sounds the shofar at the 150th anniversary celebration of Mount Zion Temple

Munsingwear

Necessity is the mother of invention

There's no denying it—without the right clothing, Minnesota winters are unbearable. Comfy outerwear is essential, of course, but we all know that it's what's underneath that really counts.

No one knew this better than entrepreneurs Frank H. Page, Edward O. Tuttle, and George D. Munsing, who founded Minneapolis's Northwestern Knitting Company in 1887 with the express purpose of making simple, comfortable undergarments. Much of the company's early success hinged on the patents filed by George Munsing, a tireless inventor. In 1888, for example, he patented a woolen knit fabric sure to please his customers: "It will be readily understood," according to the patent description, "that the desirable qualities of a fabric for this purpose are that it shall be heavy enough to be sufficiently warm; that it shall also have a fine attractive, and handsomely finished outer surface and a soft but smooth under surface that will not irritate the flesh of the wearer."

In 1919, the company was renamed Munsingwear. By then its place in the underwear industry was secure, thanks to its prodigious output of the humble yet essential union suit. Munsingwear's signature product was affordable (due to the company's well-honed production techniques), comfortable (due to Munsing's patented knitting techniques), and ubiquitous (due to Munsingwear's savvy marketing). With its 1897 advertisement in the *Ladies' Home Journal,* the company became the first to place an underwear ad in a national magazine. In 1917, the company's output was 30,000 garments a day. By 1923, Munsingwear, Inc., was the largest manufacturer in the world producing underwear under one trademark. It was also Minnesota's largest employer of women—85 percent of its 3,000 employees were female.

Business remained brisk over the years. Munsingwear made its last union suit in 1969, but by then the company had diversified and was making a range of products, from Vassarette undergarments for women to Grand Slam golf shirts for men (remember the penguin logo?). Munsingwear's Minneapolis production plant, built in 1915, closed in 1981. The building is now known as International Market Square. *Minneapolis Star and Tribune* columnist Jim Klobuchar spoke for many with his memories of the company's most notable product: "For generations, nobody made longjohns like Munsingwear. We wore them every day for seven months at a time in northern Minnesota. Every Monday was a reveille for the town's longjohns. They were marshaled in white regiments on the wash line, hanging in frozen attention."

Bing Crosby for Munsingwear

Bronko Nagurski (1908–1990)

Big man on campus

The story goes like this: Doc Spears, football coach for the University of Minnesota Gophers, made a recruiting trip to northern Minnesota in 1926. On a farm outside International Falls, he spotted a brawny young man plowing a field—without a horse. Spears soon signed the dynamo, and an athletic legend was born.

The young man's name was Bronislaw (Bronko) Nagurski. He played four positions for the university in football and in 1929 was named All-American at two of them—fullback and tackle (the only University of Minnesota player to ever do so). In 1930, he signed with the Chicago Bears. The Bears won two pro championships, in 1932 and 1933, and advanced to two more title games in 1934 and 1937, all during his tenure. Nagurski retired from professional football in 1938.

During the Depression, Bronko supplemented his football income with stints as a professional wrestler. In 1937, when he became world wrestling champion, he rated a spot in "Ripley's Believe It or Not" as the king of two sports. Two more wrestling championships in 1939 and 1941 followed before Nagurski retired and returned to his Minnesota farm. He came out of retirement just once, playing a strong final season for the depleted Bears during World War II.

The mystique didn't end when Bronko retired. Never one to toot his own horn, he refused most interviews, preferring to lead a quiet life on his farm and, after 1960, at the gas station he ran with his sons. The stories continued, of drivers pulling up at the pump and being greeted by a mountain of a man who screwed gas caps on so tightly you needed a wrench to remove them. In 1963, Bronko Nagurski was enshrined as a charter member of the Professional Football Hall of Fame.

Bronko Nagurski (left) with gubernatorial candidate Elmer L. Andersen at Nagurski Pure Oil Station, International Falls, 1960

Near v. Minnesota (1931)

A landmark case upholding freedom of speech

I n 1925, the Minnesota legislature passed the Public Nuisance Law, or "Minnesota Gag Law." Its purpose was to silence a rash of scandal sheets, including Duluth's *Rip-Saw,* the *Twin Cities Reporter,* published in both Minneapolis and St. Paul, and, especially, the *Saturday Press,* published in Minneapolis by Howard A. Guilford and Jay M. Near. With their frequent charges of government corruption and their anti-Semitic viewpoints, the publications' editors were characterized as courageous journalists or as notorious bottom-feeders, depending on one's point of view.

Two years later, Hennepin county attorney Floyd B. Olson filed a complaint against Near and Guilford's *Saturday Press,* asking for a restraining order under the Gag Law. It was granted, and the Minnesota Supreme Court later upheld the decision, ruling that the paper was a scandalous publication and that it constituted a nuisance and endangered safety.

The story might have ended there but for Near's next step, which eventually led him to the U.S. Supreme Court. He wrote to a newly founded New York organization, the American Civil Liberties Union (ACLU). Roger Baldwin, the ACLU's founder, gave Near $150 and a pledge to appeal his gag order. "We see in this new device for previous restraint a menace to the whole principle of freedom of the press," the ACLU said.

Near then garnered the support of Robert McCormick, publisher of the *Chicago Tribune.* The *Tribune*'s lawyer, Weymouth Kirkland, prepared an appeal and argued the first freedom of the press case of prior restraint before the U.S. Supreme Court. On July 31, 1931, the Supreme Court ruled that the Gag Law was unconstitutional.

As Fred W. Friendly wrote in his *Minnesota History* article (Winter 1978), "Censorship and Journalists' Privilege": "A paragraph of [Chief Justice] Hughes's majority opinion in the Near case is perhaps more relevant now than on that hot June day in 1931 when he read it aloud in the old Supreme Court chamber in the United States Capitol":

'The administration of government has become more complex, the opportunities for malfeasance and corruption have multiplied, crime has grown to most serious proportions, and the danger of its protection by criminal alliances and official neglect, emphasize the primary need of a vigilant and courageous press, especially in the great cities. The fact that the liberty of the press may be abused by miscreant purveyors of scandal does not make less necessary the immunity of the press from previous restraint in dealing with official misconduct.'"

Knute Nelson (1843–1923)

A Norwegian immigrant goes to Washington

There is a statue on the grounds of the Minnesota State Capitol that depicts U.S. senator Knute Nelson. The very embodiment of political power and prestige, the image of Nelson is flanked by two smaller sculptures: one depicting Nelson as a child with his mother and the other as a Civil War soldier. Nelson's life story is depicted through these sculptures as a reminder of the many European immigrants who arrived with little and went on to achieve much in Minnesota.

Born in Norway, Nelson was six years old when he and his widowed mother came to the United States. They eventually settled in Wisconsin; at age eighteen, Nelson enlisted in the Fourth Wisconsin Cavalry Regiment, serving from 1861 to 1865. He returned to Wisconsin and studied law in Madison, where he met his future wife, Nicolina.

The Nelson family moved to Alexandria, Minnesota, in 1871, where Knute practiced law and farmed. From there, he launched his political career, serving as Douglas County attorney, as Minnesota state senator from 1875 to 1878, and, from 1883 to 1889, as representative to the U.S. Congress from Minnesota's newly formed fifth district. It was during his time as a congressman that Nelson made one of the most significant moves of his political career. In 1889, as a member of the Committee on Indian Affairs, he drafted an act, "Relief and Civilization of the Chippewa Indians in Minnesota," commonly known as the Nelson Act, which stipulated that Ojibwe families receive "allotments" of land on the White Earth reservation. This attempt to consolidate all of Minnesota's Ojibwe people on a small land base resulted in the loss of Indian lands beyond what had already been ceded to the United States through treaties.

Nelson was elected governor of Minnesota in 1892 and 1894; he resigned to make a successful run for the U.S. Senate, where he served until his death in 1923. While in the Senate, he was involved in the creation of the Department of Commerce and Labor in 1902, as well as in the passage of the Nelson Bankruptcy Act in 1898, the first act of Congress that gave companies the option of protection from creditors. In 1908, in the midst of his senatorial career, biographer J. H. Baker summed up Nelson's career as follows: "That this plain and unassuming but earnest man, in the multitude of things which have pressed upon him in his busy life, has made some mistakes, is not to be denied. That his vigorous and decided manner has made him some enemies, is to be admitted. But take him for all in all, as a public man, for the immense practical and valuable service he has rendered to the state and nation."

Floyd B. Olson (1891–1936)

A man of the people makes it to the top

The 1920s and 1930s were hard times for Minnesota's farmers and laborers. Drought and the Great Depression had brought prices for farm goods to a low, and in the city jobs were scarce. Unions had not yet taken hold in the state. Out of this struggle came a radical political movement called the Farmer-Labor Party, and from the party came one of Minnesota's most popular governors— Floyd Bjornsterne Olson.

Born in north Minneapolis, the son of Scandinavian immigrants, Olson worked his way through a year at the University of Minnesota before heading to the Pacific Northwest to find work. He returned to Minneapolis, where he completed a law degree at Northwestern College of Law. In 1920, he became Hennepin County attorney, a position he held for ten years. He made a name for himself as a tough-talking, no-nonsense prosecutor by taking on graft among city officeholders and by challenging the Minnesota Citizens Alliance, a grassroots antiunion movement. In 1930, he was elected governor of Minnesota on the Farmer-Labor ticket.

During his time in office, Olson fought successfully against a relatively conservative legislature for unemployment relief, the enactment of a state income tax, and a moratorium on farm foreclosures. Through the strength of his personality, he helped make the Farmer-Labor Party the most successful third party in America's history. Many expected him to run for president, but cancer cut his life short. Biographer George H. Mayer said, "His pragmatic approach to problems melted the hostility of hard-headed conservatives, while his persuasive friendliness converted suspicion into open enthusiasm. An hour's conversation often won Olson a lifetime friend."

(Top) Floyd B. Olson (at right), 1932; (bottom) campaign headquarters, 1932

The Olympic Hockey Team, 1980

A Minnesota hockey legend stuns the world

If you asked Herb Brooks (1937–2003) about his greatest hockey achievement, he would answer that it was playing on St. Paul's Johnson High School team in 1955, when it won the state championship. He won that honor with a group of his best friends, he would say, and that had made all the difference.

But ask a hockey fan—or almost any Minnesotan, for that matter—that same question, and you would likely get a different answer. Herb Brooks is best known for the "Miracle on Ice," when he coached the 1980

U.S. Olympic hockey team to a gold medal. Composed mostly of college-aged players, twelve of them from Minnesota, who had been teammates and rivals for years, the U.S. team defeated Finland in the final match after beating the Soviet Union in the previous game. The Soviet Union was the odds-on favorite, having won four consecutive Olympic titles, from 1964 to 1976.

So much for the facts. The 1980 victory was one of those memorable moments that transcend sports history and become the stuff of

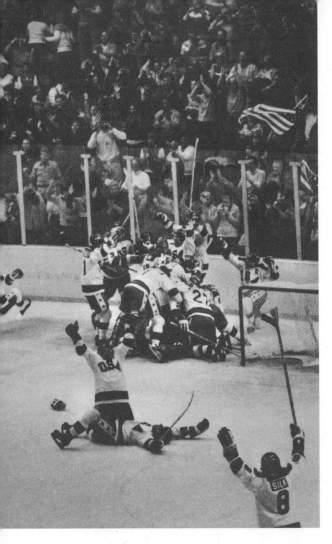

legend. Let's hear it straight from Brian Weber of Brainerd, Minnesota: "In 1980, as an eight-year-old hockey player from Virginia, Minnesota, I did not know that hockey was not the center of the universe, and that playing for the United States Olympic team was not the highest honor that could possibly be achieved in the entire world. The fact that the United States Olympic team was made up of amateur college kids, and was not seeded very high, was almost entirely lost on me. I knew that the USSR and Finland were very good. But it didn't matter—our team was mostly from Minnesota and we play hockey pretty good. We should—we've been doing it our entire lives.

"What I did not know of, or at least as an eight-year-old think too hard about, was the political and economic situation of the time. It makes me think of our neighbor, a miner with a very Finnish last name, who watched all the games with us. I'm sure he knew all about inflation, energy, unemployment, Iran hostages, Afghanistan, etc. I'm sure my dad did, too, but I've never talked to him about it. Thinking about it now, after the taconite expansion of the early to mid-1970s, this was the beginning of the end for the mines up there. And I think they knew it. But they felt they had a hockey team and a coach that was fighting for us. And hockey mattered. .

"I watched those games lying on the floor about a foot away from the TV. Nothing else I have witnessed has been so completely mesmerizing, satisfying, and above all motivating. From my viewpoint, one foot from the TV screen, in Virginia, Minnesota, on Minnesota's Iron Range, the universe was in focus."

The 1980 U.S. Olympic hockey team celebrates its upset 4–3 victory over the Soviet Union in the semifinal game

Bradford Parkinson (1935–)

Getting us all from point A to point B

They said it couldn't be done. When Bradford Parkinson first started working on a global positioning system (GPS), people were skeptical. "When I got approval to go ahead with it, most people heard the story and thought it was so incredible, they thought it was a pet rock," Parkinson later said.

Guess who got the last laugh? GPS is a navigational system that uses signals from satellites to pinpoint places with great accuracy. Originally developed for the U.S. military to guide missiles to targets, GPS is becoming a standard component of everyday life. GPS systems are found in cars and are used by air traffic controllers, farmers, and rescue workers. They are becoming widely available in mobile phones and other handheld devices.

Born in Minneapolis, Parkinson graduated from Breck School before earning a bachelor's degree in aeronautics and astronautics from the Naval Academy in 1957. He earned a PhD from Stanford University in 1966. His first GPS system was operational in 1978. Since then he has received numerous awards, including a spot in NASA's Hall of Fame and the National Association of Engineers' Draper Prize, which is akin to a Nobel Prize in the field of engineering. "Many of engineering's great achievements become so much a part of our lives that they are taken for granted," said National Association of Engineers president William A. Wulf in presenting the Draper Prize to Parkinson in 2003. "I think that, without question, GPS is destined for this distinction."

The first example of handheld GPS to be carried in airplanes, 1990

Gordon Parks (1912–2006)

A Renaissance man

Gordon Parks loved to tell the story of how he got his start as a fashion photographer—one of many paths he followed in his long, varied life. It was 1938 when he walked into Frank Murphy's, an exclusive women's clothing store in downtown St. Paul, and asked if they needed anyone to take photos of the store's runway models. He didn't mention that he didn't own a camera and that his only experience with models was a recent perusal of *Vogue* magazine. Frank Murphy turned him down, but on his way out of the store, Mrs. Murphy suggested that Parks return after the store closed. "Later I asked her why she took a chance on me, and she said she had just had an argument with Frank and was trying to get under his skin," Parks recalled. "Actually, I think she was just a woman who had a great heart."

Parks's photos caught the eye of Marva Louis, wife of heavyweight champion Joe Louis. She persuaded Parks to move to Chicago, where he quickly honed his skills. In 1941, he received a fellowship that offered a choice of photo assignments. Parks chose to work for Roy Stryker at the Farm Security Administration. From there, he went on to assignments for the Office of War Information, *Vogue, Glamour,* and, finally, *Life* magazine, where he worked as a photographer and essayist for nearly twenty-five years. His success at *Life* led to other ventures, including publishing (as a cofounder of *Essence*), writing (including *The Learning Tree* and *A Choice of Weapons*), and film (especially *Shaft,* an Oscar-winning film that was both a commercial blockbuster and a racial breakthrough).

Gordon Parks's varied interests and boundless curiosity resulted in a body of work that shed light on the poverty, racism, and powerlessness that faced African Americans. His best-known photograph, which he titled "American Gothic," depicts a black cleaning woman standing stiffly in front of an American flag. Through his photos, his writings, and his films, he made groundbreaking statements about the inequities he experienced firsthand. "I'm not proud to be the first black to do these things," he said in a 1996 interview. "There were many blacks who should have been there before me because they were more talented, but they just never got the chance."

The Phyllis Wheatley and Hallie Q. Brown Community Centers

Home away from home

In the early years of the twentieth century, community centers known as settlement houses were founded in many U.S. cities. These houses were primarily intended to help recent immigrants find their way in their new country; citizenship classes, language classes, and a host of other programs were offered.

The Phyllis Wheatley settlement house opened in Minneapolis in 1924. Serving the needs of the city's African American community, the Phyllis Wheatley performed a wider range of functions than other settlement houses. Under the direction of the powerful and visionary W. Gertrude Brown, the house offered classes not only in citizenship and English, but in recreation, music, drama, and black history. It also was a hotel for out-of-town visitors in a time when hotels did not accommodate black guests. Langston Hughes,

Marian Anderson, and other visiting artists all stayed at the Wheatley.

Meanwhile, in St. Paul, the Hallie Q. Brown Center had been serving the needs of that city's African American community since 1908 (it is currently located on Kent Street, where it is also home to Penumbra Theatre). Together, the two organizations were places where the Twin Cities' black residents could "find comfort with their own kind," as nominator James Brown puts it. Brown, who grew up in St. Paul, remembers that they offered "sewing classes, dance classes, music classes, etc. Some of the music classes turned out musicians of renown, like Percy Hughes, the Pettifords, Charles Beasley, and many more who just took an interest in learning. They had acting classes and put on

their own plays in summer camps for families to take time out from the trials of daily survival.

"The joy of these centers was that they were not only for black people. They were open to all nationalities who cared to participate. The officers and board members who ran these facilities were dedicated people who overcame unbelievable problems that challenged their sincerity daily. They were and are unsung heroes whose devotion can never be praised enough."

(Opposite bottom) Lunchtime at Phyllis Wheatley nursery school; (opposite top) bridge party, Hallie Q. Brown Center; (above) archery class at Hallie Q. Brown Center

Pilgrim Baptist Church

Minnesota's oldest African American church

The year was 1863. President Abraham Lincoln had issued the Emancipation Proclamation, an executive order declaring the freedom of all slaves in states in rebellion, and yet the Civil War raged on. It was in this climate of unrest and danger that a small group of African American men, women, and children made their way from Boone County, Missouri, to St. Paul, Minnesota, in search of employment and better lives. Not certain of their final destination, the travelers called themselves "pilgrims."

Among the group was Robert T. Hickman, a former slave whose master had taught him to read and had given him permission to preach to other slaves. On his arrival in St. Paul, Hickman began organizing prayer services in the homes of his fellow travelers. Over the next several years, the group continued to meet in rented space throughout the city.

Finally, on November 15, 1866, Robert Hickman and others held a baptismal service on the banks of the Mississippi River near downtown St. Paul, marking the formal organization of Pilgrim Baptist Church. As Minnesota's first African American church, Pilgrim Baptist soon built a gathering place, with seating for 300, on Sibley Street.

The congregation moved to its current building, at 732 Central Avenue West, in 1928. It has served over the years as a place of worship and a community center for St. Paul's African American community—"a harbor in a storm," as nominator and longtime Pilgrim Baptist member Marjorie Tendle puts it. "We are who we are because of our history," wrote Pilgrim Baptist's pastor, Dr. Earl Fredrick Miller Sr., in marking the congregation's 125th anniversary in 1988. "The challenge has been passed to us. The task of faith is always to see and move forward."

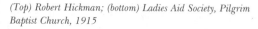

(Top) Robert Hickman; (bottom) Ladies Aid Society, Pilgrim Baptist Church, 1915

Pipestone

A national treasure

Deep below the ground in southwestern Minnesota are thick layers of ancient rocks that were deposited there more than 1.6 million years ago. Today the rocks are known as Sioux Quartzite. Sandwiched between the quartzite layers, which are harder than steel, is a soft, easy-to-carve red mineral called pipestone (known geologically as catlinite). In 1836, George Catlin published a story he had heard from Dakota Indians about the origin of pipestone: "At an ancient time the Great Spirit, in the form of a large bird, stood upon the wall of rock and called all the tribes around him, and breaking out a piece of the red stone formed it into a pipe and smoked it, the smoke rolling over the whole multitude. He then told his red children that his red stone was their flesh, that they were made from it, that they must all smoke to him through it, that they must use it for nothing but pipes: and as it belonged alike to all tribes, the ground was sacred, and no weapons must be used or brought upon it."

Tools and other evidence left behind show that people have been quarrying pipestone in what is now southwestern Minnesota for at least 3,000 years. A sacred site, the pipestone quarries draw Indian tribes from across North America, who use the stone for making pipes and effigies. Since 1937, the National Park Service has operated Pipestone National Monument on the site and kept it open to visitors, but only American Indians who have received a permit can quarry the valuable natural resource.

Chuck Derby is a Dakota pipemaker who has for many years demonstrated his art for Pipestone National Monument visitors. He began working in the quarries with his father as a young child; later he learned how to carve pipestone, a skill passed down through generations of his family members. "We grew up as pipemakers here in this town," said Derby in a 1992 interview. "We know the stone. We know what tools to use and how to use them. In the old days, there were always people who had certain skills, who were specialists in one thing or another, and there were always pipemakers."

"In late August," he continued, "I asked a medicine man to do a Sweat Lodge Ceremony. We prayed that all would go well in the quarry; that no one would get hurt; that the elderly would be taken care of. The stone I got this year was so good—a beautiful piece. When I saw it, I knew the spirits were with me. The spirits answered my prayer."

Standing Eagle working the sacred pipestone in a quarry at the Pipestone National Monument, 1970s

Veda Ponikvar (1919–)

Newsprint in her blood

She was in fifth grade when she decided she wanted to run a newspaper, and her commitment never wavered. Born in Chisholm, on Minnesota's Iron Range, in 1919, Veda Ponikvar studied journalism at Drake University; after graduation in 1942, she enlisted in the U.S. Navy WAVES. Trained as a linguist, Ponikvar spent three years in Washington, D.C., where she interpreted information on Eastern Europe and Yugoslavia for the Office of Naval Intelligence. She was discharged in 1946 as a lieutenant commander.

Ponikvar returned to Chisholm, where she started her own weekly newspaper, the *Free Press.* A decade later, she bought the town's *Tribune Press,* and until 1996 she published both, writing more than 4,000 editorials and covering all the town's news stories, big and small. Never an impartial observer of the day's events, Ponikvar used her newspapers to prod politicians and to help shape public policies. She was a player in her region's landmark events over the decades, from the 1964 Taconite Amendment to the 1978 signing of the Boundary Waters Canoe Area Wilderness Act to the creation of Chisholm's Ironworld, a living history museum that showcases the heritage of northern Minnesota.

"Publishers like Veda felt it was a legitimate function to be a leader of the community," said Bob Shaw, once head of the Minnesota Newspaper Association. Looking back over her career as she prepared for retirement in 1996, Ponikvar summed up the philosophy that informed her fifty years in the newspaper business: "I realized a newspaper was a powerful force—for good or bad," she said. "I made up my mind to be positive, but I'd be honest. I'd do my homework and get my facts straight."

> In 1965, Veda Ponikvar wrote an obituary for Dr. Archibald Graham, Chisholm's longtime community physician, who, as "Moonlight" Graham, was introduced to the world through the novel *Shoeless Joe* and later the movie *Field of Dreams* (in which Ponikvar herself had a cameo). She wrote, **"As the community grew, Doc became an integral part of the population. There were good years and lean ones. There were times when children could not afford eyeglasses, or milk, or clothing because of the economic upheavals, strikes, and depressions. Yet no child was ever denied these essentials, because in the background, there was a benevolent, understanding Doctor Graham. Without a word, without any fanfare or publicity, the glasses or the milk, or the ticket to the ball game found their way into the child's pocket."**

C. Stanley Potter (c. 1918–1988)

Making the written word available to all

Reading a best seller, flipping through the pages of a magazine, scanning the headlines of a favorite newspaper—for people with impaired vision, these experiences are difficult, if not impossible. In 1969, C. Stanley Potter, an amateur radio enthusiast with limited vision, developed a solution to this problem. With his friend Bob Watson, a former neighbor who was working for NASA as an engineer, Potter developed the Radio Reading Service, the first such service in the world, using the FM subcarriers of Minnesota Public Radio.

Stan Potter and his brother, Bill, were both legally blind. After spending time at the Minnesota School for the Blind in Faribault,

Stan and Bill persuaded their parents to move to St. Cloud, where the boys were mainstreamed in public schools. Stan went on to complete bachelor's and master's degrees at public colleges; for his dissertation, he transcribed the first Braille version of the Minnesota Multiphasic Personality Inventory.

Potter was director of the Minnesota State Services for the Blind from 1948 until 1985. It was during this time that he and Watson introduced their radio station. Nominator Cheryl Merrill of St. Paul tells us more: "His idea to establish a radio station for the sight impaired was complete genius. Since its inception, more than 160 stations worldwide have been established. The daily newspaper and current best sellers are two types of written words read on these stations each day. Minnesota Public Radio's *Talking Book* continues to provide programming twenty-four hours a day."

Powwows

An enduring celebration

Tradition and change: the two concepts are interdependent. People uphold traditions in the midst of great change, while change is often the catalyst for the establishment of new traditions.

The American Indian powwow is a tradition that has not only endured but flourished in the midst of change. Nominator Brenda Child, an enrolled member of the Red Lake Band of Chippewa Indians, explains: "'Powwow' is an Algonquin word used by Minnesota Ojibwes and many other tribal nations historically and today to describe social gatherings that emphasize song and dance. Minnesota Ojibwes are known throughout Indian Country for their great tradition of song, reflected in contemporary drum groups such as Eyabay, or the music of the older Kingbird Singers, both of Red Lake.

"At the turn of the twentieth century in the United States, when indigenous cultural traditions and spiritual practices were suppressed on reservations, powwows and many forms of American Indian dance were considered illegal. Indians celebrated the Fourth of July and other American holidays with powwows, finding a way to continue their traditional culture. Powwows are events that bring Indians together, and Dakota and Ojibwe people have a long tradition of cultural borrowing and intertribal socialization in Minnesota. Powwows combine elements of tradition and innovation to serve the needs of the Indian community. Powwows can be joyous events or very solemn, depending on the occasion, but they are always about cultural survival."

The *Circle*, an American Indian newspaper published in Minneapolis, carries a full listing of local and regional powwows. For more information, see also http://www.drumhop.com/mnpowwow.html. Various types of powwows are listed there, from those recognizing holidays such as Veterans Day and Mother's Day, to those celebrating achievements such as graduation and sobriety, to contest powwows where dancers compete for prizes.

Prince (1958–)

Creator of the Minneapolis Sound

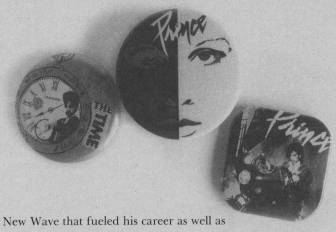

His parents named him Prince Rogers Nelson, after his pianist father's band, the Prince Rogers Trio. In 1993, he dropped his name in favor of a glyph. People began calling him "The Artist Formerly Known as Prince," "The Artist," and a host of less charitable things. He changed his name back in 2000. He has cultivated a singular, mysterious persona throughout his career and has repelled and intrigued listeners in equal measure. For all his intentional blurring of the lines, though, one thing is clear: Prince changed the course of popular music.

A devoutly Christian black man, standing 5 feet, 3 inches, and weighing 125 pounds, Prince is a most unlikely international star and sex symbol. He's credited with inspiring the Minneapolis Sound—a mix of funk, rock, R&B,

and New Wave that fueled his career as well as those of other musicians, including Jimmy Jam and Terry Lewis, Morris Day, and Sheila E. Unlike contemporaries such as Madonna and Michael Jackson, Prince is often described as being more than a commercial sensation. He is viewed as a serious musical artist, influencing everyone from George Michael to Janet Jackson to D'Angelo to Outkast. He has kept tight control over the production of his material, recording most of it in the Minneapolis metro area. Given his sexually explicit lyrics and suggestive moves, his live performances have also set a standard for others to follow.

Here's how Alex Hahn, who published a biography of Prince in 2003, sums up his influence: "As the 1980s continued, the sound Prince perfected with records like *1999* and *Purple Rain* became the most influential (and, for that matter, the most openly imitated) style of the entire decade. His artistic calling cards— minimalist production, taut funk rhythms, and salacious lyrics—were appropriated by dozens of pop artists, often with potent results. Even as important musicians like Miles Davis, Eric Clapton, and Robert Plant hailed Prince as a pop pioneer, the most convincing evidence of his influence was on the radio: it was almost impossible to spin the dial without encountering something that sounded very much like him."

145

Elizabeth C. Quinlan (1863–1947)

The Twin Cities' first fashionista

It was a brown wool dress lined with taffeta. With its long, full skirt, tight bodice, high collar and leg-o'-mutton sleeves, it was the kind of dress a fashionable woman might wear for afternoon tea in the late 1890s. It sold for fifty dollars, and when shop owner Elizabeth Quinlan introduced it to her Minneapolis clients, she made retail history.

Quinlan was the first merchant to sell women's ready-to-wear clothing west of the Mississippi. Before this, women either made their dresses themselves or paid someone to make them. Quinlan's innovation was simply the most notable of the many things she accomplished during her long tenure as one of Minneapolis's most successful businesswomen. She grew up in a working-class home in Minneapolis. At eighteen, she began selling clothes at Goodfellow and Eastman on Nicollet Avenue. Fifteen years later, and by then one of the store's top salespeople, Quinlan left Goodfellow's for a three-month stint at Fred D. Young and Company, the nation's second ready-to-wear shop, newly founded by a former Goodfellow's executive. She stayed at Young's (which in 1903 became Young-Quinlan's) for the next fifty-one years.

For Elizabeth Quinlan, 1911 was a watershed year. A devastating fire necessitated an entire remodeling of her store. Later that year, her partner, Fred Young, died at age forty-nine after a long illness. Quinlan bought his interest in the business from his relatives, thus becoming its sole owner and one of very few women business owners in Minneapolis.

In 1926, when she was sixty-three years old, Quinlan built the elegant Young-Quinlan Building at 901 Nicollet Avenue, a five-story emporium that combined elegance, luxury, and convenience. The "perfect gem," as Quinlan described it, was widely admired and copied, becoming the template for Neiman-Marcus's expansion in Dallas in the late 1920s.

Elizabeth Quinlan was well known throughout Minneapolis's civic circles. She supported charities and cultural groups and founded the Business Women's Club in 1919. In 1933, she was the only woman to serve on the board of the National Recovery Act, advising on specialty stores and advocating a raise in minimum wage. The *Saturday Evening Post* devoted a four-page spread to her in 1927, and, in the mid-1930s, *Fortune* magazine named her one of the country's top businesswomen. A winning combination of elegant socialite and shrewd manager, Quinlan was once asked if her store was the realization of her lifelong dreams. "No," she answered. "Everyone wants me to say so, but it isn't. Not really. It was just the thing for me to do."

Young-Quinlan building at night, 1963

146

Rapidan Dam

The lights go on in rural Minnesota

When the scientists in Thomas Edison's Menlo Park laboratory powered the first electric lightbulb in 1879, they were onto something big. As the decades unfolded, more and more Americans realized the benefits of electric power in their homes, at work, and throughout their communities. By 1930, nearly 70 percent of all city residents were hooked up to power lines.

In rural areas, though, it was a different story. Only 10 percent of the nation's farm families had access to electricity in 1930. Thus, in 1935, President Franklin D. Roosevelt launched the Rural Electrification Administration (REA), a New Deal program designed to help organize farmer-owned electrical cooperatives. The REA was a success, and by the 1950s most American farmers enjoyed all the benefits of electric power.

The citizens of Mankato and surrounding rural areas short-circuited the REA process by building the Rapidan Dam on the Blue Earth River. As a result, the Mankato area enjoyed a surge in electric power in the 1910s. We'll let nominator Jane Tarjeson of Good Thunder, Minnesota, take it from here: "The Rapidan Dam is significant as one of the early hydroelectric components of the power system that developed into Northern States Power Company and as an important early source of electric power for the Mankato and southern Minnesota area. Construction began in February and was completed by December 1910. Local materials and labor were utilized to build it.

"The first power was generated on March 11, 1911, and with an initial capacity of 1500 kilowatts, the power produced at the dam more than doubled the capacity of Mankato's electric system. Mankato sorely needed this boost in power to move ahead as a manufacturing center in southern Minnesota. In the following years, power was supplied to many communities in the area and fed into lines that spread across southern Minnesota.

"Rapidan Dam played an important role in the production of electricity for southern Minnesota, providing it to small communities and rural areas that otherwise would have had to wait decades for the 'wonder of electricity.' In 1966, NSP presented the dam and deed to adjoining land to Blue Earth County. In 1985, the dam was renovated and it again produced electricity. It is still producing electricity today."

Red River Trails

Rolling, rolling, rolling

RED RIVER CARTS
ON THE PEMBINA TRAIL

Today, when we think about "transportation networks," we're likely to conjure up images of freeways, gridlock, air traffic control towers, and global positioning systems. But there was a time when our region's main transportation routes were muddy trails traversed by squeaky-wheeled, overloaded carts pulled by teams of oxen. Nominator Kevin Duchschere explains: "Transportation networks were vital to the settling of the West in the nineteenth century. They began with the trailblazers and continued with the much larger group of those who followed the trails, bringing with them not just commerce but the customs and traditions that stamped a territory with its own unique identity.

"In Minnesota, no road system has proven as vital to the state's growth or as important internationally as the Red River trails, a meandering patchwork of rutted oxcart paths across the prairie and around the woods that connected St. Paul with Fort Garry and Winnipeg from the 1820s until the coming of the railroad in the 1870s. The trade in furs and other merchandise that the trails facilitated helped establish the young city of St. Paul as an important commercial center and were invaluable to the development of Winnipeg—the state's first important foreign trading partner—and, not incidentally, opened the door to the settling of the Red River Valley in both Minnesota and North Dakota.

"The trails also were the backdrop for a colorful chapter of the state's early history, filled with long trains of screeching oxcarts, colorfully dressed métis from the frontier borderlands, and the romance of stories and song from far away. One of the traders was Joe Rollette, who wielded political power in north-western Minnesota and is credited with keeping the capital in St. Paul.

"Although traces of the original trails are mostly gone, some portions of them follow the route now followed by Interstate 94. Other national trails—the Oregon and California, for instance—may be better known, but the Red River trails were the first important commercial network for settlers in Minnesota."

Religious Orders

Called to serve

Born in St. Paul in 1875, Caroline Hanggi grew up to be Sister Carmela Hanggi, a member of the community of the Sisters of St. Joseph of Carondelet. In 1921, as principal of the city's Cathedral School, Sister Carmela became increasingly concerned about the safety of her students as they crossed the busy streets near her school. After returning from a trip to New Jersey, where she saw a particularly effective school-crossing program, Sister Carmela asked the St. Paul Police Department to authorize "police boys," who would monitor the crossings near the Cathedral. Soon her School Safety Patrol program was a model for other schools across the Midwest.

Sister Carmela's story is one of hundreds that demonstrate the influence members of religious orders have had on Minnesota. The Sisters of St. Joseph of Carondelet arrived in Minnesota in 1851 to open a school. Other members of religious orders came in the second half of the nineteenth century as teachers, and, once they had established communities, their members branched out into nursing and social work and wherever else their ministries were welcomed and needed. Over the years, students at the colleges of St. Catherine in St. Paul, St. Benedict in St. Joseph, St. Teresa in Winona, and St. Scholastica in Duluth have flourished under the leadership of Minnesota's religious orders. St. Mary's Hospital, in Rochester, founded in 1889 by the Sisters of St. Francis in conjunction with Dr. William Mayo, still operates today as part of the Mayo system.

Today, there are about 1,000 female religious working in Minnesota. As an example of their many contributions to Minnesota's quality of life, members of the Sisters of St. Benedict have served on the Red Lake and White Earth Indian reservations since the 1880s. Members of the Sisters of St. Joseph of Carondelet operate Peace House, a haven for the homeless. Nuns are in addiction and recovery programs, on community farms, and in battered women's shelters. They are part of the fabric of our state.

(Left) Sisters at St. Mary's Mission, Red Lake, 1956; (above) College of St. Catherine, St. Paul, 1970

Joseph Renville (c. 1779–1846)

Building bridges between cultures

The son of a French trader and a Dakota woman, Joseph Renville was born near present-day St. Paul and lived with his Dakota relatives until he was ten, when he moved with his father to Canada. He eventually returned to Minnesota, where he was an interpreter for Lieutenant Zebulon Pike in 1805 and 1806 and for Major Stephen Long in 1823. Renville established a fur-trading post near Lac qui Parle, as an agent for the American Fur Company, in 1826. His familiarity with European and Indian culture, as well as his fluency in the Dakota, English, and French languages, made him an effective trader and a trusted intermediary among the people who lived and worked near his post.

Raised as a Catholic, Renville invited European missionaries to establish a mission and school near his fur post. Through the Lac qui Parle mission, Renville worked to further strengthen relationships among the European and Dakota peoples. With missionaries Thomas S. Williamson, Stephen R. Riggs, and Samuel and Gideon Pond, he translated the Bible and various hymnbooks into the Dakota language. The process was slow—a Bible verse would be read in French, Renville would translate it into the Dakota language, and his words would be carefully written down. Dakota is an oral language, and Renville's translations were among the first attempts to record Dakota in written form.

Martha Ripley (1843–1912)

An early advocate for women's health and welfare

When Dr. Martha Ripley and her family moved to Minneapolis in 1883, she had just completed medical training at Boston University School of Medicine. At forty-one, though, she was no newcomer to the medical profession. Born in Vermont, she was introduced to medicine through nursing victims of diphtheria epidemics. She tried to work as a nurse during the Civil War but was judged too young, and so she recruited others to nursing instead. After her marriage to William Ripley in 1867, the couple moved to Massachusetts, where she continued nursing while also embarking on her lifelong involvement in the woman suffrage movement. After a young child in her care died of croup, she enrolled in medical school.

Ripley established Maternity Hospital in Minneapolis in 1886. At that time, unwed mothers were generally denied hospital admission. Ripley's hospital was open to any woman, regardless of her marital or financial status. As the hospital grew, so did its services. It housed destitute children and unwed mothers and their infants; it provided adoption services; and it provided training and job assistance for single mothers.

From 1883 to 1889, Ripley was president of the Minnesota Woman Suffrage Association. Throughout her life, she was an outspoken advocate for women. She insisted that there be matrons on the Minneapolis police force; she lobbied for the right of female domestic workers to unionize; and she pushed for public health reforms, including better sanitation and clean water. She wore her skirts and hair short to minimize the spread of disease. Her hospital had an enviable rate of infant mortality—only 25 percent that of the national average.

Martha Ripley died in 1912, just as her new hospital on Minneapolis's Glenwood Avenue was being completed. The hospital buildings, now listed on the National Register of Historic Places, are currently being renovated to provide rental and housing units for low- and moderate-income residents. She wouldn't have wanted it any other way.

(Top right) Dr. Martha Ripley, ca. 1905; (top left) Ripley Memorial Maternity Hospital, Minneapolis, ca. 1905

> **"In all these long years it has been like a wise and loving mother to all who have come through its doors. Many girls have said it was the only real home they have ever known."** Martha Ripley, 1911

Henry Hastings Sibley (1811–1891)

First governor of the state of Minnesota

Born in Detroit, Michigan, the son of a Michigan Supreme Court justice, Henry Sibley abandoned his own legal training at eighteen to pursue "a more active and stirring life." When he died some sixty years later, Sibley could look back on a truly active life that included stints as a fur trader, politician, military leader, and, finally, president of the St. Paul Gas Light Company.

Sibley arrived in Minnesota in 1834, settling in St. Peter's (now Mendota), where the house he built for himself still stands. Sibley was in charge of regional affairs for the American Fur Company and oversaw trade with Dakota Indians, from the Falls of St. Anthony to the Dubuque River and west to the headwaters of the Missouri River. Already fluent in French,

during his time in Mendota Sibley also learned the Dakota language and forged friendships with missionaries, settlers, and Indians active in the fur trade.

Sibley's political career began in 1838 when he was appointed the first justice of the peace west of the Mississippi River. He was elected a delegate from Wisconsin Territory to the U.S. Congress in 1849, where he worked to ensure passage of an act recognizing Minnesota Territory. He insisted that his adopted home be named "Minnesota" rather than "Itasca," the name preferred by the territorial bill's sponsor, Stephen A. Douglas.

Sibley later served in the Minnesota legislature and was elected the state's first governor in 1858. He chose not to run for reelection, and for the rest of his life he pursued a range of interests—as a military commander, president of the University of Minnesota's Board of Regents, president of the Minnesota Historical Society, and president of the St. Paul Chamber of Commerce. He served as president of several banks and railroads, among other interests.

Like so many of his contemporaries who were active in shaping Minnesota, Sibley seems to us today to have conducted a life filled with contradictions. His years as a fur trader made him a trusted friend and advisor of Dakota

went off quietly." Sibley's biographer, Rhoda Gilman, notes that in Sibley's writings she has "sensed a silent admission that there were things he could not say. . . . Like the rest of the country, he never questioned the moral superiority of European civilization and he saw assimilation with it as uplifting the 'savage.' Yet this easy justification for conquest, when contrasted with the reality of the Indians' fate, left an unhealed wound upon both man and nation."

Indians, yet in 1851 he headed a group of traders who negotiated the acquisition of vast tracts of Dakota land through the Treaties of Mendota and of Traverse des Sioux. In 1862, he was appointed commander of an emergency force of volunteer militia that fought Dakota Indians in the bloody U.S.–Dakota War. Later that year, after thirty-eight Dakota Indians had been hanged, it was Sibley who telegraphed President Abraham Lincoln that "everything

Henry Hastings Sibley portrait by Thomas Cantwell Healy, 1860; (opposite) Sibley House today

Skyways

Rising above the cold

There comes a time in every Minnesotan's life when a single truth becomes crystal clear: It's cold here. Sometimes very cold.

Reactions to this realization can vary. Some people just put on an extra layer of clothing and tough it out. Hardier sorts embrace winter sports and try to act like they're having fun. Many people just give up and move away. Then there are the few who seek to improve the hand we were dealt eons ago, back when the glaciers didn't recede quite far enough.

One of those visionaries was Edward Baker, known as "the father of the skyway system." He designed the first skyway, which spanned Seventh Street South between Marquette and Second avenues in downtown Minneapolis, in 1962. Today there are miles of skyways in Minneapolis and in St. Paul, and both systems support a thriving second-story retail world catering mostly to downtown workers.

Since the 1960s, skyways have been built throughout the country. They're not without their detractors—critics in many cities charge that they have led to the demise of street-level storefronts and have sucked the life out of downtown neighborhoods. But here in Minnesota they're still going strong. They've become such a part of life, in fact, that a website catering to Twin Cities visitors recently posted an article, "Acceptable Behavior in Minneapolis Downtown Skyways." The author offers pointers on opening doors safely, steering clear of children, and avoiding uncomfortably close quarters. The most quintessentially Minnesotan tip, though, is this one: "Unavoidable transgressions should be apologized for, but more often than not, the person inconvenienced will apologize to you. If someone says, 'excuse me,' and you don't think he has done anything wrong, try to figure out what you did."

(Top) Edward Baker, "the father of the Minneapolis skyways," in the skyway of Nicollet Mall, June 11, 1990; (bottom) skyway across Sixth Street South, Minneapolis, 1975

Snowmobiles

Whoosh!

Although we think of them today as recreational vehicles, the first patent for a snowmobile was awarded to R. H. Muscott of Waters, Michigan, for a vehicle with rear tracks and front sleds to be used for rural mail delivery. For the next several decades, snowmobiles were used for work—to carry mail and schoolchildren, to move groups of people through snowy passages, and as ambulances.

In January 1956, David Johnson, Paul Knochenmus, and Orlen Johnson of Roseau, Minnesota, built the first Polaris Snow Cat, using a grain elevator conveyor belt for a track and pieces of a Chevy bumper for skis. With their Snow Cat, Polaris proved that it was possible to build a sturdy, reliable vehicle that could negotiate snowy fields and forests faster than cross-country skis. But it wasn't yet ready for production. Polaris founder Edgar Hetteen sold the first Snow Cat to a local lumberyard and used the proceeds to meet payroll for his company, which made farm equipment. Then he, his brother Allan, and his brother-in-law David Johnson kept tinkering.

Meanwhile, in Valcourt, Quebec, an inventor named Joseph-Armand Bombardier was hard at work. He had introduced a large vehicle propelled by a caterpillar track in 1937. More than two decades later, in 1959, Bombardier introduced the vehicle that would earn him the title "Father of the Snowmobile." Called the Ski-Doo, it was a relatively light-weight, open-cab model that seated only one or two passengers.

In March 1960, Edgar Hetteen set out to prove that snowmobiles were more than just curiosities. Edgar and three others set out on three Polaris Sno-Travelers, for a 1,200-mile trek across the Alaskan wilderness. The twenty-one-day trip was a success and changed popular opinions on winter travel. Within a few years, Polaris introduced the Colt and Mustang, small-profile snowmobiles designed for recreation. The company was a national leader in the recreational industry by the mid-1960s.

Allan Hetteen took over as president of Polaris later in 1960, when Edgar moved to Thief River Falls to found Arctic Cat. Together, Polaris and Arctic Cat revolutionized the sport of snowmobiling and helped seal Minnesota's reputation as a place where snow and cold are not just endured but enjoyed.

Socialist Opera House

The stage is set for social change

"Remodeling Plans for Old Opera House Will Leave Only Memories of Range's Colorful Cultural Center of Yesterday," declared a headline in the Virginia, Minnesota, *Mesabi Daily News* on January 30, 1958. The article explained that the city's Socialist Opera House was being renovated as a retail and office building by its owners, the local chapter of the United Brotherhood of Carpenters and Joiners, who had bought it in 1955 for $125,000: "The gilt has worn away and once-gleaming white boxes and balcony sections are discolored. . . . Up in the rafters, above the stage rigging, is lashed a wooden boat which once sailed a water-tank in the stage floor."

The article described the building's significance for its community: "Old timers recall the famous names who appeared there, the productions in which live horses were used on the stage, the countless plays produced by local actors and the stormy political meetings held during one of its most controversial eras." Virginia's Socialist Opera House was one of many halls built in communities across the nation where concentrations of Finnish immigrants had settled. Most of the halls served a dual purpose, encapsulated in the unusual pairing of the words "socialist" and "opera" carved over the Virginia hall's entrance. Used for dances, gymnastic performances, and stage plays, they also provided meeting places for like-minded Finns, many of them laborers who embraced socialist ideals. The Socialist Workers' Organization of Virginia built the Virginia hall. Its mission statement outlined its goals: With the help of plays "it was possible to draw audiences unaware of the [socialist] movement to hear agitators' speeches, poems, songs and such material with which it was possible to elevate their knowledge."

The most significant moment in the building's long history came in 1916, during a miners' strike that rocked the Iron Range. The Socialist Opera became the headquarters for the local strike committee and for the Industrial Workers of the World (IWW), a national organization that had come to town to direct the strike effort. Fiery, emotionally charged speeches and rallies were staged at the Opera House, with IWW leaders' speeches translated into the workers' many languages. The strike was considered lost by many, and mining companies throughout the Iron Range blacklisted Finnish workers. But the IWW held out at the Opera House and supported a loggers' strike later that year. For many, the building came to symbolize workers' struggles for equality, and for the rest of its tenure as a public building it remained in the hands of workers' organizations, from cooperatives to, eventually, unions.

Sound 80

Listen carefully

Want to impress someone the next time you're at a party? If there's a CD playing in the background, comment on its superb sound quality, then segue smoothly into this little-known fact: it is widely believed that the first digital audio recordings to be commercially released were made at Sound 80 studio in Minneapolis.

Sound 80 was founded in 1969 by Tom Jung and Herb Pilhofer. In the spring of 1978, a 3M engineer presented the partners with a digital tape machine. Head engineer Jung recorded the studio's landmark digital recordings—a jazz album with Flim and the BB's and two albums by the St. Paul Chamber Orchestra. One of the SPCO recordings, with Aaron Copland's *Appalachian Spring* and Charles Ives's *Three Places in New England,* won a Grammy for Best Chamber Orchestra Recording in 1979 and was nominated for Best Engineered Classical Recording.

In a 2004 interview, Tom Jung described how and why he got involved in digital recording. "I could never get my head past all the noise and distortion coming off the surface of the disc. . . . It was always so hard to make something quiet. Some people's brains allow them to create a filter and hear through this and just listen to the music. Nothing's perfect, but good or bad, I made a conscious decision to go digital and leave analog behind. I jumped in with both feet and didn't look back.

"The thing that grabbed me in that first playback was the absence of wow and flutter. Most of the recordings we were doing included a piano, and getting a piano sound was always a real struggle. Doing it direct to disc or on digital tape, I could get a lot closer to what I was after."

Two more details, just in case you need some more conversation starters: The 3M people called their digital recorder "Herbie," after Jung's partner, Herb Pilhofer. And the building that housed Studio 80, which was sold in 1990, is now the home of Orfield Laboratories, Inc. It now contains an anechoic chamber (a room with no echoes) that is listed as "the quietest place on earth" in the *Guinness Book of World Records.*

Southdale Center

A retail revolution

onald Dayton, head of Minneapolis-based Dayton's department stores, once commissioned a study that reinforced what most Minnesotans have experienced first-hand: the state has only 126 "ideal shopping weather" days each year. Rather than give up and relocate to more temperate climes, Dayton took action and teamed up with designer Victor Gruen to create a comfortable, convenient setting for Minnesota shoppers. In 1952, Dayton and Gruen unveiled their plans for Southdale, the nation's first enclosed, weatherproofed mall.

Gruen's aspirations went far beyond retail bliss. A Jewish Viennese citizen who had escaped his homeland during the Nazi takeover, Gruen hoped to create a new kind of American community inspired by the best of European urban life. The Dayton Corporation bought 500 acres of land in Edina, and Gruen drew up plans that placed the mall at the core of a new

development of apartment buildings, houses, schools, a medical center, a park, and a lake. Gruen's vision was, as one writer later described, "the Minneapolis downtown you would get if you started over and corrected all the mistakes that were made the first time around."

Southdale Center was built at a cost of $20 million and had 800,000 square feet; it opened with 72 stores and 2 anchors, Dayton's and Donaldson's. 75,000 people attended the gala opening on October 8, 1956. Another 188,000 visited the complex the following weekend, most taking advantage of the mall's 5,000 free parking spaces (organized into lots identified by clever animal symbols—an innovation, like the mall itself, that would inspire countless imitators). What did visitors see? Gruen's interpretation of the best of European cities: "streets," cafes, two department stores, and many smaller boutiques surrounding a "town square" with a garden court spotlighted by an enormous skylight. A fishpond, mature trees, and a twenty-one-foot cage filled with brightly colored birds. In short, a prototype for the malls that would fuel suburban growth throughout the country.

What of the rest of Gruen's vision? The medical center opened in 1965; eventually, the corporation sold the remaining land for housing. With his dreams only partially realized, Gruen came to detest shopping malls, decrying the suburban sprawl often associated with them. Love them or hate them, though, there's no denying their impact on American life. Southdale changed more than shopping habits; it led to the transformation of the American landscape.

> **From Southdale's 1956 press release:** "Southdale shopping center could be called in psychological terms 'an introvert center.' On the outside it presents a quiet and dignified appearance, inviting the shopper to enter through one of ten huge all-glass entrances into the interior. . . . Here he finds himself in an atmosphere of unparalleled liveliness, colorfulness, and beauty. Between shopping activities there is an opportunity for rest in the sidewalk café and on the many rest benches. Here is a chance to amble and promenade, to window shop, to chat with friends, and a large array of features arouses interest and invites contemplation. Trees, tropical plants, flowers, a bird cage, sculptures, and other work of important artists, a pond, a fountain, a juice bar, a cigar and newsstand are some of them."

SPAM

Fuel for American troops worldwide

One of the most maligned products in American culinary history, SPAM started out as anything but a joke. Hormel Foods, of Austin, Minnesota, made a name for itself in 1926 by marketing the nation's first canned ham. Eleven years later, in 1937, Jay C. Hormel, son of company founder George Hormel, developed SPAM luncheon meat, the first canned meat product that did not require refrigeration. It's a fully cooked combination of chopped pork shoulder and ham, salt, water, sugar, and sodium nitrate. Countless lame jokes to the contrary (for example, "Some Parts Are Meat"), its name is derived from the "sp" in "spiced" and the "am" in "ham."

SPAM's ability to stay fresh without refrigeration made it a useful commodity during World War II, when it became a staple of GIs' diets. Today it remains popular in countries where it was widely available during war years. It is sold in forty-one countries. The largest consumers after the United States are the United Kingdom (not coincidentally the home of comedy troupe Monty Python, who parlayed SPAM mockery into a memorable sketch and a Broadway musical) and South Korea, where it gained popularity due to the large presence of American troops there during the Korean War.

SPAM's popularity in South Korea is particularly intriguing. Far from being a joke there, it is a luxury item—a delicacy that is popular during Chusok, the biggest gift-giving occasion of the year for Koreans. For decades after the end of the Korean War, South Koreans bought SPAM on the black market, from supplies that had been diverted from U.S. military bases. Then, in 1987, CJ Corporation bought the rights from Hormel and began producing SPAM at a factory south of Seoul. South Korean SPAM has less salt and slightly different spices than its American counterpart. It's fried with rice or mixed into soups and stews. Sometimes it appears in kimbab, the Korean version of sushi.

Arguably Minnesota's most famous—or infamous—international export, SPAM has secured its place in the world's popular culture.

Allan Spear (1937–)

A longtime activist makes political history

In 1993, the Minnesota legislature amended the Human Rights Act to prohibit discrimination in housing, employment, and other areas for gay, lesbian, bisexual, and transgender (GLBT) people. State senator Allan Spear, the nation's first gay man in public office to acknowledge his sexual orientation, sponsored the legislation in the Senate. "That was a twenty-year struggle," Spear said of the legislation. In 1978, St. Paul had rejected a citywide ordinance guaranteeing GLBT rights, but in 1991 the city's voters passed the ordinance. That move helped clear the way for the statewide law. "People realized the world was not going to end, and I was able to put together a coalition to pass a state law that I hadn't been able to do before."

Allan Spear moved to Minneapolis in 1964 to join the faculty of the University of Minnesota's History Department. He had been involved in civil rights actions during his student days at Oberlin College and at Yale University and quickly became active in Minnesota's DFL party. He was first elected to the Minnesota State Senate in 1972. Two years later, he announced that he was gay. "It seemed to me it was going to come out anyway," he later said. "I chose the reporter I gave the story to."

Spear was elected president of the Minnesota State Senate in 1992 and served in that role until his retirement in 2000. He left public office as the longest-serving openly gay state legislator in the nation.

Split Rock Lighthouse

The symbol of Minnesota's North Shore

In the early years of the twentieth century, iron ore shipments on Lake Superior boomed. U.S. Steel's bulk ore carriers were among the world's largest fleets, and with their increasing presence came increased demand for a lighthouse on the lake's North Shore. A fierce storm on November 28, 1905, damaged twenty-nine ships, a third of which were owned by U.S. Steel. A delegation led by the steamship company's president lobbied the U.S. Congress, and, in early 1907, $75,000 was appropriated for a lighthouse and fog signal near Split Rock.

The U.S. Lighthouse Service completed the lighthouse and surrounding buildings in 1910 and operated the site until 1939, when the U.S. Coast Guard took over. By that time, Split Rock's location near the North Shore highway (completed in 1924) made it one of the most visited lighthouses in the country. The station closed in 1969 when modern navigational equipment made it obsolete; today it is a historic site operated by the Minnesota Historical Society and is also on the National Register of Historic Places.

For many Minnesotans, Split Rock Lighthouse symbolizes Lake Superior's North Shore. It is a place to return to on annual vacations, a place to snap photos, a place that reminds us of the area's rich past. "On a personal note," writes nominator Sally Wojtowicz of Forest Lake, Minnesota, "it was where my parents took me on my first vacation as a child. I fell in love with lighthouses at that moment. Surely, at that early age, I thought I was looking out at the ocean below! Forty-six years later, and with visits to many other lighthouses behind me, I can truly state that nothing can compare to her."

Harold E. Stassen (1907–2001)

He started early and never gave up

10 reasons why I am for

HAROLD STASSEN FOR PRESIDENT

1. He is forthright, courageous and con-
   we need.

2. He is an exceptional administrator . . .

He ran for president in 1948, and really didn't stop." That's how Chris Georgacas, a longtime member of the Metropolitan Council, once described Harold Stassen in the second half of his long political career. But to characterize Stassen as only a perennial presidential candidate—he ran nine times—is to leave out the most significant details of his life story.

Harold Stassen grew up on a farm in what is now West St. Paul and finished high school when he was fourteen. He graduated from the University of Minnesota at nineteen; by the time he was twenty-one, he had completed his law degree. In 1930, at age twenty-three, Stassen was elected Dakota County attorney. He was a moderate Republican who shared beliefs with members of the Democratic and Farmer-Labor parties that then dominated Minnesota politics. "I was always an advocate of the right of labor to organize, and more liberal and humanitarian policies for the country," Stassen said in 1997.

A charismatic public speaker with a passion for politics, Stassen was only thirty-one when he was elected governor of Minnesota in 1938. He was reelected twice; in 1943, four months into his third term, he resigned and enlisted in the U.S. Navy. He distinguished himself as a soldier and as a statesman during the war years, serving as Admiral William F. Halsey's assistant chief of staff, receiving six major battle stars, and heading the navy's prisoner evacuation program in Japan.

Stassen's most significant moment during his military service, however, came when President Franklin Roosevelt picked him as one of eight American delegates to the United Nations charter conference in 1945. Long an advocate for world peace, Stassen had spoken of a world association of free nations in his 1940 keynote address at the Republican National Convention. After addressing the U.S. Senate on the topic in 1943, he authored "We Need a World Government" for the *Saturday Evening Post*. Stassen was a key player as the UN charter took shape, later being named one of the group's two most effective delegates by a journalists' group, and on June 26, 1945, he signed the charter. Stassen died in 2001 and he was the last living American signer of that historic document.

Harold Stassen was a strong contender for the 1948 Republican presidential nomination but lost to Thomas Dewey. He was president of the University of Pennsylvania from 1948 to 1953 and then served under Dwight Eisenhower as a cabinet member and on the National Security Council until 1958. He returned to St. Paul in 1978, where he maintained a law practice until his death at age ninety-three.

State of Minnesota v. Philip Morris

A landmark victory for nonsmokers

In August 1994, the State of Minnesota, represented by Secretary of State Hubert "Skip" Humphrey III, and Blue Cross and Blue Shield of Minnesota filed suit against Philip Morris, R. J. Reynolds, Brown and Williamson, and a host of other tobacco companies and research groups. The unprecedented suit alleged a fifty-year conspiracy to mislead Americans about the hazards of smoking, to stifle development of safer cigarettes, and to target children as new customers. Cigarette manufacturers had been sued by hundreds of smokers in previous decades but had won every case. This time around, the outcome was different.

The largest case in Minnesota history, *Minnesota v. Morris,* eventually involved hundreds of legal motions and a dozen appeals, including two to the U.S. Supreme Court. After years of effort, a fifteen-week trial, and testimony by health experts and tobacco company CEOs, the case resulted in 1998 in the fourth-largest tobacco settlement, anytime, anywhere. The tobacco companies were ordered to stop targeting children, cease billboard advertising, end marketing of branded merchandise, end paid product placement in movies, and more. The State of Minnesota was to receive more than $6 billion dollars over the first twenty-five years and about $200 million dollars annually thereafter.

A public health foundation was formed, funded by $200 million from the settlement. And thirty-five million pages of documents were opened for public scrutiny, fueling hundreds of scientific articles and government reports.

The impact of *Minnesota v. Morris* continues to be felt. In 2005, the World Health Organization adopted the Framework Convention on Tobacco Control, the world's first public health treaty. It has been ratified by 146 countries, representing three-quarters of the world's population, and is transforming the way the world deals with the epidemic of tobacco use.

> **"A more-than-year-long series of briefings and hearings . . . eventually led to the U.S. Supreme Court and to the historic release, during trial, of never-before-seen documents which had been improperly shielded through assertion of the attorney-client privilege and work product doctrines. Those documents revealed what the tobacco companies knew, when they knew it, and how they conspired to cover up and fraudulently mislead the public."**
> Michael V. Ciresi, counsel for the plaintiff

Ten Thousand Lakes of Minnesota Association

A catchy, if inaccurate, slogan is born

Here's a stumper, found on Minnesota North Star, the state's official website:

FAQ: How many lakes are there in the Land of 10,000 Lakes?

Answer: According to the Department of Natural Resources there are over 11,842 lakes (10 acres or larger) in Minnesota.

Notice a slight discrepancy here? Is this just an extreme example of our oft-cited propensity for understatement?

The answer goes back to the first decades of the 1900s, when it dawned on the state's movers and shakers that the northern forests, which had been depleted through logging and were being replanted, could be transformed into huge state parks. At the same time, the rise of automobile tourism led to a growing public interest in marketing the state's recreational advantages.

Thus, in 1917, the Ten Thousand Lakes of Minnesota Association was formed to promote tourism. With contributions from fifty communities throughout the state, the association placed advertisements nationwide, funded a movie about canoeing on the Mississippi River, and published a range of beautifully illustrated pamphlets and postcards touting Minnesota's obvious and varied vacation opportunities. The association's hard work paid off. In 1926, Ten Thousand Lakes president

Arthur Roberts of Winona reported that "the expenditure of $50,000 . . . was one of the best investments ever made by the citizens of the state. It not only brought us more tourists than we have ever had before, but it has started people in other states to talking about Minnesota." After expanding on this idea, Roberts got down to the heart of the matter: "Tourists are good business stimulators. Most of them are good buyers and they have cash. . . . They are splendid customers and I believe that we do not fully appreciate what they are worth to our state."

The Ten Thousand Lakes of Minnesota Association went strong until the 1930s, when the Bureau of Tourism in the Department of Conservation was formed. Today, the state's tourism promotion branch, Explore Minnesota, reports that the industry brings $10 billion into the state annually.

John Thomas (1907–2002)

His compassion knew no boundaries

John Thomas was born in north Minneapolis in 1907; his mother was a Swedish immigrant and his father was the son of a slave. "His early world," writes nominator Mick Caouette, "was filled with people who were integrated by the boundaries of segregation— immigrant families with names like Piazza, Finkelstein, and Johnson. His early world consisted of streetcars, gaslights, and outdoor bathrooms in subzero weather. He was poor but hardly knew it."

Thomas served in the U.S. Army during World War II. After the war, he joined the newly formed United Nations' massive effort to rebuild Europe. He arrived in Germany in 1945. "I was shocked to see that everything I had heard was true," he later said of his visits to internment camps and devastated communities. It was in Germany that Thomas first helped create systems for providing international relief. Along with workers from European countries, he ran displaced-persons camps throughout Germany and relocated thousands of people.

In 1956, Thomas was called to the Austrian-Hungarian border during a Russian invasion. Wading in waist-high water with Russian soldiers close at hand, he helped 200,000 Hungarian refugees cross the border into Austria to safety, one at a time. In 1963, President John Kennedy appointed him director of the Cuban Refugee Program, resulting in the resettlement of 30,000 Cuban families. Three years later, President Lyndon Johnson named him director of the U.S. Vietnam Refugee Program. Thomas settled nearly five million people before and after the 1968 Tet Offensive.

In 1969, John Thomas became the first African American to head an international organization—the International Committee for European Migration, headquartered in Geneva, Switzerland. As director, he came to the aid of the two million Ugandans who were forced to flee by the regime of Idi Amin and was involved in every major world refugee flow until his retirement in 1978.

John Thomas died in New York City in 2002. At his memorial service in Minneapolis, Mick Caouette spoke: "It is estimated that the kid from the north side, who had limited opportunities but never acknowledged his own limitations, helped to save as many as six million people during the forty years of the Cold War. In the words of his friend, Senator Ted Kennedy, 'You have embraced the cares of the world's deprived and dispossessed as your own. Your compassionate commitment will always be an inspiration to us all.'"

John Thomas (at right) with Vietnamese camp leader

Tonka Trucks

Transforming the sandbox into a construction site

I love dumpin', I love diggin', I love haulin', I love liftin', I love dirt and rocks and sand and mud and muck. I love my Tonka—man, I love my truck."

That's the jingle used by Hasbro to market one of its best-selling lines—brightly colored, rugged Tonka trucks. Today's Tonkas come in a variety of models, from dump trucks to fire trucks to pickups, all made of highly durable plastic. Their predecessors—red, yellow, and blue models made of steel— are now highly desirable collectibles cherished by baby boomers whose formative years were spent building sandbox cities. Nominator Matt Bjurstrom of Minneapolis explains: "Tonka toy trucks were created by Mound Metalcraft Company in 1947 in a schoolhouse basement near Lake Minnetonka and were an immediate success. A half-dozen employees produced 37,000 toy trucks that first year alone. Since then, entire generations of children have grown up with Tonka trucks. These durable, bright yellow toys may well be seen as an iconic symbol of childhood in the post–World War II era. Millions of us have fond memories of the Tonka truck received as a birthday or Christmas present."

The first trucks offered by Mound Metalcraft were the Model 100 steam shovel and the Model 150 "crane and clam." Over the years, the company—which became Tonka Toys in 1956—developed a reputation for durability and attention to realistic detail, all the while keeping up with changes in the real-life construction and transportation industries. A pickup premiered in 1955, followed by a jeep in 1962. The bright yellow Mighty Dump Truck came on the scene in 1965 and was Tonka's best seller for the rest of the century. Today's Tonkas are made by Hasbro, which acquired the company in 1991. "Lemme tell ya, buddy, if ya got one you're in luck. I love my Tonka—man, I love my truck."

Treaty of 1837

An unfair exchange

On July 29, 1837, the United States entered into a treaty with several bands of Ojibwe Indians. Under the terms of the treaty, the Indians ceded the northern third of present-day Wisconsin and more than three million acres of land between the St. Croix and Mississippi rivers and south of Lake Mille Lacs in what would become Minnesota to the United States. The United States, in turn, guaranteed to respect certain Indian hunting, fishing, and gathering rights on the ceded land and made payment of annuities for twenty years. According to nominator Joe Niznik of Minneapolis, among other things the treaty "opened the great white pine forest in the St. Croix River valley to lumbermen from the eastern United States. Easy to harvest, with strong and durable wood, the white pine was the lumberman's tree of choice. For over half a century, white pine lumber fueled the economic development and settlement of Minnesota."

In August 1990, the Mille Lacs Band of Chippewa Indians filed suit in federal district court against the State of Minnesota, seeking a judgment that it retained the right to hunt, fish, and gather on the land ceded in 1837. At issue were fishing rights in Lake Mille Lacs. After years of litigation, a ruling was made in favor of the Mille Lacs Band in 1994. The U.S. Supreme Court upheld the ruling in 1999.

Ann River Logging Company's load of logs on a sled near the
St. Croix River, 1892

The Treaty of 1837 and the subsequent
litigation illustrate that one group's loss can
be another's gain and that governmental acts
can have lasting consequences. It also raises a
fundamental question—why were treaties made
in the first place? Do Minnesota's Indians have
special rights?

A treaty is an agreement, binding and legal,
between two or more sovereign nations. When
Europeans first came to America, they dealt
with native Indian tribes as sovereign nations—
that is, as political entities on a par with
European nations. As time went on and the
United States gained independence from
England, the new U.S. government continued to
deal with Indian nations as sovereign bodies.
Today, federally recognized tribes still maintain
sovereignty. The U.S. Constitution upholds
treaties as "the supreme law of the land."

In Minnesota and across the country, treaties
had and continue to have tremendous impact
on the lives of American Indians. The first
treaties were made to preserve peace and to
make alliances between Indians and Europeans.
As Europeans gained power, "treaties of
removal," like the Treaty of 1837, allowed
European settlers access to land and resources.
Finally, "reservation treaties" set aside lands for
exclusive use and occupancy by Indians.

Clara Ueland (1860–1927)

Campaigning for women's rights

I f I can be, in any small way, instrumental in gaining the franchise for the women of Minnesota, I shall feel that I have been allowed to be of real use," Clara Ueland once said. The "franchise" she referred to was the right to vote, and Ueland's contribution to the cause turned out to be anything but small. "Her interest began at a convention of the National American Woman Suffrage Association in Minneapolis in 1901," writes nominator Jean Fideler. "By that time she was already a mother of seven children, yet it was through her daughters' interest in woman suffrage that she came to be involved." In 1913, Ueland invited a small group of women to gather at her home to organize the Equal Suffrage Association of Minnesota, a club open to both men and women interested in a systematic, organized approach to building support for their cause.

The next year, Ueland was elected president of the Minnesota Woman Suffrage Association. Her task was accomplished when Minnesota ratified the Nineteenth Amendment to the U.S. Constitution on September 18, 1919, making Minnesota the fifteenth state to give women the right to vote. In 1919, she became the first president of the Minnesota League of Women Voters. "Ueland was definitely ahead of her time in terms of balancing the raising of children and working toward improving her own life and the community as well," writes Fideler. "She basically created the kindergarten model for the Minneapolis Public School District. She was also an activist who promoted multiculturalism in the arts and preservation of immigrant cultures during a time when few even considered such an idea. She cared about clean water and encroachment on the environment due to industrialization, and she strongly promoted women's rights in all situations.

"Once the state League of Women Voters began, she set the pace for what the future actions of the league would be. The league now dedicates time and effort to many issues that reach far beyond the initial right of women to have access to the voting booth.

"My interest in joining the league was based on my frustration with the disparities I see in my government and in my community, and I believe those were exactly the reasons why Ueland became involved. I'm always humbled when I think of how she influenced and empowered so many women going forward while doing so much for her own family. She truly was a visionary who cared for people and community."

(Opposite) Clara Ueland, 1920; (right) women seated in front of an early suffrage banner, April 1937

University of Minnesota Fruit-Breeding Program

One a day keeps the doctor away

During the 2006 Minnesota legislative session, six fourth-graders from Andersen Elementary School in Bayport, Minnesota, testified before the Senate's State and Local Government Operations Committee, asking that Minnesota adopt the Honeycrisp apple as the state fruit. The committee voted unanimously to forward the bill to the Senate floor, where, on May 10, the unusually crisp and tasty cultivar made the cut. "It's pretty hard to vote against kids and the University of Minnesota at the same time," said Senator Brian LeClair, a Republican from Woodbury, one of the bill's sponsors.

Professor Jim Luby and scientist David Bedford of the University of Minnesota's Agricultural Experiment Station introduced the Honeycrisp to the public in 1991, after years of careful tasting and cross-breeding. Their goal was to develop an apple that could stand up to Minnesota weather. No problem there—the Honeycrisp can last up to ten months in the refrigerator. Plus it needed to taste good. To ensure that, Luby and Bedford bred it to have a slightly tart, slightly sweet flavor along with unusually large cells that account for its crisp, crunchy texture.

About 80 percent of the apples grown in Minnesota today are varieties developed by the university's fruit-breeding program—the only such program in the upper Midwest and one of only four nationwide. The program began in 1908 as the Fruit Breeding Farm on eighty acres near Victoria, Minnesota. In 1978, it merged with the Minnesota Landscape Arboretum. Over its history, the program has developed more than one hundred cold-weather varieties of fruits, from grapes, cherries, and strawberries to pears and apricots. These fruits thrive not only in Minnesota but throughout the northern United States and in Canada.

The fruit-breeding program isn't just good for our appetites—it's good for the region's economy, too. Each Honeycrisp tree puts an estimated $1,000 into the pocket of its grower each year, many of whom are small-business owners just one bad crop away from financial hardship. Take Doug Shefelbine of Holmen, Wisconsin: "Eighty percent of my customers will buy nothing but Honeycrisp," he says. "I don't think we'd be growing apples if we didn't grow Honeycrisp."

Unknown Champions

Thanks, and more thanks

Nominator Doug Wilhide of Minneapolis makes a strong case for the kinds of people we often forget to acknowledge when formulating lists like the Minnesota 150: "These are the people who may not be remembered by history, even in their own communities, but who were essential to building Minnesota and making it what it is. They include the people who built the churches, hockey arenas, first schools, community centers, town parks, ball parks, and downtowns. Each of these projects required someone—often acting on his or her own initiative and out of a passion for building a working society—to get the job done. Committees helped, as did official organizations and governments. But behind every major structure, physical and otherwise, in every town in Minnesota, there is someone who decided to just go ahead and do it."

Nominator Jan MacKenzie-Polanski, Minneapolis, describes one of these projects: "Plymouth Congregational Church in Minneapolis has a marvelous project that has been going on for decades. Many women of the church have collaborated to stitch large tapestries. The images include themes depicting church history, Christmas, spring, and the newest, a patriotic theme. In addition to the four large tapestries, they have made numerous wall hangings and covered many sofas and chairs with their works of art. It is the longevity of the project and the quality of these pieces that I feel make them so amazing."

And from nominator Julia Crozier, Fountain City, Wisconsin: "John Latsch has been a quiet hero for many people in southeastern Minnesota and beyond. He lived in the late 1800s and was a very successful businessman. He lived a simple, frugal life, and his favorite pastime was to canoe on the Mississippi. One day while canoeing, a terrible thunderstorm caused Latsch to take shelter on the shore. He was soon surprised to see the landowner next to him screaming for him to get off his land. This upsetting experience prompted Latsch to start buying up as much land as possible in order to make it possible for him to turn those parcels of land into parks, so that a similar experience would be less likely to happen to other people. The lands that he purchased and subsequently donated are the Winona Golf Course, Latsch Island, Latsch and Blufflands state parks in Minnesota, and Merrick and Perrot state parks in Wisconsin. John Latsch is a good example of the far-ranging influence one person can have on the world."

U.S.–Dakota War

Minnesota's darkest hour

It has been known by many names over the years, from the Great Sioux Uprising to the Dakota Conflict to the U.S.–Dakota War. It is one of Minnesota's most tragic, most notorious moments in time, and its effects are still felt today.

In 1851, the Treaty of Mendota and the Treaty of Traverse des Sioux resulted in the ceding of all but 4 percent of Dakota lands in Minnesota Territory to the United States. Over the next nine years, some Dakota families managed to adapt to the government's policy that they establish farms on their reservation lands, but tensions continued to rise as annuity payments promised through the treaty were delayed. Crop failures in 1861 made a bad situation worse, and by the summer of 1862, Minnesota's Dakota families were starving.

On the morning of August 18, 1862, a group of Dakota men attacked the Lower Sioux Agency, a U.S. government establishment near Redwood Falls. The United States retaliated, and for the next six weeks a series of battles broke out throughout southern Minnesota. Nominator Kristian Berg picks up the story from here: "The war resulted in hundreds dead, farms and homes abandoned, and the

(Right) Six Dakota men in prison compound at Fort Snelling, 1864; (opposite) white settlers escaping from the Indian attacks of 1862

People escaping from the Indian Massacre of 1862, in Minnesota, at Dinner on a Prairie. Photographed by one of the party.

WHITNEY'S GALLERY.   SAINT PAUL.

forced exile of the Dakota people from the state. A military court condemned over 300 Dakota men, many in 15-minute trials. President Abraham Lincoln reviewed the cases and pardoned all but 38, who were hanged on the day after Christmas, 1862, in Mankato, Minnesota. To heighten the effect of their execution, all 38 were hanged simultaneously in a single drop—the largest mass execution in U.S. history."

For many years, the Dakota perspective on the war was ignored. Today, the inhumane treatment of the Dakota people—before the hangings they were forced into a concentration camp at Fort Snelling, and after the hangings they were exiled from Minnesota—is widely acknowledged, and ceremonies seeking reparation and reconciliation have taken place. The first was a powwow held near Mankato in 1972. Organized by Amos Owen, a Dakota spiritual leader, and Bud Lawrence, a white businessman from Mankato, the powwow helped spur a campaign to replace an outdated granite marker near the site of the hangings

with a bronze tablet that explains the executions within the context of the war. On the twenty-fifth anniversary of the first powwow Reconciliation Park was dedicated in Mankato, with a thirty-five-ton bison sculpture as its centerpiece. Amos Owen offered a prayer at the powwow that is now inscribed on a plaque near the sculpture:

Grandfather I come to you this day
in a humble way to offer prayers
for the thirty eight Dakota who perished
in Mankato in the year 1862.
To the West, I pray to the Horse Nation
and to the North, I pray to the Elk People.
To the East, I pray to the Buffalo Nation,
and to the South, the Spirit People.
To the Heavens, I pray to the Great Spirit
and to the Spotted Eagle.
And Below, I pray to Mother Earth
to help us in this time of reconciliation.
Grandfather, I offer these prayers
in my humble way.
To all my relations.

Xang Vang (1950–)

Helping people establish new roots

Born in Laos, Xang Vang came to the United States in 1975. He eventually settled in St. Paul, where he became a respected teacher and community organizer. In 1980, he was elected director of the Lao Family Community of Minnesota. After two years, though, Vang left his secure job to take a risk that paid big dividends for his community. Xang Vang left his job to plant a garden.

Through the help of the Ramsey County agricultural extension office, Vang leased land in Oakdale, a St. Paul suburb. He used his own money to clear and plow the land, and his own car to haul water to the site and to drive Hmong families to buy seeds and plants that they planted and tended in the garden. The following year, the University of Minnesota Agricultural Extension Department recognized Vang's work, and he became codirector of an

agricultural training program based on his plan. Hmong farmers, according to Vang, "were used to slash-and-burn agricultural practices. We were all skilled in intensive labor and in using manual tools. Now, mechanical equipment and pesticides were readily available. Never before were we aware of poison on food production. Now we have to be sure that it is well cleaned for the consumer."

Vang's garden was the first step in helping Hmong farmers participate in Twin Cities farmers' markets. He started the training with 20 families; three years later, 200 Hmong families were selling produce at the markets. Vang's years as a community organizer paid off in his latest enterprise: "I spent countless hours fighting to have the Hmong be a part of the farmers' markets and local chain grocery stores."

Xang Vang didn't stop there. According to nominator Tzianeng Vang, "He then turned entrepreneur, investing in the Frogtown neighborhood as well as in the University Avenue business corridor. And true to form, he and his family were again a part of another proud chapter in Minnesota history by committing and contributing $20,000 to the Center for Hmong Studies at Concordia University–St. Paul."

(Bottom) Xang Vang, 1985; (top) Hmong vendors at the St. Paul Farmers Market

Jesse Ventura (1951–)

A wrestler turned politician "shocks the world"

Details of his life story were repeated early and often throughout his gubernatorial campaign. Born into a working-class family in Minneapolis, James George Janos served six years in the U.S. Navy before embarking on a career as a professional wrestler. Going by the name of Jesse "The Body" Ventura, he was one of the American Wrestling Association's "bad boys," a flamboyant, bullying sort who often spouted the motto: "Win if you can, lose if you must, but always cheat." After retiring from the ring in the mid-1980s, he worked as a wrestling commentator and appeared in a few movies. He ran successfully for mayor of Brooklyn Park, Minnesota, in 1990, and served until 1995. After that first stint in politics, he had a radio call-in show on KFAN, a Twin Cities sports radio station.

In 1998, the former wrestler, talk-show host, and Navy Seal was elected to be Minnesota's thirty-eighth governor. Running as a Reform Party candidate, Ventura claimed 37 percent of the vote, besting St. Paul mayor Norm Coleman's 34 percent and Minnesota attorney general Hubert H. "Skip" Humphrey III's 28 percent. The pugnacious, earthy persona he crafted in his earlier careers served him well throughout the campaign, as he denounced politics as usual and managed to present his self-described lack of knowledge of key issues as a virtue. He was the voice of the people, a candidate for those who were tired of bipartisan gridlock and ready for a fresh start. When he rode into his postelection party on a Harley, pink feather boa streaming, Minnesotans knew that, for better or worse, change was in the works.

In the end, it was Ventura's talent for grabbing headlines, rather than his strong leadership while in the governor's office, that resulted in lasting change. He was a player on the national stage, and because of him folks across the country saw Minnesota in a new light. If we—the mild-mannered, cautious citizens of flyover land—were capable of voting a mouthy, independent candidate into office, what might we do next?

(Bottom) Former governor Jesse Ventura speaking with reporters at the Great Wall of China, 2002; (top) Jesse Ventura "Volunteer Football Coach/Man of Action" doll

Owen H. Wangensteen (1898–1981)

Making the impossible almost commonplace

Young Owen Wangensteen wanted to be a farmer. He grew up on a farm in Becker County in western Minnesota, a lifestyle that agreed with him. But Owen's father wanted his son to go to college instead, so he handed him a shovel and directed him to move manure from one building to another. After that formative experience, the would-be farmer was college bound.

Score one for tough love. Owen Wangensteen grew up to be a groundbreaking surgeon and researcher who headed the University of Minnesota's Department of Surgery from 1930 to 1967. Wangensteen once said that the best teachers are those who inspire excellence in others, and in fact his greatest contribution to his profession may have been as a mentor. C. Walton Lillehei, one of Wangensteen's protégés, who, with F. John Lewis, performed the world's first successful open-heart surgery in 1952, credited

> **"Plant a tree for prosperity in the orchard of your profession. It will give you enduring satisfaction though you may never live to see it mature; its growth can project your image and wishes far into time and space."**
> Owen Wangensteen, in the *Journal of the American Medical Association*

Wangensteen with supporting bold research that yielded impressive results. "He was a very firm believer that where knowledge was lacking, it could often be rapidly broadened in the experimental laboratory," Lillehei once said. In 1955, Richard DeWall, also a Wangensteen trainee, introduced the bubble oxygenator, an artificial heart-lung machine that sent oxygen through the heart during operations and is the prototype of equipment still in use today.

And the list goes on. Christiaan Barnard, the South African surgeon who performed the first human heart transplant in 1967, received his PhD at the University of Minnesota during Wangensteen's tenure, as did Norman Shumway, who devised techniques for successful heart surgeries. "He was never jealous," said J. Ernesto Molina, the last student to earn his PhD under Wangensteen. "I had never seen a doctor like him. He considered himself just the helper to get everyone ahead."

Washburn Center for Children

Establishing a culture of concern that has grown with the city

On the morning of May 2, 1878, a huge explosion at Minneapolis's Washburn A Mill killed eighteen workers, injured many more, and flattened buildings in a large area radiating from the riverfront. Mill owner Cadwallader Washburn immediately set to work rebuilding his nearly ruined business by hiring scientists to determine the cause of the explosion and by building a state-of-the-art replacement for the old mill that incorporated the latest safety features.

But something more than business was on Washburn's mind after the explosion. He became increasingly concerned about the families of workers injured or killed in industrial accidents. He died four years later, and he designated $375,000 in his will for the founding and endowment of Washburn Memorial Orphan Asylum. From 1886 through 1924, 942 children lived at the orphanage, located at Fiftieth Street and Nicollet Avenue, then on the outskirts of Minneapolis. The children were also given an education, both on-site and at public schools. In 1927, due to increasing costs for child care and changing community needs, the orphanage and grounds were sold to the Minneapolis Board of Education, which soon built Washburn High School on the site.

But Washburn's dream didn't end there. In response to unmet needs in Minneapolis, the

MINNEAPOLIS.—THE WASHBURN HOME FOR ORPHAN CHILDREN.—[From a photo by Chas. F. Barber.

organization's trustees founded the Washburn Foster Home to coordinate the placement in foster homes of "children who, because of temperament, environment, unfortunate experiences or health problems[,] required a more careful and thoughtful handling than the average agency could give." In 1951, the board of trustees again changed the home's name and mission; as Washburn Memorial Clinic, it responded to a growing need for mental health services for at-risk children.

Since 1975, as the Washburn Child Guidance Center, and through its 2007 change to Washburn Center for Children, the organization has maintained Cadwallader Washburn's original focus on children who are at the highest risk within the community.

WCAL

The nation's first public radio station

Minnesota's own WCAL 89.3 FM was our nation's first listener-supported radio station and a cofounder of National Public Radio. It began with a physics experiment in 1918, when five students and a professor at St. Olaf College in Northfield, Minnesota, built a small radio transmitter on the campus. Using a wire antenna strung between the campus chapel and another building, the students sent signals that were picked up as far away as New Zealand. Four years later, St. Olaf was granted the WCAL call sign and began broadcasting two programs a week at 770 on the AM dial.

In 1924, a financial crunch threatened the station. When listeners sent donations in response, WCAL achieved its pioneering "listener-supported" status. The station was granted an FM license in 1968.

Three years later, WCAL became one of ninety founding members of National Public Radio.

WCAL developed a core group of dedicated listeners who appreciated the diversity of its classical programming and its knowledgeable, genial hosts. "Classical 89.3" became a welcome alternative to Minnesota Public Radio's (MPR) more mainstream classical station, and for more than a decade the nation's first public radio station shared a market with one of the nation's largest public radio networks.

On August 11, 2004, St. Olaf announced its decision to sell WCAL to MPR. Although two other broadcasters submitted offers for the station, college officials said at the time that MPR, "with its own strong focus on classical music and on news, as well as its 37-year history in public radio and public service," was the best buyer to carry on the legacy.

At the time of its sale, WCAL had 80,000 listeners. Some of those people formed a grassroots group called SaveWCAL, which petitioned the Federal Communications Commission to block the sale. But the FCC dismissed the group's petition, calling parts of it "frivolous and irrelevant." The station stopped broadcasting from its Northfield studios on November 21, 2004. On January 24, 2005, listeners tuning in to 89.3 FM heard "Shhh" by the local hip-hop group Atmosphere, the first song to air on KCMP, Minnesota Public Radio's new alternative music station, popularly known as "The Current." Three months later, The Current was voted "best radio station" by *City Pages* readers.

Webster Cooperative Dairy Association

Making a profit on Minnesota farms

Nominator Merle Fossum connects the dots between his family's history and the story of Minnesota farming. "I often heard that the Webster Co-op Dairy Association was the largest co-op creamery in Minnesota for some period of time. Our grandfather, John Fossum, moved from farmer to being manager of the creamery in Webster, and our other grandfather, Fred Sandmann, was on the board of directors. Big fish in a little pond. The bigger picture is that the rural cooperative movement in Minnesota was the financial organization created by small farmers to market their products. Over time, the hundreds of small co-ops have been bought up by Land O' Lakes, etc.—or just went out of business—but it was the movement that sustained agriculture in Minnesota for generations."

Well said, Merle. Any farmer who has ever tried to raise crops or livestock for profit has faced the problem of how best to sell his or her wares. A century ago, poor roads and trucks without refrigeration made things particularly hard for dairy farmers. Their solution was to form cooperatives—members delivered milk to a local dairy and then shared in its profits. The state's first dairy cooperative was organized at Clarks Grove in Freeborn County in 1889–1890, and it quickly became a model for other farming communities, including Webster.

Minnesota became a national leader in the cooperative movement; by the early 1900s, the state's 671 cooperative creameries represented about half of all those in the United States.

It wasn't just milk and cheese that was sold through cooperatives, of course. In fact, by 1919, Minnesota had more than 2,600 cooperatives, selling products ranging from livestock to sugar to wheat. In 1999, Minnesota led the nation in net business volume of agricultural co-ops, with $9.3 billion. There were thirty-five dairy co-ops.

(Top) Posing in front of the Webster Co-op; (bottom) milk wagon, Minneapolis, 1922

Paul Wellstone (1944–2002)

A life of service ends too soon

Born in Washington, D.C., the son of Ukrainian Jewish immigrants, Paul Wellstone arrived in Minnesota in 1969, when he accepted a teaching job at Carleton College in Northfield. A newly minted PhD in political science and an outspoken political activist, the twenty-four-year-old professor focused on questions of economic justice and poverty and began engaging in campus activism by organizing protests and criticizing the school's administration for its corporate ties. Wellstone was a popular, charismatic teacher who became the youngest faculty member ever to receive tenure.

In 1989, Wellstone announced his candidacy for the U.S. Senate. Virtually unknown to Minnesota voters but with a loyal following from his years as a community organizer, he hit the campaign trail hard—knocking on doors, making phone calls, and crisscrossing the state in a rickety green bus that became the symbol of his grassroots campaign. He went on to become the only candidate in the 1990 election to unseat an incumbent when he defeated his Republican opponent, Rudy Boschwitz. He was reelected to the Senate in 1996.

Wellstone brought his outspoken, unapologetically combative style to Washington

Paul and Sheila Wellstone arrive at victory party

(provoking President George H. W. Bush to ask, "Who is that little chickenshit?" after encountering him at a White House reception), where he took on ethics issues, passing a sweeping reform bill that limited gifts to senators from lobbyists. He also championed a liberal agenda on health care, the environment, and children's issues. He gained a national reputation for his work supporting veterans, the Hmong community, mental health care, and poverty programs. His wife, Sheila, also gained a higher profile during their time on the national scene, becoming a national spokesperson on domestic violence. With Paul, she was a key factor in getting the Violence against Women Prevention Act passed in 1998.

Wellstone was seeking his third term in the Senate when, on October 25, 2002, a plane carrying Paul and Sheila Wellstone, their daughter Marcia, and three campaign staff members crashed near the Eveleth airport in

"I will never forget the first time I saw Paul Wellstone, at the 1992 Minnesota DFL convention in Duluth. In walked an energetic and buoyant man who stood behind a podium that was too tall for him. His speech reminded me of a Hubert Humphrey speech. It began with a recitation of principles and ideals he espoused and what he felt was lacking in the current political arena. Soon he began to wind up and passionately proclaimed to the audience his vision for America and the changes he would like to make. I swear the man was almost levitating by the end of the speech! When he left the podium he shook as many hands as he could, meanwhile smiling and waving to the audience. And that was Paul Wellstone." **Nominator Brenda S. Hagen, North Mankato, Minnesota**

northern Minnesota. There were no survivors. Over the course of his life in Minnesota, he had evolved from an outspoken young community activist into the embodiment of a long-standing Minnesota tradition of Populist politics that went back to the Grange movement, Floyd B. Olson and the Farmer-Labor Party, Hubert Humphrey, and Eugene McCarthy.

Wheat

A staple, a commodity, and a way of life

I n 1880, almost 70 percent of Minnesota's farmland was planted in wheat. That's 4.4 million acres, producing more than 34 million bushels of wheat that year. By 1900, that figure had dropped to 50 percent—southern and central Minnesota farmers had shifted to dairy farming and raising beef cattle and hogs— but the state's wheat output remained the highest in the nation. Thanks to increased mechanization and the development of better, stronger hybrids, production had increased to 95 million bushels a year.

This rural revolution was matched by the rapid rise of flour milling—first, wherever waterpower could be harnessed to power a mill, and, increasingly, in Minneapolis, which became known as the Mill City. At the Washburn Crosby Company A Mill, one of the city's largest, more than 175 railroad cars of wheat were processed each day, translating into 12 million loaves of bread made daily from 1880 to 1930. Multiply those figures by the dozens of flour mills that lined the Mississippi River during milling's heyday, and you have some idea of the supply and demand cycle that kept wheat prices high and led to the establishment of huge bonanza farms in the Red River Valley in northwestern Minnesota.

All those farmers, all those millers, all the grain traders and bakers and merchants and admen and factory workers connected to that one grain—wheat—transformed Minnesota. People came to Minnesota from abroad—first from northern Europe and later from Eastern Europe—to work in the fields and the factories. They built houses, schools, churches, families, and communities. They brought with them traditions from their homelands that are still manifest across the state. And they have not been forgotten. As nominator Rebecca Ridgeway, whose great-grandparents, grandparents, and parents were all wheat farmers, puts it, "I would not be here without wheat."

Wheat field, Aitkin County, 1910

Henry B. Whipple (1822–1901)

A strong voice in troubled times

enry Whipple was born in Adams, New York, and began his religious training in the nearby community of Rome, where he was rector of Zion Episcopal Church. He later moved to a post as first rector of the Church of the Holy Communion in Chicago. Throughout his early career as an Episcopal priest, Whipple dedicated himself to the struggles of the poorest members of his congregations.

On June 30, 1859, Henry Whipple was named the first Episcopal bishop of Minnesota. He established the Episcopal see at Faribault and was instrumental in founding three schools in the town—Shattuck for boys, St. Mary's for girls, and Seabury Divinity for seminary students—as well as a mission school for Ojibwe at White Earth. From his earliest days in Minnesota, Whipple befriended and supported American Indians. He made regular visits throughout his diocese, often supporting missionary clergy with his own money. Through his travels, he became dedicated to the welfare of the state's Dakota and Ojibwe people, a stance that earned him the enmity of many European settlers, particularly as the racial divides that resulted in the U.S.–Dakota War were being formed. "Bishop Whipple informed himself of the condition and prospects of both [Indian] nations," wrote historian William Watts Folwell, who saw firsthand the fear and suspicion that divided the state, "and soon became satisfied that much of their wretchedness was chargeable to the indifference . . . of white men."

Although Whipple has often been credited with influencing President Lincoln's decision to commute the sentences of 265 Dakota men convicted of war crimes as a result of the U.S.–Dakota War, his attempts to seek justice were in fact limited. In his diary and in a letter to a friend, Bishop Whipple recorded an attempt to meet with Lincoln in 1862, following the August outbreak of the war. Of Whipple, Lincoln later told a friend, "He came here the other day and talked with me about the rascality of this Indian business until I felt it down to my boots. If we get through this war, and I live, this Indian system shall be reformed!"

White Pine Trees

A natural resource feeds an industry

A white pine tree can grow to be more than one hundred feet tall, with a trunk diameter of more than forty inches. There was a time when Minnesota's forests were dense with white pines, which flourish in the cool shade and fine soils of the north.

New Englanders schooled in logging and sawmilling began looking to the pine forests of Minnesota as early as the 1830s. The first easterners established their logging operations along the St. Croix River, where they found white pines that were light enough to float on log drives, soft enough to mill easily, and were strong, durable, and resistant to decay. Commercial lumbering began in Minnesota in 1839 when a group of New England businessmen started a sawmill at what soon became a small town, Marine on St. Croix. A year later, a second commercial mill was built, at Stillwater, which within a decade became Minnesota Territory's milling capital.

Over time, logging camps spread northward, becoming larger and more efficient in the process. Oxen were replaced with draft horses, and logs moved ever more quickly from the woods to sawmills to lumberyards. The years from 1890 to 1910 were the heyday of logging in Minnesota; lumber companies' combined output was valued at $1 billion. Production peaked in 1905, when the lumber harvested in Minnesota would have filled 240,000 railroad cars.

"For all this a price was paid," wrote Agnes Larson in her *History of the White Pine Industry in Minnesota,* published in 1949. "One cannot with impunity rob Mother Nature of her treasures, for truly the sins of the fathers are avenged unto the third or fourth generation. The price we must pay for the rapid use of our forests is a vast area of wasteland for generations, or else a wise and vigorous policy of reforestation." Since 1997, the Minnesota Department of Natural Resources has overseen the White Pine Initiative to protect and replant this valuable resource.

The Willmar 8

Taking a stand when the stakes are high

Doris Boshart, Sylvia Erickson, Jane Harguth, Teren Novotny, Shirley Solyntjes, Glennis Ter Wisscha, Sandi Treml, and Irene Wallin. You may not recognize their individual names, but collectively they stirred up controversy in their Minnesota town and across the country in the late 1970s. Known as the Willmar 8, they came to symbolize the uphill climb many American women faced when seeking pay commensurate with their experience and equal to that of their male peers.

The women had been hired at Citizens' National Bank in Willmar at $400 a month. Starting monthly salaries for men averaged $700. Women were expected to work overtime without pay. The bank's sole female officer earned $4,000 less per year than her male supervisees. The last straw, though, came when the women were directed to train a young man right out of college to become their boss. When they pointed out this inequity to bank president Leo Pirsch, his reply spoke volumes: "We're not all equal, you know." They filed a gender discrimination complaint with the Equal Employment Opportunity Commission (EEOC) and an unfair labor practice charge with the National Labor Relations Board. In June 1977, they formed Minnesota's first bank union, the Willmar Bank Employees' Association Local 1.

The EEOC took up their cause, but negotiations with bank management broke down. Finally, on December 16, 1977, the women zipped up their snowmobile suits and stepped out into the seventy-degree-below-zero windchill with their picket signs to begin the nation's first bank strike.

They hoped a new contract could be negotiated within a few weeks. After two years, they still hadn't reached an agreement, but sympathizers nationwide had heard their voices loud and clear. Feminist concerns were making headlines everywhere, and the Willmar 8, a group of plainspoken wives, daughters, and mothers, struck a chord. Representatives from the National Organization for Women joined them on the line, as did members of the United Auto Workers. In 1980, actress Lee Grant filmed a documentary about them. "It was the first labor strike that really brought together issues of the labor movement and the women's movement," says Renee Vaughan, who teaches at Metropolitan State University in St. Paul. "Before the Willmar 8, the labor movement didn't see gender discrimination as part of the platform. The eight of them really did create social change."

In September 1978, the EEOC negotiated a settlement and the women dropped the lawsuit and agreed to work without a contract. One by one, as their demands went unmet and the bank refused to rehire them, the women found other jobs. Doris Boshart was the only member of the Willmar 8 called back to work immediately; eventually, three others joined her, but only for a few months. Boshart was the only one who stuck it out, even though she was demoted from head bookkeeper to teller and was harassed by coworkers. The National Labor Relations Board issued a ruling in 1979 that did not support the women's position in regard to discrimination. Ter Wisscha, now living in St. Paul, still gets letters and phone calls from students. "That's what fuels my belief that we're not done winning yet," she says. "People are still asking the questions. People still want to try to understand."

The Willmar 8 begin their strike, December 16, 1977

August Wilson (1945–2005)

An emerging star finds his voice in Minnesota

Born in Pittsburgh, August Wilson had published a few poems and had begun writing some plays in 1977 when he came to St. Paul to rewrite a play a friend was directing at the newly founded Penumbra Theatre. The next year, Wilson settled in St. Paul, where he stayed until moving to Seattle in 1990. During his years in St. Paul, especially through his association with Penumbra and with Minneapolis's Playwrights' Center, Wilson wrote an exceptional number of groundbreaking plays that illuminated African American culture, including Pulitzer Prize winners *Fences* and *The Piano Lesson.* He later told the *New York Times,* "Having moved from Pittsburgh to St. Paul, I felt I could hear voices for the first time accurately."

The pivotal moment in Wilson's career came in 1980, when he was awarded a $2,400 grant for a year's "membership" in the Playwrights' Center, funded by the Jerome Foundation. At the time, there were few organizations like the Playwrights' Center in the country, where emerging talents could hone their skills and have their works produced and critiqued by peers and mentors. Wilson used his time at the Playwrights' Center wisely, drafting and rewriting two plays: *Fullerton Street* and *Jitney.* John Fenn, who moderated a reading of *Jitney,* later recalled, "There was a general agreement that this was something pretty hefty. . . . We knew it was bound for glory." For his part, Wilson said, "The workshop I had with John Richardson on *Fullerton Street* opened up the world of playwriting as nothing had before, and armed with that glimpse of its possibilities and the confidence gained from my acceptance as a Jerome Fellow, I sat down and wrote *Ma Rainey.*"

Ma Rainey's Black Bottom was the first of Wilson's plays to gain national recognition; it debuted on Broadway in 1984. After its success, Wilson remained active in the Twin Cities theatrical community and a regular at several St. Paul bars and restaurants, where he wrote many of his plays. August Wilson moved to Seattle in 1990 but kept close ties to his adopted midwestern home. St. Paul's Penumbra Theatre regularly produced his work, dedicating a whole season to his plays in 2002–2003. Before he died, in 2005, he chose the Playwrights' Center as one of four national institutions to receive donations in his name.

Wind Turbines

Transforming the landscape by harnessing a natural resource

The growing availability of electricity in rural Minnesota made the windmills that once dotted the landscape all but obsolete. In recent years, though, rising fuel prices and environmental concerns have sparked renewed interest in the power of wind. Today, thousands of tall, gleaming wind turbines stand across Buffalo Ridge in southwestern Minnesota. Here's how nominator Raymond Crippen of Worthington, Minnesota, describes the change:

"Buffalo Ridge has been determined to be one of the most windswept sites on the North American continent. The nearly constant Buffalo Ridge winds match or exceed the winds at Pacific Coast sites where ocean zephyrs break over the shores. So it came to be, in 1993, that a cluster of more than seventy wind turbines was erected near Hendricks and Lake Benton in Lincoln County, as the U.S. government, the State of Minnesota, and several energy conglomerates began a serious effort to create electricity from wind. Southwest Minnesota's landscape has been transformed, just as the search for energy has been transformed. Minnesota's southwest corner, in particular, has become an American center for the production of electricity. The sleek, nearly silent wind turbines are all about 250 feet high. Each turbine weighs nearly 100 tons. Most have three blades with a rotor diameter of more than 150 feet. They are awesome structures. Each turbine may supply the annual electrical needs of up to 250 homes.

"Lincoln County has become an emblem of the future for energy production and attendant financial benefits. Winds that sweep the state from the Lake Superior shores to the relentless zephyrs of Buffalo Ridge are making Minnesota a center of electrical production, supplanting old-time coal-burning plants of decades gone by and bringing a new boon to the state's economy."

"Most natives and all visitors will tell you that southwestern Minnesota is as flat as a pancake. But there are greater extremes of terrain here than anywhere else in Minnesota. Here is some of the state's highest ground, along Buffalo Ridge, the backbone of the coteau. . . . The sweep of the horizon in any direction is infinite. There is no telling where earth and sky meet. Here one can get some sense of the milieu of the prairie as it was not so long ago, when it was a treeless expanse of waving grass, visited only occasionally by nomads, deathly still because even the wind has no sound except when it is interrupted." Paul Gruchow, "This Prairie, This Terrible Place," reprinted in *The North Country Reader,* 1979

Theodore Wirth (1863–1949)

Making the City of Lakes a delight for all

I n the northwest corner of Minneapolis lies the Quaking Bog, a five-acre wetland shaded by tamaracks. The bog is a delicate ecosystem where rare plants, frogs, and dragonflies flourish. A boardwalk extends over the bog, so that park visitors can stroll through the unique setting without damaging it.

The Quaking Bog is a part of Theodore Wirth Park. It is fitting that this picturesque spot has been preserved within the city park named for Wirth, a gardener by training who is credited with creating Minneapolis's park system. Born in Switzerland, Wirth apprenticed in London and Paris before moving to the United States in 1888. Once here, he found work as a tree trimmer in New York's Central Park, working his way up to sub-superintendent of Riverside Park. Wirth became superintendent of parks in Hartford, Connecticut, in 1896,

where he developed a park system from plans sketched by Central Park designer Frederick Law Olmsted that included the nation's first municipal rose garden.

Wirth took over as Minneapolis Park Board superintendent in 1906. Following plans by Olmsted and by Horace Cleveland, designer of the Twin Cities' system of parkways, Wirth dredged lakes, eliminated swampy sections, and developed parks, golf courses, and boulevards, all oriented around the Chain of Lakes. He designed the nation's second municipal rose garden, near Lake Harriet, and increased park board land from 1,810 to 5,241 acres. He believed that parks were for public recreation, not just passive enjoyment of nature, and so he removed fences and installed "Please Walk on Grass" signs. His goal was simple, but it spoke volumes about a philosophy that remains in place today: he wanted every home in Minneapolis to be within six blocks of green space.

(Top) Theodore Wirth reading the newspaper, 1930;
(bottom) Wirth Park today

Essay on Sources

Several key sources on Minnesota history cover many of the topics listed below, including Clifford E. Clark Jr., ed., *Minnesota in a Century of Change: The State and Its People since 1900* (St. Paul: Minnesota Historical Society Press, 1989); June Drenning Holmquist, ed., *They Chose Minnesota: A Survey of the State's Ethnic Groups* (St. Paul: Minnesota Historical Society Press, 1981); Norman K. Risjord, *A Popular History of Minnesota* (St. Paul: Minnesota Historical Society Press, 2005); Anne J. Aby, ed., *The North Star State: A Minnesota History Reader* (St. Paul: Minnesota Historical Society Press, 2002).

The MHS website, www.mnhs.org, is also full of leads on a number of topics, and more sources are being added all the time. See also the index to *Minnesota History* magazine, published by MHS since 1915, at http://www.mnhs.org/market/mhspress/MinnesotaHistory/index/. The MHS visual resources database, accessed through the website, contains a rich assortment of pictorial images. Other key sites for visual research include the Minneapolis Public Library's Minneapolis Photo Collection at http://204.169.52.41/dbtw-wpd/phosrc.htm, the University of Minnesota's Digital Collections at http://digital.lib.umn.edu/, and the Minnesota Reflections digital library at http://reflections.mndigital.org/.

Resources specific to each of the Minnesota 150 are as follows:

American Indian Movement:

For the founders' viewpoints, see Peter Nabokov, ed., *Native American Testimony: A Chronicle of Indian-White Relations from Prophecy to the Present* (New York: Penguin Books, 1978; revised edition, 1992). See also the AIM website at http://www.aimovement.org; the MHS website contains a useful resource on this and other subjects on its History Topics page at http://www.mnhs.org/library/tips/history_topics/index.htm (hereafter MHS History Topics).

Ancient Tropical Sea:

Warren Upham, *Minnesota Place Names: A Geographical Encyclopedia* (St. Paul: Minnesota Historical Society Press, 2001).

Elmer L. Andersen:

Lori Sturdevant, ed., *A Man's Reach* (Minneapolis: University of Minnesota Press, 2000); http://www1.umn.edu/umnnews/Feature_Stories/Elmer_L._Andersen.html; there is also an informative exhibit at the Elmer L. Andersen Human Services Building in St. Paul; the MHS website contains source material on each of the state's governors at http://www.mnhs.org/people/governors/governors.htm (hereafter MHS Minnesota Governors).

Arrival of Major League Sports:

Joel A. Rippel, *75 Memorable Moments in Minnesota Sports* (St. Paul: Minnesota Historical Society Press, 2003); Stew Thornley, *Baseball in Minnesota: The Definitive History* (St. Paul: Minnesota Historical Society Press, 2006); Jim Klobuchar, *Knights and Knaves of Autumn: 40 Years of Pro Football and the Minnesota Vikings* (Cambridge, MN: Adventure Publications, 2000).

Atmosphere:

See http://www.rhymesayers.com/ and articles in *City Pages* (Peter S. Scholtes, "Rhyme Out of Joint," July 5, 2000, and "One Nation, Invisible," August 18, 2004) and the *Star Tribune* (Chris Riemenschneider, "Ice Hot: The Atmosphere Is Finally Right for Minnesota Rappers," March 27, 2004).

Ann Bancroft:

See http://www.yourexpedition.com/explore/ArcticOcean2007/index.jsp.

Margaret Culkin Banning:

See http://www.catholicauthors/com/banning/html and http://people.mnhs.org/authors/biog_detail.cfm?PersonID=Bann136. The Karal Ann Marling quote is in Clark, ed., *Minnesota in a Century of Change*. The Minnesota Authors Biography Project at http://people.mnhs.org/authors/index.cfm contains many references to Banning and her work (hereafter MHS Minnesota Authors).

John Beargrease:

For this entry, I relied heavily on a training manual for the MHS History Players program. The quotation about Beargrease is from Willis H. Raff, *Pioneers in the Wilderness: Minnesota's Cook County, Grand Marais, and the Gunflint in the 19th Century* (Grand Marais: Cook County Historical Society, 1981).

Charles Albert Bender:

Minnesota writer Tom Swift has a book on Bender coming out in 2008; until then, check out Swift's essay about Bender at http://www.nickelcurves.com/essays_comments.php?id=38_0_5_0_C. See also Bender's page on the National Baseball Hall of Fame website at http://www.baseballhalloffame.org/hofers_and_honorees/hofer_bios/bender_chief.htm; Thornley, *Baseball in Minnesota*.

Patty Berg:

See Rhonda Glenn's moving tribute to Patty Berg at http://www.usga.org/news/2005/february/berg.html; Rippel, *75 Memorable Moments*.

Harriet Bishop:

Barbara Stuhler and Gretchen Kreuter, eds., *Women of Minnesota: Selected Biographical Essays* (St. Paul: Minnesota Historical Society Press, 1998); MHS History Topics.

Charles K. Blandin:

Donald L. Boese, *Papermakers: The Blandin Paper Company and Grand Rapids, Minnesota* (Grand Rapids, MN: Charles K. Blandin Foundation, 1984); http://www.blandinfoundation.org/html/about.cfm.

Norman Borlaug:

Leon Hesser, *The Man Who Fed the World* (Dallas, TX: Durban House, 2006); an English translation of Mrs. Aase Lionaes's 1970 Nobel Prize presentation speech is at http://www.nobelprize.org/peace/laureates/1970/press.html.

Boundary Waters Canoe Area:

R. Newell Searle, *Saving Quetico-Superior: A Land Set Apart* (St. Paul: Minnesota Historical Society Press, 1977); Joe Paddock, *Keeper of the Wild: The Life of Ernest Oberholtzer* (St. Paul: Minnesota Historical Society Press, 2001); MHS History Topics; for Sigurd Olson, see MHS Minnesota Authors; quote from Bill Hansen is at http://news.minnesota.publicradio.org/features/2003/10/21_kelleherb_bwca/.

Fanny Brin:

Stuhler and Kreuter, *Women of Minnesota*; for this entry I also relied heavily on a training manual for the MHS History Players program, prepared by Linda Cameron in 2004.

Bryan v. Itasca County:

Most of the information for this entry came directly from nominator Kevin Washburn; see also the website of the Minnesota Indian Gaming Association at http://mnindiangaming.com.

Paul Bunyan:

Risjord, *Popular History*; there are many online resources on this topic, including http://www.wisconsinhistory.org/topics/bunyan/index.asp.

Burma-Shave Road Signs:

Tom Gilsenan, "Signs Meant Sales: Burma-Shave into the Sixties," *Hennepin History* (Fall 1994); Bill Vossler, *Burma-Shave: The Rhymes, the Signs, the Times* (St. Cloud, MN: North Star Press of St. Cloud, 1997). Frank Rowsome, *The Verse by the Side of the Road: The Story of the Burma-Shave Signs and Jingles* (Brattleboro, VT: S. Greene Press, 1965), contains all known slogans from 1927 to 1963.

Center for Victims of Torture:

See the organization's website at http://www.cvt.org/.

Charter Schools:

See the Minnesota Association of Charter Schools website at http://www.mncharterschools.org/; David Kraft's story is in Jessica Flannigan, "Midway's Avalon School Takes State Academic Decathlon," in *Midway Como Monitor* (April 2006).

F. Melius Christiansen:

Joseph M. Shaw, *The St. Olaf Choir: A Narrative* (Northfield, MN: St. Olaf College, 1997); the Hoekstra quote is at http://www.stolaf.edu/offices/communications/magazine/2004winter/benediction.pdf.

The Cloquet/Moose Lake Fires of 1918:

Christine Skalko and Marlene Wisuri, *Fire Storm: The Great Fires of 1918* (Cloquet, MN: Carlton County Historical Society, 2003); Francis M. Carroll and Franklin R. Raiter, *The Fires of Autumn: The Cloque–Moose Lake Disaster of 1918* (St. Paul: Minnesota Historical Society Press, 1990).

Confluence of Mississippi and Minnesota Rivers:

See Upham, *Minnesota Place Names.*

Gratia Alta Countryman:

Quotes are from Jane Pejsa, *Gratia Countryman: Her Life, Her Loves and Her Library* (Minneapolis: Nodin Press, 1995). See also Bruce Weird Benidt, *The Library Book: Centennial History of the Minneapolis Public Library* (Minneapolis: Minneapolis Public Library and Information Center, 1984); Stuhler and Kreuter, *Women of Minnesota.*

Courage Center:

Mavis A. Voigt, *Courage: The Story of Courage Center* (Golden Valley, MN: Courage Center, 1989).

Seymour Cray:

The University of California, San Francisco, has an extensive tribute to Seymour Cray at http://www.cgl.ucsf.edu/home/tef/cray. The Chippewa Falls Museum of Industry and Technology maintains a large collection of Cray supercomputers and other materials; see http://my.execpc.com/~cfmit/.

Betty Crocker:

Susan Marks, *Finding Betty Crocker: The Secret Life of America's First Lady of Food* (New York: Simon and Schuster, 2005); http://www.bettycrocker.com/.

Dan Patch:

D. R. Martin, "The Most Wonderful Horse in the World," *American Heritage* (July/August 1990); Jack El-Hai, "The King of Sport," *Minnesota Monthly* (July 2003); City of Savage website at http://www.ci.savage.mn.us/history_dan_patch.html; for a fictionalized account, see the 1949 film *The Great Dan Patch.*

Danza Mexica Cuauhtemoc:

See the organization's website at http://cuauhtemoc.org.

Destruction of the Metropolitan Building:

Larry Millett, *Lost Twin Cities* (St. Paul: Minnesota Historical Society Press, 1992); the *Minneapolis Journal* quote is from May 31, 1890.

Walter H. Deubener:

Paul Ceplecha, "It's in the Bag," *Grand Gazette* (June 1992).

Don Miguel (Howard H. Hathaway):

Information about Don Miguel came directly from his wife, Dorrie Hathaway.

Ignatius Donnelly:

Martin Ridge, *Ignatius Donnelly: The Portrait of a Politician* (St. Paul: Minnesota Historical Society Press, 1991).

Duluth Lynchings:

Michael Fedo, *The Lynchings in Duluth* (St. Paul: Minnesota Historical Society Press, 1993); quotes are taken from the MHS's extensive website on this topic at http://collections.mnhs.org/duluthlynchings/html/purpose.htm.

Bob Dylan:

Bob Dylan, *Chronicles: Volume One* (New York: Simon and Schuster, 2005); "55746 Zip USA, Hibbing, Minnesota," *National Geographic* (October 2002); MHS History Topics.

Ensilage Harvester:

The Adolph Ronning Collection, Volume One: The Ensilage Harvester and Farmall System, DVD (Firestorm Films, 2002).

Ethnic Presses:

Holmquist, *They Chose Minnesota*.

Wilford H. Fawcett:

The most comprehensive information I could find about *Captain Billy's Whiz Bang* is the Wikipedia entry on Fawcett Publications at http://en.wikipedia.org/wiki/Fawcett_Publications.

Finkelstein and Ruben:

Kirk J. Besse, *Show Houses, Twin Cities Style* (Minneapolis: Victoria Publications, 1981); Dave Kenney, *Twin Cities Picture Show: A Century of Moviegoing* (St. Paul: Minnesota Historical Society Press, 2007).

First Minnesota Volunteer Infantry Regiment:

Richard Moe, *The Last Full Measure: The Life and Death of the First Minnesota Volunteers* (St. Paul: Minnesota Historical Society Press, 1993); James A. Wright, *No More Gallant a Deed: A Civil War Memoir of the First Minnesota Volunteers* (St. Paul: Minnesota Historical Society Press, 2001);

Brian Leehan, *Pale Horse at Plum Run: The First Minnesota at Gettysburg* (St. Paul: Minnesota Historical Society Press, 2002).

F. Scott Fitzgerald:

Matthew J. Bruccoli, *Classes on F. Scott Fitzgerald* (Columbia, SC: Thomas Cooper Library, University of South Carolina, 2001); Patricia Hampl, *The Saint Paul Stories of F. Scott Fitzgerald* (St. Paul: Minnesota Historical Society Press, 2004); Arthur Mizener, *The Far Side of Paradise: A Biography of F. Scott Fitzgerald* (Boston: Houghton Mifflin, 1949); MHS Minnesota Authors.

William Watts Folwell:

See the University of Minnesota's biographies of past presidents at http://www1.umn.edu/pres/05_hist_folwell.html; Folwell's inaugural address is quoted in Clark, *Minnesota in a Century of Change.*

Wanda Gág:

Gwenyth Swain, *Wanda Gág: Storybook Artist* (St. Paul: Borealis Books, 2005); Wanda Gág, *Growing Pains: Diaries and Drawings for the Years 1908–1917* (New York: Coward-McCann, 1940); MHS History Topics; MHS Minnesota Authors.

Verne Gagne:

See the Professional Wrestling Hall of Fame and Museum website at http://pwhf.org/halloffamers/bios/gagne.asp; Joel A. Rippel, *Minnesota Sports Almanac* (St. Paul: Minnesota Historical Society Press, 2006).

Cass Gilbert:

Geoffrey Blodgett, *Cass Gilbert: The Early Years* (St. Paul: Minnesota Historical Society Press, 2001); Neil B. Thompson, *Minnesota's State Capitol: The Art and Politics of a Public Building* (St. Paul: Minnesota Historical Society Press, 2005).

Robert R. Gilruth:

Much of our information about Gilruth came from his nominator, Art Wright. Quotes are from the NASA website at http://www.nasa.gov/centers/johnson.

Glaciation:

See Upham, *Minnesota Place Names.*

James Madison Goodhue:

For this entry, I relied heavily on a training manual for the MHS History Players program.

Grand Portage:

Carolyn Gilman, *Where Two Worlds Meet: The Great Lakes Fur Trade* (St. Paul: Minnesota Historical Society Press, 1982); Carolyn Gilman, *The Grand Portage Story* (St. Paul: Minnesota Historical Society Press, 1992).

Grasshoppers:

Annette Atkins, *Harvest of Grief: Grasshopper Plagues and Public Assistance in Minnesota, 1873–78* (St. Paul: Minnesota Historical Society Press, 1984).

Greyhound Bus Company:

For a comprehensive timeline of company history, see the Greyhound website at http://www.greyhound.com/company/media/history.shtml; Margaret Walsh, "Tracing the Hound: The Minnesota Roots of the Greyhound Bus Company," *Minnesota History* 49, no. 8 (Winter 1985).

Wendelin Grimm:

See the Three Rivers Park District website at http://www.threeriversparkdistrict.org/parks/grimmfarm.cfm.

Guthrie Theater:

The Tyrone Guthrie quote is in Peg Guilfoyle, *The Guthrie Theater: Images, History, and Inside Stories* (Minneapolis: Nodin Press, 2006); the Sullivan quote is in the *Minneapolis Tribune*, May 8, 1963; the Dowling quote is in Stephen Graubard, ed., *Minnesota Real and Imagined* (St. Paul: Minnesota Historical Society Press, 2000); MHS History Topics.

Hall Brothers New Orleans Jazz Band:

Most of the information here is directly from the nominator, Dick Parker, and from Hall Brothers member Mike Polad.

Hazelden:

For a history of Hazelden, see the organization's website at http://www.hazelden.org/web/public/history.page; the Moyers quote is from http://www.pbs.org/kcet/tavissmiley/archive/200610/20061019_transcript.html#2.

Herter's, Inc.:

A history of Herter's has yet to be compiled. For primary source research, the MHS collections contain a number of Herter's catalogs and objects.

Highway 61 along the North Shore:

For maps, history, and guides to attractions along Highway 61, see the National Scenic Byways Program website at http://www.byways.org/explore/byways/11185/index.html.

James J. Hill:

Albro Martin, *James J. Hill and the Opening of the Northwest* (St. Paul: Minnesota Historical Society Press, 1991); Craig Johnson, *James J. Hill House* (St. Paul: Minnesota Historical Society Press, 1993).

The Honeywell Project:

Most information on this topic came directly from Marv Davidov.

The Honeywell Round Thermostat:

Judy Haaversen, ed., *All Together Now, Happy Centennial* (Minneapolis, Honeywell, Inc., 1985); an inventory of Honeywell, Inc., archives at MHS is at http://www.mnhs.org/library/findaids/00051.html; MHS History Topics.

Hubert H. Humphrey:

Carl Solberg, *Hubert Humphrey: A Biography* (St. Paul: Borealis Books, 2003); MHS History Topics.

Immigrants:

Holmquist, *They Chose Minnesota*; see also the Hmong Today website at http://www.hmongtoday.com/index.asp.

Indian Boarding Schools:

Brenda J. Child, *Boarding School Seasons: American Indian Families, 1900–1940* (Lincoln: University of Nebraska Press, 1998); Northrup quote is from the *Indian Country Today* website at http://www.indiancountry.com/content.cfm?id=1065111954.

John Ireland:

Ann Regan, *Irish in Minnesota* (St. Paul: Minnesota Historical Society Press, 2002); Marvin R. O'Connell, *John Ireland and the American Catholic Church* (St. Paul: Minnesota Historical Society Press, 1988).

Iron Ore:

Denis P. Gardner, *Minnesota Treasures: Stories behind the State's Historic Places* (St. Paul: Minnesota Historical Society Press, 2004); David Allan Walker, *Iron Frontier: The Discovery and Early Development of Minnesota's Three Ranges* (St. Paul: Minnesota Historical Society Press, 1979).

Itasca State Park:

Roy W. Meyer, *Everyone's Country Estate: A History of Minnesota's State Parks* (St. Paul: Minnesota Historical Society Press, 1991).

Jeffers Petroglyphs:

Gardner, *Minnesota Treasures*; website for Jeffers Petroglyphs Historic Site at http://www.mnhs.org/places/sites/jp/.

Frederick McKinley Jones:

Virginia Ott and Gloria Swanson, *Man with a Million Ideas: Frederick Jones, Genius/Inventor* (Minneapolis: Lerner Publications, 1977); David Vassar Taylor, *African Americans in Minnesota* (St. Paul: Minnesota Historical Society Press, 2002); MHS History Topics.

J. R. Watkins Medical Company:

See http://www.watkinsonline.com/history/; http://jrwatkins.com; Chris Serres, "Winona's Watkins Takes Leap from Door to Store," *Minneapolis Star Tribune* (December 19, 2005).

Hamilton Harris Judson:

The best source I located on Judson is on a website maintained by the Farmington Area Historical Society, at http://www.geocities.com/fahsmn/post_office_history.htm.

Garrison Keillor:

There is a good analysis of Keillor's style and appeal at http://www.slate.com/id/2143763; the blogger's quote was found at http://prairiehome.forum.publicradio.org/article.pl?sid=06/09/14/1127233 (site no longer active); MHS Minnesota Authors.

Oliver H. Kelley:

The Oliver H. Kelley Farm page on the MHS website contains links to a number of resources; see http://www.mnhs.org/places/sites/ohkf/; see also the National Grange website at http://www.nationalgrange.org.

Sister Elizabeth Kenny:

For an overview of Kenny's life and career, see http://news.minnesota.publicradio.org/features/200208/22_olsond_sisterkinney/; for current programs offered at the Sister Kenny Institute, see http://www.allina.com/ahs/ski.nsf/page/aboutus; MHS History Topics; see also *Sister Kenny*, a 1946 movie starring Rosalind Russell.

Kensington Runestone:

For a recent overview of the history and current thinking about the Runestone, see Rhoda R. Gilman, "Kensington Runestone Revisited: Recent Developments, Recent Publications," *Minnesota History* 60, no. 2 (Summer 2006).

Theodore F. Koch:

Robert Schoone-Jongen, "Cheap Land and Community: Theodore F. Koch, Dutch Colonizer," *Minnesota History* 53, no. 6 (Summer 1993); Koch's papers are at the University of Texas at Austin; for a summary see http://www.tsha.utexas.edu/handbook/online/articles/KK/fko7.html.

Sinclair Lewis:

Mark Schorer, *Sinclair Lewis* (Minneapolis: University of Minnesota Press, 1963); Richard Lingeman, *Sinclair Lewis: Rebel from Main Street* (St. Paul: Borealis Books, 2005); MHS Minnesota Authors.

Charles A. Lindbergh Jr.:

Charles A. Lindbergh Jr., *The Spirit of St. Louis* (New York: Scribner's, 1953); A. Scott Berg, *Lindbergh* (New York: Berkley Books, 1999); Jim Fisher, *Ghosts of Hopewell: Setting the Record Straight in the Lindbergh Case* (Carbondale: Southern Illinois University Press, 1999); Paula Fass, *Kidnapped: Child Abduction in America* (New York: Oxford, 1997); MHS History Topics.

Ron and Al Lindner:

The best way to learn about the Lindners is to learn from them, by reading their books, looking at back issues of their *In-Fisherman* magazine, and watching their DVDs; for information on their latest ventures, see http://www.anglingedge.com.

Maud Hart Lovelace:

The Mankato-based Betsy-Tacy Society maintains a website at http://www.betsy-tacysociety.org/mhl.htm; see also http://www.geocities.com/navaho59/maud.html for links to Lovelace biographies and more; MHS Minnesota Authors; Stuhler and Kreuter, *Women of Minnesota*.

Lutheranism:

Anne Gillespie Lewis, *Swedes in Minnesota* (St. Paul: Minnesota Historical Society Press, 2004); the Lutheran Social Service website is at http://www.lssmn.org/.

Warren MacKenzie:

In 2002, University of Minnesota art history professor Robert Silberman interviewed Warren MacKenzie for the Archives of American Art, Smithsonian Institution. A transcript of the interview is at http://www.aaa.si.edu/collections/oralhistories/transcripts/macken02.htm; David Lewis, *Warren MacKenzie, an American Potter* (Tokyo: Kodansha International, 1991). A number of exhibition catalogs also feature MacKenzie's work; for an example, see *Warren MacKenzie, Potter: A Retrospective* (Minneapolis: University Art Museum, University of Minnesota, 1989).

Paul Manship:

Paul Manship: Changing Taste in America (St. Paul: Minnesota Museum of Art, 1985); Susan Rather, *Archaism, Modernism, and the Art of Paul Manship* (Austin: University of Texas Press, 1993); the collections of the Minnesota Museum of American Art in St. Paul contain many Manship works; see the museum's website at http://www.mmaa.org/Manship.html.

Market Hunting:

Mark H. Davis, "Market Hunters vs. Sportsmen on the Prairie: The Case of William Kerr and Robert Poole," *Minnesota History* 60, no. 2 (Summer 2006); David and Jim Kimball, *The Market Hunter* (Minneapolis: Dillon Press, 1969); Dave Sonnenburg, "Minnesota Market Hunting," *Minnesota Sportsman* (September 1980); the Minnesota Department of Natural Resources website contains a section on Heron Lake at http://www.dnr.state.mn.us/rprp/heronlake/index.html.

Mayo Clinic:

The most comprehensive information about Mayo's history and current practices is on the clinic's website at http://www.mayoclinic.org/tradition-heritage/.

Eugene J. McCarthy:

A number of tributes to McCarthy appeared after his death in 2005 and are still available online; a particularly poignant remembrance by James Kilpatrick is at http://www.lawcrossing.com/article/index.php?id=1296; Minnesota Public Radio has produced a number of features on McCarthy, collected on their website at http://news.minnesota.publicradio.org/features/2005/06/15_olsond_genemccarthy/; see also the 2001 documentary about McCarthy, "I'm Sorry I Was Right," directed by Mike Hazard; MHS History Topics covers standard print references for McCarthy and 1960s politics; MHS Minnesota Authors.

Fredrick L. McGhee:

Paul Nelson, *Fredrick L. McGhee: A Life on the Color Line, 1861–1912* (St. Paul: Minnesota Historical Society Press, 2002).

L. David Mech:

Two websites contain a great deal of information about Mech and the International Wolf Center: see the center's site at http://www.wolf.org/wolves/index.asp; and Mech's website at http://www.davemech.com/.

Minneapolis Truckers' Strike, 1934:

William Millikan, *A Union against Unions: The Minneapolis Citizens Alliance and Its Fight against Organized Labor, 1903–1947* (St. Paul: Minnesota Historical Society Press, 2001); MHS History Topics.

Minnesota Mining and Manufacturing:

The company's early history is outlined in *Our Story So Far: Notes from the First 75 Years of 3M Company* (St. Paul: 3M, 1977); the stories of recent innovations, including Scotch Tape and Post-it Notes, are available at http://www.3m.com; for a visual history of 3M, see Loralee J. Bloom, "Mining the Archives," *Minnesota History* 58, no. 3 (Fall 2002).

Minnesota Multiphasic Personality Inventory:

The University of Minnesota maintains a website about the MMPI that contains a brief history and information about current developments at http://www1.umn.edu/mmpi/index.php.

Minnesota Orchestra:

Sandra Hyslop, ed., *Minnesota Orchestra at 100: A Collection of Essays and Images* (Minneapolis: Minnesota Orchestral Association, 2002); the orchestra website is at http://www.minnesotaorchestra.org/about/index.cfm.

Minnesota State Fair:

Karal Ann Marling, *Blue Ribbon: A Social and Pictorial History of the Minnesota State Fair* (St. Paul: Minnesota Historical Society Press, 1990); the fair's website is at http://mnstatefair.org.

Vilhelm Moberg and Ole E. Rølvaag:

J. R. Christianson, ed., *Scandinavians in America: Literary Life* (Decorah, IA: Symra Literary Society, 1985). Dorothy Burton Skardal, *Double Heritage: Scandinavian Immigrant Experience through Literary*

Sources (PhD thesis, Radcliffe College, 1962), contains a useful bibliography of works by Moberg, Rølvaag, and their contemporaries. MHS Minnesota Authors.

Walter F. Mondale:

Richard Moe, "The Making of the Modern Vice Presidency: A Personal Reflection," *Minnesota History* 60, no. 3 (Fall 2006); Walter F. Mondale, *The Accountability of Power: Toward a Responsible Presidency* (New York: D. McKay, 1975); the University of Minnesota and MHS both have extensive collections of Mondale's records from his many years in public service; MHS History Topics.

George Morrison:

George Morrison as told to Margo Fortunato Galt, *Turning the Feather Around: My Life in Art* (St. Paul: Minnesota Historical Society Press, 1998).

Mount Zion Hebrew Congregation:

W. Gunther Plaut, *Mount Zion, 1856–1956: The First Hundred Years* (St. Paul: North Central Publishing, 1956); a *Minneapolis Star Tribune* article on the 150th anniversary of Mount Zion is at http://www.startribune.com/614/story/932668.html; see also the congregation's website at http://www.mzion.org/Secondary.cfm?PageID=10200.

Munsingwear:

Quotes taken from Marcia Anderson, "Munsingwear: An Underwear for America," *Minnesota History* 50, no. 4 (Winter 1986); MHS has a comprehensive collection of Munsingwear garments and company records; a finding aid for the records is at http://www.mnhs.org/library/findaids/00206.html.

Bronko Nagurski:

See http://bronkonagurski.com; Rippel, *75 Memorable Moments*.

Near v. Minnesota:

Fred W. Friendly, *Minnesota Rag: Corruption, Yellow Journalism, and the Case That Saved Freedom of the Press* (Minneapolis: University of Minnesota Press, 2003); the opinion is available on the U.S. Supreme Court website at http://www.oyez.org/cases/1901-1939/1929/1929_91/; "Censorship and Journalists' Privilege: The Case of Near versus Minnesota—A Half Century Later." *Minnesota History* 46, no. 4 (Winter 1978).

Knute Nelson:

Millard L. Gieske and Steven J. Keillor, *Norwegian Yankee: Knute Nelson and the Failure of American Politics* (Northfield, MN: Norwegian-American Historical Association, 1995); Holmquist, *They Chose Minnesota*; Aby, *The North Star State*; MHS Minnesota Governors.

Floyd B. Olson:

George H. Mayer, *The Political Career of Floyd B. Olson* (St. Paul: Minnesota Historical Society Press, 1987); MHS Minnesota Governors.

The Olympic Hockey Team:

Wayne Coffey, *The Boys of Winter: The Untold Story of a Coach, a Dream, and the 1980 U.S. Olympic Hockey Team* (New York: Three Rivers Press, 2005); Rippel, *75 Memorable Moments*. For some great game footage, see *Do You Believe in Miracles? The Story of the 1980 U.S. Hockey Team* (HBO: 2001); and *Miracle* (Walt Disney Video: 2004), a fictional account starring Kurt Russell as Herb Brooks.

Bradford Parkinson:

Information on Parkinson was supplied by his sister (and nominator), Brenda Parkinson Hauschild; see also Stanford University's website at http://newsservice.stanford.edu/news/2004/february18/parkinson-218.html; an interview with Dr. Parkinson is at http://www.aero.org/corporation/parkinson.html.

Gordon Parks:

Gordon Parks, *A Choice of Weapons* (St. Paul: Minnesota Historical Society Press, 1986), *Voices in the Mirror: An Autobiography* (New York: Doubleday, 1990), and *A Hungry Heart: A Memoir* (New York: Atria Books, 2005). See also the documentary *Half Past Autumn: The Life and Works of Gordon Parks* (HBO, 1999).

The Phyllis Wheatley and Hallie Q. Brown Community Centers:

Taylor, *African Americans in Minnesota*. See also Mick Caouette's documentary *The Heart of Bassett Place: W. Gertrude Brown and the Wheatley House* (1999); Caroline Arnold, *Children of the Settlement Houses* (Minneapolis: Carolrhoda Books, 1998).

Pilgrim Baptist Church:

Quote is taken from *Pilgrim Baptist Church, St. Paul, Minnesota, 125th Anniversary Book, 1863–1988* (Marcelline, MO: Walsworth Publishing, 1988). Taylor, *African Americans in Minnesota*; the church's website is at http://www.pilgrimbaptistchurch.org/history.htm.

Pipestone:

The National Park Service maintains a comprehensive website on this topic at http://www.nps.gov/pipe/index.htm; the Derby quote is in Jacqueline Wiora Sletto, "Pipestone," *Native Peoples* (Winter 1992).

Veda Ponikvar:

An interview with Veda Ponikvar was conducted at MHS as part of the 20th Century Radicalism project (transcript available in the MHS Research Library); see also Bob von Sternberg, "She Ran a Powerful Press," *Minneapolis Star Tribune* (January 22, 1996, 1B); excerpts from Veda Ponikvar are included in Thomas Saylor, *Remembering the Good War: Minnesota's Greatest Generation* (St. Paul: Minnesota Historical Society Press, 2005).

C. Stanley Potter:

Information about Potter was provided by his nominator, Cheryl Merrill.

Powwows:

The Circle's powwow listings are at http://thecirclenews.org/powwow_calendar_2007.html; Tara Browner, *Heartbeat of the People: Music and Dance of the Northern Pow-Wow* (Urbana: University of Illinois Press, 2002).

Prince:

Quote is from Alex Hahn, *Possessed: The Rise and Fall of Prince* (New York: Billboard Books, 2003); Julie Baumgold, "Glitter Slave: Amid Pomp and Circumspection, Rock's Crown Prince Extends His Purple Reign," *Esquire* (Autumn 1995); Michaelangelo Matos, *Sign "O" the Times* (New York: Continuum International Publishing Group, 2004).

Elizabeth C. Quinlan:

Marilyn Revell DeLong, ed., *Minnesota Creates: Fashion for a Century* (St. Paul: Goldstein Museum of Design, University of Minnesota, 2000); Catherine Oglesby, "The Real Miss Quinlan," undated pamphlet.

Rapidan Dam:

Rapidan Hydroelectric Project (Litchfield, MN: Indeco, 1984); a brief history of the dam is at http://mrbdc.mnsu.edu/reports/bluearth/rapidan2004/rapidan04.html.

Red River Trails:

Rhoda R. Gilman, Carolyn Gilman, and Deborah M. Stultz, *The Red River Trails: Oxcart Routes between St. Paul and the Selkirk Settlement, 1820–1870* (St. Paul: Minnesota Historical Society Press, 1979); Gardner, *Minnesota Treasures.*

Religious Orders:

Laurent Cantwell, CSJ, *A Design for Living: A History of the Sisters of St. Joseph of Carondelet in the Northwest* (St. Paul: North Central Publishing, 1973); Annabelle Raiche, CSJ, and Ann Marie Biermaier, OSB, *They Came to Teach* (St. Cloud, MN: North Star Press of St. Cloud, 1994). Each of Minnesota's religious orders maintains a web presence; see, for example, http://www.sbm.osb.org/OurMinistry/BeyondtheMonastery/tabid/139/Default.aspx.

Joseph Renville:

Warren Upham, *Minnesota Biographies, 1655–1912* (St. Paul: Minnesota Historical Society Press, 1912); for information on Renville and his relatives, see http://www.geocities.com/renville_newsletter/Renvilles_in_the_us.html; information on Lac qui Parle Mission is at http://www.montechamber.com/cchs/lqpmissn.htm.

Martha Ripley:

The Central Community Housing Trust, which is overseeing the renovation of the Maternity Hospital buildings, has a website with information on Ripley at http://www.ccht.org/Site_History.html; the records of the Ripley Memorial Foundation are housed at MHS; see http://www.mnhs.org/library/findaids/00467.html.

Henry Hastings Sibley:

Rhoda R. Gilman, *Henry Hastings Sibley: Divided Heart* (St. Paul: Minnesota Historical Society Press, 2004), is an exhaustive survey of Sibley's life and career; MHS Minnesota Governors.

Skyways:

The skyway web reference is at http://www.minneapolis.about.com/od/shoppingservices/a/ skywayetiquette.htm; *Time* magazine ran a cover story on Minnesota in 1973 that included a discussion of skyways; see http://www.time.com/time/archive/preview/0,10987,907665,00.html; see also Mike Meyers, "Edward Baker, 80, City's Skyway Designer," *Minneapolis Star Tribune* (June 19, 2006).

Snowmobiles:

See http://www.polarisindustries.com/en-us/ourcompany/aboutpolaris/historyandheritage.html; MHS History Topics.

Socialist Opera House:

James A. Roe, "Virginia, Minnesota's Socialist Opera: Showplace of Iron Range Radicalism," copy in author's possession; a version of this paper was published in *Finnish Americana* 9 (1991/1992); quote is from Clarence W. Ivonen, "Remodeling Plans for Old Opera House Will Leave Only Memories of Range's Colorful Cultural Center of Yesterday," *Mesabi Daily News* (January 30, 1958), 1.

Sound 80:

Larry Millett, *AIA Guide to the Twin Cities* (St. Paul: Minnesota Historical Society Press, 2007); Jung quote is at http://www.stereophile.com/interviews/604jung/index.html.

Southdale Center:

Quote about Southdale is from Malcolm Gladwell, "The Terrazzo Jungle," New Yorker (March 15, 2004); Southdale press release is at http://www.southdale.com/static/node2231.jsp; Edgerton Martin, "From Southdale to the Mall of America: Urban Models for Cities of Our Time," *Hennepin History* (Summer 1992).

SPAM:

See http://hormel.com; http://spam.com; for more on SPAM's popularity abroad, see Barbara Demick, "When Only Slabs of Pink, Jellied Byproduct Will Do," *Los Angeles Times* (October 15, 2005).

Allan Spear:

Most information came directly from Senator Spear and from his nominator, Senator D. Scott Dibble; the quote is from an oral history conducted by the Oberlin College GLBT Community Project, at http://www.oberlinlgbt.org/personal-histories/spear/.

Split Rock Lighthouse:

Split Rock is an MHS Historic Site; see the website at http://www.mnhs.org/places/sites/srl/; Stephen P. Hall, *Split Rock: Epoch of a Lighthouse* (St. Paul: Minnesota Historical Society Press, 1978).

Harold E. Stassen:

Harold Stassen, *Man Was Meant to Be Free: Selected Statements, 1940–51* (Garden City, NY: Doubleday, 1951); Alec Kirby, "A Major Contender: Harold Stassen and the Politics of American Presidential Nominations," *Minnesota History* 55, no. 4 (Winter 1996/1997). MHS has a large collection of Stassen's documents; see http://www.mnhs.org/library/findaids/00202.html; MHS Minnesota Governors.

State of Minnesota v. Philip Morris:

Most of the information included here was supplied by nominator Doug Blanke, director, Tobacco Law Center, http://www.tobaccolawcenter.org; quote is from *Tobacco: A Catalog of Minnesota Tobacco Case Related Materials,* developed and compiled by Robins, Kaplan, Miller & Ciresi LLP (1998); information on the World Health Organization initiatives is at http://www.who.int/tobacco/en/.

Ten Thousand Lakes of Minnesota Association:

Quote is from Linda Lorentzen, "View from the Lake," *Paynesville Press* (May 30, 2001); Clark, *Minnesota in a Century of Change*; http://www.exploreminnesota.com.

John Thomas:

Information came from nominator Mick Caouette, a filmmaker who is currently finishing a documentary on John Thomas.

Tonka Trucks:

MHS has a collection of Tonka Toys catalogs and promotional materials; search http://www.mnpals.net/ under Tonka Corporation; a 1956 company overview is at http://www.neatoldtoys.com/; jingle is from http://www.hasbro.com/tonka.

Treaty of 1837:

James M. McClurken, *The 1837 Treaty of St. Peters Preserving the Rights of the Mille Lacs Ojibwa to Hunt, Fish, and Gather: The Effect of Treaties and Agreements since 1855* (East Lansing, MI: J. M. McClurken, 1993); Bruce M. White, *Early Game and Fish Regulation and Enforcement in Minnesota, 1858–1920: A Report Prepared for the Mille Lacs Band of Ojibwe* (St. Paul: Bruce White, 1995); see MHS holdings related to the Save Lake Mille Lacs Association at http://www.mnhs.org/library/findaids/00577.html.

Clara Ueland:

Clara Ueland, *The Advantages of Equal Suffrage* (Minneapolis: Minnesota Equal Suffrage Association, 1914); Barbara Stuhler, *Gentle Warriors: Clara Ueland and the Minnesota Struggle for Woman Suffrage* (St. Paul: Minnesota Historical Society Press, 1995); for woman suffrage, see MHS History Topics.

University of Minnesota Fruit-Breeding Program:

See http://www.arboretum.umn.edu; quote from Senator Brian LeClair is at http://wcco.com/local/local_story_084174522.html; quote from Doug Shefelbine is at http://www.apples.umn.edu/assets/betterworldreport.pdf.

U.S.–Dakota War:

Waziyatawin Angela Wilson, ed., *In the Footsteps of Our Ancestors: The Dakota Commemorative Marches of the 21st Century* (St. Paul: Living Justice Press, 2006); Gary Clayton Anderson, *Kinsmen of Another Kind: Dakota-White Relations in the Upper Mississippi Valley, 1650–1862* (St. Paul: Minnesota Historical Society Press, 1984); Gary Clayton Anderson and Alan Woolworth, eds., *Through Dakota Eyes: Narrative Accounts of the Minnesota Indian War of 1862* (St. Paul: Minnesota Historical Society Press, 1988); MHS History Topics.

Xang Vang:

Information for this topic came from Xang Vang and from his nominator, Tzianeng Vang; a biography of Xang Vang is at http://www.hamaa.org/Bios/xang.htm; see the results of Xang Vang's work with the University of Minnesota Extension Service at http://www.extension.umn.edu/distribution/horticulture/DG7475.html.

Jesse Ventura:

Graubard, *Minnesota Real and Imagined*; MHS Minnesota Governors.

Owen H. Wangensteen:

See http://www.mmf.umn.edu/bulletin/fall2005/lookback/; the Lillehei quote is at http://www.ctsnet.org/sections/residents/pioneerinterviews/article-8.html; interviews with Earl Bakken, inventor of the electronic pacemaker, DeWall, and Lillehei are at http://www.mnhs.org/collections/medTech/bio_bakken.html; for the pacemaker, see MHS History Topics.

Washburn Center for Children:

Thomas Balcom, *Washburn's Century of Helping Children: From Orphanage to Child Guidance Center, 1883–1983* (Minneapolis: Washburn Child Guidance Center, 1983).

WCAL:

Joseph M. Shaw, *Dear Old Hill: The Story of Manitou Heights, The Campus of St. Olaf College* (Northfield, MN: St. Olaf College, 1992); other information came from Jeff Sauve, associate archivist, and Janet Kringen Thompson, interim vice president for college relations, St. Olaf College.

Webster Cooperative Dairy Association:

Steven J. Keillor, *Cooperative Commonwealth: Co-ops in Rural Minnesota, 1859–1939* (St. Paul: Minnesota Historical Society Press, 2000); for current statistics, see http://www.rurdev.usda.gov/rbs/pub/mar01/minn. MHS collections include the records of many individual co-ops, as well as those of the Minnesota Association of Cooperatives; see http://www.mnhs.org/library/findaids/00200.html.

Paul Wellstone:

See Paul Wellstone, *The Conscience of a Liberal: Reclaiming the Compassionate Agenda* (Minneapolis: University of Minnesota Press, 2002); http://bioguide.congress.gov; http://www.wellstone.org/archive; http://www.pbs.org/newshour/vote2002/races/mn_wellstone.html.

Wheat:

Clark, *Minnesota in a Century of Change*; see also the Mill City Museum website at http://www.millcitymuseum.org/history.html; for bonanza farms, see MHS History Topics.

Henry B. Whipple:

William Watts Folwell, *A History of Minnesota* (St. Paul: Minnesota Historical Society Press, 1921–1930); Phillips Endecott Osgood, *Straight Tongue: A Story of Henry Benjamin Whipple, First Episcopal Bishop of Minnesota* (Minneapolis: T. S. Denison, 1958); information on the timing of Whipple's visit with Lincoln was supplied by Carrie R. Zeman, scholar of nineteenth-century Minnesota history.

White Pine Trees:

Agnes M. Larson, *History of the White Pine Industry in Minnesota* (Minneapolis: University of Minnesota Press, 1949); information on the White Pine Initiative is at http://www.dnr.mn.gov/fid/june98/06309808.html.

The Willmar 8:

Quotes are in Asa Wilson, "Twenty-five Years Late, Willmar 8 Are Heroes to a New Generation," *Workday Minnesota* (August 6, 2006); see also the documentary by Lee Grant, *Willmar 8* (1981).

August Wilson:

Quotes are in Justin Maxwell, "Reciprocal Relationships: August Wilson and the Playwrights' Center," *Minnesota History* 60, no. 4 (Winter 2006/2007); see also Penumbra Theatre's bibliography of articles related to August Wilson, at http://penumbratheatre.org/content/blogcategory/48/60/.

Wind Turbines:

"Buffalo Ridge: Is Minnesota the 'Saudi Arabia of Wind Power'?" *Rake* (April 2005); Minnesota Public Radio has done a number of features on wind turbines over the past decade, including http://news.minnesota.publicradio.org/features/2003/09/29_galballye_windthree/.

Theodore Wirth:

Conrad Wirth, *Parks, Politics, and the People*, at http://www.cr.nps.gov/history/online_books/wirth2/chap1.htm; http://www.mpls.lib.mn.us/history/cg4.asp; http://www.minneapolisparks.org/default.asp?PageID=70.

Credits and Permissions

For institutional and other listings, the name of the photographer, when known, is given in parentheses, as is additional information about the source of the item.

American Public Media
Page 94. Photo by Brian Velenchenko.

Liv Arnesen
Page 9 (both). Photo © Liv Arnesen. Used with permission. See http://www.yourexpedition.com.

The Beargrease Foundation Board of Directors
Page 11 (bottom). Photo © Gary Meinz.

Judith Brin-Ingber
Page 20

Mick Caouette
Page 166 (both)

Center for Victims of Torture
Page 24, all photographs © Stephanie Hynes.

Chisago County Historical Society
Page 124

Cook County Historical Society
Page 11 (top). Used with permission.

Corbis
Page 135. Copyright © Bettmann/Corbis.

Courage Center
Page 32 (both)

Marv Davidov
Page 76 (both)

El Centro International de Mejoramiento de Maiz y Trigo
Page 17

Tania Galaviz de Epinoza
Page 36 (costume headdress photo by Eric Mortenson)

Farmington Area Historical Society
Page 93, from *Over the Years* (47:1), April 2006. Used with permission.

Beth Ann Gaede
Page 19 (top)

Brian Gardner
Pages 22 (bottom), 25, 67 (bottom). All images © Brian Gardner.

General Mills Archives
Page 34. Used with permission.

Getty Images
Page 45, photo © John Cohen, Hulton Archive. Used with permission.

Terry Gydesen Photography
Pages 144, 145 (bottom), 183. All images © copyright Terry Gydesen.

Mrs. Howard H. (Dorie) Hathaway
Page 40

Hazelden
Page 69. Used with permission. http://www.hazelden.org

Robert Jacobson
Page 37 (both). All images © Robert Jacobson and used with permission.

Charlie Maguire
Page 88, "Itasca: A Place of Beginnings," music and lyrics by Charlie Maguire. From the album *Stepping Stones*. Copyright © Mell-Jamin Music. All rights reserved. Used with permission.

Family of Eugene J. McCarthy
Kind permission to reprint poem "The Maple Tree."

L. David Mech
Page 115 (top). Image © L. David Mech.

Susan Miller Photography
Pages 122, 123 (top), 160. All images © Susan Miller.

Minneapolis Public Library, Special Collections
Pages 30 (left), 130 (bottom; *Minneapolis Journal*)

Minneapolis Star Tribune
Page 154 (top; photo by Mike Zerby), 176 (bottom), 189

Minnesota Historical Society Collections, St. Paul
Pages 6–7, 10, 14, 15 (top: engraving by J. C. Buttre), 16 (Northwestern Photographic Studio, Inc.), 18 (left), 21, 22 (top), 23 (top; Eric Mortenson), 23 (bottom),

Index